West Academic Publishing's Law School Advisory Board

Criminal Law

Joseph E. Kennedy
Professor of Law
University of North Carolina
School of Law

A SHORT & HAPPY GUIDE® SERIES

WEST
ACADEMIC
PUBLISHING

a short & happy guide series is a trademark registered in the U.S. Patent and Trademark Office.

© 2016 LEG, Inc. d/b/a West Academic

    444 Cedar Street, Suite 700
    St. Paul, MN 55101
    1-877-888-1330

Printed in the United States of America

ISBN: 978-0-314-28761-8

For Maria, who is my guide to a happy life.

Preface

Congratulations! You are "living the dream," or you are living *your dream*, to be more precise. If you are a first year law student, you might be feeling tired, stressed and a little bit overwhelmed right about now. That is why you wandered into an online or virtual bookstore looking for a study guide on criminal law. Before I say another word about what this guide will and won't do for you, I do want to remind you that you dreamed of this moment. Well, not this exact moment of feeling tired, stressed and overwhelmed. You dreamed of attending law school, of passing the bar, and of becoming a lawyer. And becoming a lawyer is a great thing, so congratulations! You are on your way to achieving a great goal. But before you deliver thundering closing arguments to juries in nationally televised cases or brilliantly parry impossible questions from Supreme Court justices in a landmark constitutional case or close mega-billion dollar deals with Beyoncé or Donald Trump over lunch, you have to graduate law school. And in your first year of law school, you will take criminal law.

This isn't the study guide you deserve; this is the study guide you need. I have adapted that line, of course, from the movie *The Dark Knight*. You rightfully feel at this point that you deserve all the help you can get. So you are understandably attracted to big, thick study guides with lots and lots of rules—often distilled in outline form—including tons and tons of examples, usually involving "A killing B," or "John stealing from Betty." Whether you realize it or not, that is not the study guide you need.

The study guide you need is shorter and easier to remember. Any criminal law course will cover only a fraction of the countless rules included in the larger guides. Even if a professor includes some of those smaller rules in reading or class discussion, they almost never make them the central issues of their exam questions. Instead, professors do their utmost to teach students the fundamental rules and issues that govern each area of criminal law. I know it feels more comforting to hold a big, heavy study guide in your hand that takes a more encyclopedic approach, but that comforting feeling is an illusion. You need a study guide that focuses on the fundamentals, not a security blanket made of paper.

You also need a study guide that does this in a memorable way. Many of these fundamental rules and issues simply won't stick to your brain easily. They are complex and not always intuitive. One of the scariest things for first year law students is that they can read something really closely the night before class (or even worse the night before the exam) and then be completely unable to remember or understand it the next day. So I use quirky, sometimes bizarre, examples that are easy to remember, yet examples that all illustrate something central and fundamental about the doctrine discussed. I learned years ago that even bad jokes will help students remember a rule better than no joke at all. And boy, do I know a lot of bad jokes.

This book has a different look and feel than your average study guide. It uses less of an outline format and more of a story approach. But here is the key: your brain is not constructed to remember outlines. It naturally remembers stories, especially quirky ones that make you either smile or grimace. That is why I use one story as a main thread whenever possible to explain a particular doctrine, changing and riffing off it as I work through different issues. The rules will hang together in your mind, connected by memorable hypotheticals.

Einstein once said that the important thing is to make things as simple as possible, but no simpler. Don't think for a minute though that I have dumbed things down. I teach at a great law school where really smart students demand to be challenged. I have also lectured for years for bar review courses that require me to explain even the most difficult concepts to ensure that their students don't get caught short on the bar exam. I hit the fundamental concepts hard in the pages that follow. I don't oversimplify these fundamental concepts. The criminal law is messy in parts, and while I explain the mess as clearly as possible, I have resisted the temptation that some authors fall into of making the law tidier than it is.

I also include not just the rules but the main ideas behind those rules. Law, as you will soon learn to your delight, is shaped by big ideas. Understanding the interplay between those big ideas and the small rules that govern any particular issue is difficult but absolutely essential to success as a law student and a lawyer. I do my best in the space that we have to give you a feel for the big ideas that animate each area of the criminal law.

Finally, I take the "guide" part of this book's title seriously. The way the law is taught—how its classes are structured and its textbooks written—often mystifies students. Different professors and different textbook authors make different decisions about what areas to emphasize and about how to approach the material. As your guide, I will try to explain these choices as we go along.

In The Dark Knight, Batman ignores lots and lots of society's rules, but he pays close attention to the most important ones. I do the same. And I promise to do it in a way that helps you remember them. (Sort of like what I did in this preface with the Batman quote. ☺)

JOSEPH E. KENNEDY

August 2015

Acknowledgments

Thanks are owed to Bonnie Karlen of West Publishing for her patience and enthusiasm in helping me see this project through to its completion, Andrew Swanson of UNC Law School for his skill and thoroughness in editing the manuscript, Maria Savasta-Kennedy and Maxine Eichner for reviewing portions of the manuscript and countless UNC Law students and colleagues who helped me find my voice in teaching criminal law. I also acknowledge a debt to the numerous criminal law scholars whose work I have learned from over the years. Among them are four giants who deserve mention by name: Joshua Dressler, Wayne LaFave, Arnold Loewy, and Paul Robinson. Without their longer, more painstakingly detailed surveys, this short and happy guide to the field would not have been possible.

Table of Contents

A Short & Happy Guide to
Criminal Law

CHAPTER 1

Thinking Like a Lawyer and Learning Like a Law Student

> *"If you don't know where you are going, you'll end up somewhere else."*
>
> *Yogi Berra*

Yogi Berra was a Major League Baseball player, coach and manager who remains famous for saying things that were either stupefying or brilliant in their simplicity. As Yogi memorably suggested, if you don't know where you are going you might not get there. Understanding the goals that professors and textbook authors have for you as a student is essential to learning the law as efficiently and as well as you can.

You might think, "law school is about learning the law, and the law is a body of rules." Well, that is both true and false. Learning rules is a key part of law school, but it is the easiest part. I can teach my twelve year old daughter to memorize a set of rules, but the hard part is learning what to do with those rules (I could probably teach her that, too, but she would have to drop out

1

of middle school, which she probably would not be too happy about). Learning how to do complicated tasks with rules is really what law school is all about, and the most important stage of that learning takes place in the first year.

This chapter begins with some cautionary words about what makes law school particularly difficult for most people. It then explains law school by working backwards from the end. It begins with a discussion of what "thinking like a lawyer means." Then it explains the role law school exams play in helping students learn to think like a lawyer. Next, it discusses the role that an outline plays in helping students prepare for an exam and concludes with an explanation of how reading cases and participating in class is key to creating a truly effective outline. A later chapter will offer more specific tips on exam-writing. I conclude with a few words of advice about how best to survive and thrive under the pressures of law school's first year.

Law School Is Difficult Because It Is Different

Let's start with the good news. Law is not rocket science. Saying that something is rocket science, of course, is a catch phrase for saying that something is inherently difficult and can only be learned by crazy smart people. Whether this is true or not of rocket scientists, it is not true of the law. Law is not inherently difficult to learn. It does not involve mental operations that are more difficult to perform than other complicated things that you have learned before. Doing complex things with rules is something that anybody who is willing to work hard can learn to do. I think I really could turn my twelve year old into a lawyer, but can you imagine dealing with a legally trained teenager?

Now for the bad news. What might actually make the law harder for you to learn than for my twelve year old daughter is that law is different from anything else you have studied. Let me say that again (and even italicize it for emphasis). *Law is difficult because it is different.* If you accept and embrace this fact, you are on your way to succeeding at the study of law because you will be open to thinking about reading and writing and thinking in a different way.

Ok, "I get it," you might be thinking. Can we move on now to discussing those differences? Not quite yet. Because over the course of twenty years of teaching law school I have learned that the vast majority of law students struggle with accepting that the law is really different. Instead they tell themselves sometime during the stress and pressure of the first semester that the law is really not all that different from something else. That something else is always something that the student has studied before and is usually something they feel comfortable learning. They are wrong, of course, but understanding how and why they go wrong is key to making sure that you don't make the same mistake. So stay with me for a few more paragraphs while I talk about this mistake in terms that you will easily remember when your own time comes.

The Blind Men and the Elephant

I am sure you have heard of the story of the blind men and the elephant. A group of blind men approach an elephant. Each touches a different part of the elephant and tries to describe for the others what an elephant is like. One person touches the trunk, another the tail, another the side, another the ear. You get the idea.

Well, the law is like an elephant. It has a lot of very different parts. One moment in class we will be doing the sort of close textual analysis that English majors feel comfortable with. The next moment we will be manipulating rules in a highly formal way that seems right and comfortable to logicians and the more mathematically minded. The next moment we will be engaging in wide ranging philosophical discussions, and the very next we will be discussing the social and economic conditions that shape the law and influence how it is applied. Well, students often latch onto what is familiar and assumes that this is what learning the law is all about. The English major/mathematician/philosopher/ social scientists thinks, "I can do this because it just happens to be exactly like something I have already learned to do well!" Gee, what a coincidence.

What has happened, of course, is that under the pressure of learning a new thing they have comforted themselves with the illusion that it is not really all that new. They are each grasping onto the part of the elephant that feels familiar and comfortable, and they are each missing the bigger picture.

One advantage that my precocious twelve year old daughter would have over you in studying the law is that she has not yet had to master a discipline that changes the way she thinks in a fundamental way. Most of you have. She would not be tempted to assume that she already knows how to think in the way that law requires. She would be writing on a blank slate, which is an advantage when drawing something unfamiliar (such as an elephant).

Are you ready for some good news? This really is good news. The unique nature of legal study means that *no one comes in with an advantage.* It does not matter what your undergraduate major was. In fact, the people who are most at risk of making the "elephant mistake" are often people who have been to graduate school. They have learned one way of thinking so well that it is sometimes more difficult to put aside their way of thinking and embrace the *inherent difference of learning the law.*

Even more good news. The eclectic elephant-like nature of learning the law also makes thinking like a lawyer FASCINATING! It is simply inherently interesting to switch from thinking like an English major to a mathematician, to a philosopher, to a social scientist all in the course of one class discussion.

Learning to be able to think this way is also incredibly USEFUL! The real world is full of elephant-like problems that require this sort of eclectic thinking. There is a reason why so many leaders in our society—CEO's, politicians, and authors—have been to law school and/or practiced law. The world is a complicated place, and it often requires more than one way of thinking to solve problems. That is why lawyers often get asked to help solve all sorts of problems, not just legal ones.

So now that you are ready to embrace the difference of learning the law, let's talk in more detail about what thinking like a lawyer and learning like a law student really means.

Thinking Like a Lawyer

Nothing is more mystifying—and ultimately more terrifying—to first year law students than their professors' regular references to the importance of learning to "think like a lawyer." Students immediately understand that thinking like a lawyer is central to their immediate academic as well as their ultimate professional success, but they often wait in vain for a clear and complete definition of what thinking like a lawyer means.

Thinking like a lawyer is *a collection of mental habits* that practicing lawyers must have in order to be successful. Specifically, there are three core mental habits that lawyers must have that the first year of law school develops.

1. **Thinking Systematically**

2. **Imagining More than One Side of an Argument or Issue**

3. **Striking a Balance between Competing Interests and Perspectives**

Thinking Systematically

"When you come to a fork in the road, take it."

Yogi Berra

Imagine a math class where you are forced to solve the same math problem over and over again in multiple different ways. That would be annoying. You solved it! Why solve it two or three times? Well, that is exactly the sort of thinking that lawyers must do routinely. They must think their way through a multitude of different possible outcomes to a particular problem. In math the answer to the problem will always be the same. In the messy real world in which lawyers operate things can turn out very differently each time for a whole variety of reasons. Think of a movie you have seen or a book you have read in which multiple versions of a story exist based on some slight change earlier in the plot. Well, lawyers are tasked with imagining those various worlds when preparing a case for court, structuring an agreement, or helping a client plan for the future. The key to being able to do this well is thinking systematically.

The key to thinking systematically is that when you come to a fork in the road that you take both paths—you think through all the choices and possible outcomes of going in either direction. More specifically, when analyzing a criminal law fact pattern you don't stop after identifying the first crime or the first defense or the first theory of liability. You think through all of them.

Lawyers and law professors call this ability to think systematically in the context of the law *issue spotting*. If a lawyer cannot spot an issue then she cannot prepare to address that issue in court, draft her away around it in a document, or counsel her client about the choice that it requires.

This does not really come naturally to most people. Most people want to find "an answer," not multiple possible answers. Well, you can't prepare a case for court or write an agreement that will still be useful when things change over time unless you think through multiple possible outcomes. Welcome to the world of maybe and if and perhaps.

People joke about lawyers being "multi-handed advisors" ("on the one hand, but on the other hand, but on the other, other hand"). Well, after they are done joking about it they take out their checkbook and hire exactly that type of lawyer because nobody likes surprises—especially in court! So get ready to become a "mental octopus" as you learn to go from one hand to another and another and another.

Imagining Both Sides of an Argument

"I'd give my right arm to be ambidextrous."

Yogi Berra

Once you have identified an "issue," your client will probably want you to do two related things. First, prepare the best possible argument for resolving the issue in her favor. Second, give the most accurate possible prediction of how that issue will be resolved by the judge, jury, or other decision maker.

At this point some of you are probably thinking, "duh! Of course lawyers need to be able to think about both sides of the argument." Please, please, please, take it from me that doing this as well as a law student/lawyer needs to is harder than you think. First of all, "thinking about both sides" does not nearly go far enough. You need to be able to really *argue* both sides. When I practiced law the most successful lawyers I worked with told me that lawyers are not ready to argue a case until they can give the other side's argument at least as well as the opposing lawyer can. This requires you not just to *think* about the other side, but to *sympathetically imagine* the other side. You get all the way into the other side's shoes as if you were representing their client, and then you give it your all.

Doing this is hard. We all have our points of view. We also like to think that right and wrong exists, and that means that there must be a *right answer*. Really and truly trying to "argue yourself to a draw" does not come naturally to most, but it can be learned by all with a lot of practice. So prepare to become mentally ambidextrous, to learn to make arguments left and right!

Striking a Balance

> "It's tough to make predictions, especially about the future."
>
> Yogi Berra

A famous legal philosopher was fond of saying "at the end of the day we must act." Well, the legal system requires decisions by judges and juries and by parties. What the legal decision maker must often do is to strike a balance between competing interests, perspectives, or versions of an event. Judges confronting cutting edge legal issues must often formulate rules that balance competing interests, reconcile separate lines of legal precedent, or synthesize discrete rulings into a more general rule. Juries often must reconcile different versions of what happened in a particular case. Lawyers seeking to form an agreement must propose language that finds common ground acceptable to all.

Wait, you might think, I am learning to be a lawyer, not a judge or a jury. Putting aside the fact that judges are lawyers, a lawyer must be able to think about how a judge or jury might strike the balance for two reasons. First, doing so is essential to thinking up the best possible arguments for striking the balance in your client's favor. Second, doing so is essential to making good *predictions* about how a particular issue will be resolved. Such predictions lie at the heart of good legal advice. Clients look to their lawyer to tell them how a judge or jury might strike the balance in their particular case.

This means that many times in your first year your professor will push you to articulate what the rule should be, or how a particular case should be resolved. Rather than resist (and wait to find out what the often non-existent "right answer" is), give it your best shot. You will only get better by trying.

Mental Habits

> *"In theory there is no difference between theory and practice. But in practice there is."*
>
> *Yogi Berra*

Now that you know what thinking like a lawyer means I want to talk about how you can begin learning to think like a lawyer in your first year of law school. The key is to understand that thinking like a lawyer is a set of *mental habits*. Learning to think like a lawyer is not something that you "know." It is something that you learn to "do." More specifically, it is something that you learn to do involving increasingly difficult problems, over and over again, and often under great pressure.

The good news is that the mental habits that constitute thinking like a lawyer can be developed by repetition. The bad news is that the only way you can develop these habits is by repetition. There is simply no substitute for "just doing it," to borrow the slogan of the famous shoe company. I stress this because many people think of mental operations in terms of something you "know," not something you "do."

In the movie "The Matrix" people are able to learn to do all sorts of cool things—Kung Fu, flying a helicopter, shooting machine guns—simply by plugging a giant computer wire into a hole in the back of their head and directly uploading the neural pathways required into their brains. Well, reach your hands to the back of your head and feel around for a terminal jack. If you don't feel one, then you are just going to have to learn how to do things the old fashioned way—by doing them. (Unless, of course, you think you, like Neo, are "the one.")

Learning to think like a lawyer is more like learning to play the piano or to dribble a soccer ball than most law students realize. You can't learn it by watching or by reading about it; you must "just do it." Accepting that learning to think like a lawyer involves developing mental habits is key to learning to study effectively as a law student, doing well on the exam, and preparing yourself to be an excellent attorney.

Law School Exams

A later chapter will focus on exam-writing specifically. For the moment, I just want to explain enough about law school exams for you to understand how the nature of the law school exam shapes how you should study during the semester.

The typical law school exam, especially in the first year, is a series of essay questions that require a student to analyze a fairly complicated fact pattern. (Some professors use short answer or multiple choice questions, but this is more common in the second and third year.) The fact pattern will sometimes be followed by sections of a statute that the student is to use in analyzing the problem. Then one or more very general questions will follow.

Some professors will simply ask the student to discuss or analyze all legal issues arising under the law studied in the course. A typical question in a criminal law course might be to analyze all criminal liability although sometimes the question will be limited to certain potential defendants or certain types of crimes.

What the typical essay question requires the student to do is to *issue spot*, to *argue both sides* of issues that have no clear resolution, and sometimes to offer an analysis of how the judge or fact finder might *strike the balance* in deciding the issue. It bears emphasis that most law school essay questions involve multiple issues. In a later chapter I will discuss in some detail how to effectively write about multiple issues at once. (Spoiler alert: you don't write about them all at once; you learn to write very efficiently and concisely about them *one at a time*.)

Outlines

Unless you truly are "the One," you will need to prepare an outline of the major rules and doctrines in order to do well on a law school exam during your first year. An outline is a distillation of the legal rules learned in the course organized in a logical way that makes it easy to use on an exam. A good outline can serve as a checklist for helping you spot issues, an organized list of the legal rules that you may need to apply to the fact pattern, and a series of personalized notes to yourself to jog your memory about particularly difficult or important points.

There are a lot of different ways to write an outline, but no one right way. There can't be one right way because the whole point of the outline is to be useful to you, and what is useful to one person may not be useful to another.

What is *really, super duper important* is that *you truly understand everything that you write down in your outline*. That might seem incomprehensibly obvious, but it is not. Under the pressure of learning this very difficult-because-it-is-very-different thing that is the law, many students will mindlessly copy into their outline rules from commercial outlines, or the outlines of their classmates, or the outlines that "A" students from past years have given them. These *copied* rules usually do first year students little or no good.

Let me explain. Every year some number of my first year students come to see me after they get their final grade back. We go over their exam. Each year at least one (and often more) student will say "that was in my outline" as we go over some issue that they missed on the exam. In fact, the students who come see me after the exam about their grades almost always have very complete and detailed outlines. Often they have their outline memorized and can recite any part of it when asked. Their problem is that they did not have a *working knowledge* of these rules.

Having a working knowledge of a legal rule means that you can recognize the issue that it governs when you see it buried in a set of unfamiliar facts. Outlines are efficient ways for you to collect and memorialize the rules you have a working knowledge of. Preparing the outline will also help you spot gaps in your knowledge of the rules and organize your thinking in a way that allows you to analyze a problem rapidly and efficiently. But simply writing down a rule in an outline does not give you a working knowledge of it. Developing that working knowledge happens earlier in the study process.

Preparing for, Participating in, and Learning from Class Discussions

The Law School Class Discussion as Video Game. Being called upon in class to answer difficult questions about the assigned reading is the most challenging but also often the most rewarding part of the law school experience. While some professors lecture for part or even all of the class period that is not the norm. Most professors teach class by asking students questions. Some professors rely on volunteers to answer the questions. Some professors "cold-call" students who have not raised their hands. Many professors do some of both.

This method of teaching through questions is referred to in law schools as the Socratic method. It is named after Socrates, the classical Greek philosopher whom engaged in such questioning with all of his pupils and challengers. You may recall that Socrates was eventually sentenced to death by poison, a sentence that some number of law students come to think of as not all that unreasonable after suffering through a few Socratic interrogations at the hands of their professors.

Many students find the Socratic method a difficult way to learn. They think their professors are "just hiding the ball" or trying to make themselves look smart at the student's expense. Some students wonder why the professor can't just tell them what the case means and then lead an open-ended discussion about why the case was decided the way it was.

Well, think of practicing law as a very complicated and interactive multiplayer video game where the scenarios are constantly changing. Would you try to teach someone to play a video game by simply telling them what to do? That would not work for a number of reasons. First, it is hard to explain or understand all of the possible variations that the player might encounter. Second, since much depends on what your opponent does and the identity of your opponent often changes from one game to another, what works against one opponent might fail against another. Third, and most fundamentally, you cannot learn how to *do* something by listening to someone else talk about it.

You need to take the controller in your hand and get blown up or eaten a couple of dozen times before you get the hang of even the basic moves. Well the same is true of learning to reason about legal rules. The Socratic discussion the professor creates in the classroom where the questions asked and the arguments raised are constantly shifting and where students are often asked to address the arguments of their fellow students creates the same sort of learning experience. Except learning to play this video game will allow you to graduate with a J.D., become a lawyer, and earn a good living while helping people. So get in the game!

Thinking Hypothetically

Let me tell you right now what will drive many of you nuts about law school class discussions. You will have read the cases assigned incredibly carefully. You will have made detailed notes about every aspect of the case. You may be able to answer every question asked about the case's facts, reasoning, and rule. In class, however, the professor will ask you a question about a hypothetical case. Maybe the hypothetical will be an altered version of the case you read, or maybe it will be about an entirely different case. Either way, you will want to cry foul because the professor is changing the facts on you.

You should rejoice when the professor asks you (or the class as a whole) such a hypothetical question (not curse her silently under your breath). These hypothetical questions are one of the best ways for you to develop that *working knowledge* of the rule being discussed. Only by having to apply the rule from the case to a different set of facts can you really hope to understand how that rule might apply to future cases.

The Greek philosopher Heraclitus said that you can't ever step into the same river twice. Well, no two cases are ever the same, and difficult cases will involve important differences. So you only really understand a legal rule if you can make arguments for and against applying or modifying it in some future case. This is the working knowledge of the rule that you need both as a law student taking an exam and as a lawyer working with the rule in real life. The key to developing such an understanding is learning to play with rules in this hypothetical way.

Participating in Class

Your class discussions are the easiest time and place to learn to think hypothetically. Theoretically, you could just do it on your own, but as Yogi Berra observed what works in theory and in practice are two different things. Over time you will learn to think about rules in this hypothetical way on your own, but in your first year it is easiest to do so in the midst of a discussion with other people that is guided by a professor who generates the hypotheticals.

Now everyone who has ever set foot in a law school has heard stories about the "silent gunner." A gunner is a very intense law student who does very well on the exam. A silent gunner is such a student who speaks very little in class—often only when called upon. Some students conclude that the existence of silent gunners means that talking in class is a waste of time, and that the time and energy is better spent writing down everything that everyone is saying. This is WRONG.

Would you try to learn how to play the piano just by watching someone play without ever touching the keys yourself? Would you try to learn to hit a baseball by just watching batting practice without ever taking a swing yourself? What sets the silent gunner apart from most other human beings is that she is able to fully participate in the discussion *in her own head*. Most of us can't. If we don't at least think about offering our own answers to the questions posed we lapse into a passive mode of thinking where we stop wrestling with the rule being discussed and just wait for some indication from the professor of what the "right answer" is. (Or we just space out altogether—especially if we have a laptop that we can web surf on right in front of us.)

Look, your class discussion is batting practice, and you want to swing the bat. Raise your hand! "But I might miss the pitch in front of all these people?" Who cares? You just don't want to miss a curve ball on the exam, and the only way to get better at hitting the curve balls your professor throws at you is to practice swinging at them. Even if you don't get called on, the fact that you formulated a tentative answer to the question in your mind is the equivalent of taking a swing at the ball. It would of course be better if the professor did call on you though because that way you would be guaranteed of learning her reaction to your particular response to the question asked. So get in the game!

Actively participating in class discussions offer two closely related benefits. First, you will develop your general ability to analyze cases and play with rules. Second, playing with the specific rule being studied will help burn the rule into your brain. I mean this literally. You literally form a neural pathway in your brain that is more likely to light up when you confront a similar issue in a future fact pattern. So it is not just that you learn to get better at dealing with curve balls in general—which you do— but that you also get used to facing that particular pitcher (dealing with that particular issue) in a way that makes you more likely to be successful in the future.

Taking Notes

I ban laptops in my first year class because they tend to turn students into passive stenographers rather than active thinkers (putting entirely aside the students who fall prey to web surfing during class). Beware if you find yourself simply typing or writing down everything that the professor and your classmates say. You can't write down what someone else is saying and think at the same time.

Students defending the "stenography approach" tell me that they will think about what is being said later.   Really?   Even assuming that you have the time (which you won't) to reread your inevitably partial and sometimes cryptic notes and recreate the entire class discussion in your mind, will you really be willing or able to think hard about these questions after the class has ended? That would be like not swinging the bat at batting practice but going home and swinging the bat in your living room at imaginary pitches that you remember being thrown.

So the time to think about the rule that is being discussed in class is right there and then as it is being discussed. That means that you should spend way more time thinking—or even better speaking—in class than taking notes.

The Ten Minutes After Class

The single most inefficient thing that most law students do (not just first years mind you) is that they spend more time taking notes before class and during class than after class.   This is woefully inefficient and ineffective. The best time to take notes is *after class*.   If you have stayed engaged in the discussion you should have a much better idea about the main points covered after the class than during it.   Odds are that a few things will seem really clear, and you will have a few questions about things that you don't fully understand.   TAKE TEN MINUTES SOON AFTER EACH CLASS AND WRITE DOWN BOTH THE MAIN POINTS YOU LEARNED AND THE QUESTIONS THAT REMAIN! These notes will be the truly valuable ones that you will use when you begin putting together your outline. If you follow this habit you will be ridiculously happy with yourself when you do sit down to outline the course. If you don't spend ten minutes after each class writing down these main points and questions you will kick yourself as you spend hours later in the semester trying to remember what was so clear right after the class ended.

Reading Cases

Before you can apply a rule to new hypothetical cases you have to first come up a working understanding of what the rule says. In law school you learn the most important rules by reading excerpts from cases that formulated or adopted those rules. Learning to distill the rule (or "holding") from the case is a key skill.

Reading cases is where the rubber first hits the road for most first year law students. The actual legal decisions excerpted in law school textbooks were not written for student consumption. They are the real thing and are primarily intended for lawyers. There are literally entire books written about how to read a legal decision, and I don't even have the space in a short guide such as this to devote a chapter to it. Doubtless your professors in the first semester will spend a fair bit of time talking about this critical legal skill. In the pages that follow I will give a quick summary of the standard approach to case reading, offer a more user-friendly way of covering the same points, and describe at some length the key step that many first year law students skip in their preparation for class.

A Tale of Three Stories

A published criminal case really contains three different stories interwoven together. You need to understand all three in order to be able to make arguments about what the case means. Separating out these three stories as you read will help you keep things straight.

1. *The legal story of what happened during the trial phase of the case.* This is often where appellate opinion begins. What happened in the trial court? What was the defendant charged with? What motions and objections were made by the parties, and what decisions were made by the trial judge? What did the jury decide? What issues did the parties raise in the appeal? This story is where you will find the *procedural posture* and the *issue* described.

2. *The factual story of what happened before the case ever came to court.* What was the evidence that a crime was or was not committed? Who did and said what? These are what we refer to as the *facts* of the case. Usually this story will be taken from the testimony that was offered at trial, but often the judge will write the facts in story form. Instead of saying that "Witness A said this" and "Witness B said that" the appellate court will instead say something like "the facts of the case are these" while noting important points of dispute.

3. *The legal story of how this case fits into the existing law.* No one really writes on a blank slate anymore because there is nothing (completely) new under the sun. So the appellate justice must describe how the case at hand fits into the law as it already exists. This often means describing earlier cases that are similar enough to be considered *precedents*. Whenever possible an appellate court will decide the present case in a way that is consistent with the earlier cases. But often cases

are chosen for a textbook because they deal with novel issues that have not already been decided. This means that the appellate court must reason about what would be the best way of deciding the new issue. All of this constitutes the court's *reasoning*. After reasoning through the issues raised the appellate court will decide the present case by articulating a rule that resolves the issue. This decision and rule constitute the holding of the case.

So the key to understanding a case is breaking it down into its component parts.

1. The Procedural Posture: how the case came to be before the appellate court.

2. The Issue: the specific question or questions the appellate court is asked to address.

3. The Facts: the version(s) of what happened that was presented at trial.

4. The Reasoning: how the appellate court thought about the issue(s) raised and the reasons given for deciding things the way they did.

5. The Holding: the rule that the court announces to decide the issue raised.

Often professors will actually frame their questions in class in terms of these components: asking a student to begin with the facts, issue, and procedural posture and then asking about the holding and reasoning.

Procedural Posture and Issue

The decisions you read in your textbook will largely be appellate decisions, not decisions written by the judge who presided over the trial. An appeal must raise a particular issue or set of issues. A lawyer can't simply appeal on the ground that "the judge made a mistake" or "the verdict is unfair" or "the law is wrong." The lawyer must identify a particular mistake that was made and articulate the particular issue raised by the mistake. The nature of the mistake raised is called the procedural posture. Common procedural postures in criminal cases will be discussed in the next chapter. For example, one common procedural posture in criminal cases is that the judge makes a mistake in instructing the jury on the law they are to apply to the facts of the case. The particular issue raised by the mistake varies greatly. A failure to state in a jury instruction in a first degree murder case that premeditation and deliberation requires cool reason undisturbed by hot blood, for example, might raise an issue in a particular jurisdiction about the proper definition of premeditation and deliberation.

The Facts of the Case

Most first year law students underestimate the importance of the facts. They assume that they are merely background for the statement of the rule. In reality the facts of the case shape and limit the meaning and scope of the case's holding. Not all of the facts of the case are essential to the holding, but some of them are. Deciding which is which determines the scope of the holding and requires that you consider the reasoning of the court.

The Reasoning

The reasoning of the case is simply the part of the opinion that describes why the court ruled as it did. A close reading of the reasoning should provide some evidence of how narrowly or broadly the court intended the holding to apply to future cases.

The Holding of the Case

This is the bottom line. What the court "holds" is the rule that the court uses to decide the case. Sometimes a court will literally state "this court holds . . . " Other times the court won't identify the holding so explicitly. Either way you cannot really understand the holding of a case without considering the procedural posture, issue, facts, and reasoning of the decision.

The hardest part of reading a case is figuring out the holding. What makes it so hard is that there is usually more than one possible answer. Specifically there are usually broad and narrow ways to read the holding of a case. Broad holdings are more general statements that apply to many more future cases. Narrow holdings are more tied to the particular facts of the case before the court and will apply only to future cases sharing those particular facts. There are often alternate ways of reading the same case.

The difference between these different versions of a case's holding usually lie in deciding which of the facts of the case are considered to be *material* (necessary) to the result. A narrower holding will include more facts; a broader holding will include less facts; alternate holdings will include different facts. Reading the court's *reasoning* in light of the *facts of the case* is the key to generating arguments for and against different versions of the holding.

Example: The Holding of the **Dudley and Stephens** _Case_

Let's use a case commonly used in criminal law textbooks to illustrate this process. The case of _Regina v. Dudley and Stephens_ involved killing and cannibalism on the high seas. Four English sailors were marooned in a lifeboat with almost no food and water. They all faced imminent death from dehydration and starvation, but one, a cabin boy by the name of Parker, was weaker and much closer to dying than all the others. Dudley initially proposed that they all draw lots with the understanding that the loser would be killed and eaten by the rest, the idea being that it would be better for one to die than for all to perish. No lots were drawn though and subsequently Dudley decided with Stephens' agreement to kill the ailing Parker. They all then feasted on Parker and survived as a result until rescue a few days later.

The procedural posture of the case was that of a special verdict, which is too unusual to merit discussion. The issue raised though was simple. Was the killing of one innocent man to save the lives of three others justified under the criminal law doctrine of necessity as the lesser of two evils, or were Dudley and Stephens simply guilty of murder. The court decided that Dudley and Stephens were guilty of murder.

A broad holding from the Dudley and Stephens case would be that one may not take an innocent human life to save one's own or that of another person. A narrower holding from the case would be that one may not take an innocent human live to save your own life or that of another _in the absence of a fair method of selecting the person to be sacrificed._ Note that the narrower holding treats as material to the holding the additional fact that the sailors never drew lots but simply killed the person who was weakest and nearest death. We will return to Dudley and Stephens a bit later to discuss how to argue for and against each holding.

Anticipating Hypothetical Questions

Your most important job is to come to class aware of alternate readings of the holding of the case and prepared to make arguments for and against each. The most efficient and effective way to do this is to apply the rule the court states to a range of hypothetical cases. I call this "playing with the holding." It is the step that most students skip in favor of writing ever more detailed notes about the case. Well, the facts of the case you read will not actually be tested on the exam. What will be tested on the exam will be your ability to apply the rule illustrated by the case to *different facts*. So doesn't it make more sense to use your class preparation and class discussion time doing the same?

Playing with the holding is essential to *really* understanding what the case says and is the best way to prepare for the hypothetical questions that the professor will throw at the class. Coming up with the hypotheticals will force you to identify things about the holding that you find ambiguous. Coming up with answers to those hypothetical questions will lead you to read back through the facts and reasoning of the case with a sharper eye.

Bouncing back and forth between these hypotheticals and the text of the case will help you achieve three important goals as a law student. First, it will focus you on key aspects of what you have read in a way that will better enable you to answer tough questions from your professor. Second, it will help you clarify what you don't understand and therefor need to figure out about the rule. Third, it will actually begin the process of burning the rule into your brain in a way that will allow you to recognize a related issue when it is buried in an unfamiliar fact pattern on the exam.

Doing this will also help you to learn to think like a lawyer. Lawyers ask themselves hypothetical questions when they read a case because they know that a judge will ask them hypothetical questions about any rule that they argue is the holding of the case. More generally, reading cases in this way will develop your ability to think systematically, argue both sides of an issue, and reconcile competing interests and perspectives.

Dudley and Stephens *Revisited*

What sorts of hypotheticals might your law school professor ask about the Dudley and Stephens case, and how might you argue for and against them? What if the sailors had drawn lots, and the sailor killed had drawn the short straw? Would that be murder, or would it then come within the defense of necessity? One would look to the court's reasoning for answers, of course. Well, in some passages the court speaks eloquently of the sanctity of innocent life. Those passages support a broad holding that innocent life cannot be taken even to save a greater number of lives. In other passages, however, the court stresses the fact that lots were never drawn and observes that no legitimate reason existed to kill the boy as opposed to any of the other sailors. These passages support the narrower holding that one cannot kill an innocent life out of legal necessity in the absence of a fair method of selection.

Yet a different hypothetical would take the discussion in a somewhat different direction. What if the person killed had agreed to be killed—had offered himself up in sacrifice to save his shipmates? One would have to at this point resort to law outside the text of the case, to the rule that one cannot ordinarily legally consent to one's own murder. Does that rule apply to a case where all involved will die if someone does not consent? Is the difference between one person agreeing to die and all persons agreeing to take a one in four chance of being killed by drawing lots one of degree rather than one of kind? Little in the reasoning of the court's decision bears upon such a question, so arguments for and against finding murder in such a scenario would resort to general philosophical arguments about the purpose of punishment or policy arguments grounded in the sociological conditions (discussed in a later chapter).

Briefing a Case

First year law students are often well advised to prepare written "briefs" of a case. A brief is simply a document that states the procedural posture, issue, facts, holding and reasoning of the case in clear, concise language under separate labeled headings. Writing legal briefs force students unfamiliar with legal case reading to break each decision into its basic components.

Written case briefs are like training wheels on a bicycle. Most people need them to start with but everyone eventually dispenses with them in order to go faster and with less effort. After you have written a few dozen of them the components of a legal case will become more familiar, and you will start to simply "book brief," which means highlighting the key passages and writing things in the margin to label and explain the component parts of the decision.

Canned Briefs

Some students fall into the trap of relying solely on "canned briefs" that they obtain for commercial publishers or from other students to get through being called upon in class. This is a huge mistake. Using a brief written by someone else will not burn anything new into your brain, will not develop your ability to spot the issues involved in the case on the exam, and will do nothing to help you learn how to read a case in the future. It also will only allow you to answer cursory questions by your professor. If you have a day when you simply cannot get the reading done and are afraid of being called upon you should simply ask your professor for a pass.

How to Use Your Law School Textbook

The focus thus far in terms of class preparation has been upon case reading, but most law school textbooks contain more than simply edited cases. Introductory and summarizing material is usually included although far less than most law students would like to see. More typically the edited cases—which are generally referred to as principal cases—are followed by a series of numbered notes.

What confuses many law students is that these notes serve different purposes, and the purposes can vary from case to case. Some of these notes present hypothetical cases to which the rule of the principal case read should be applied. Others introduce summaries of cases that decided a similar issue in a different way. Still others seek to place the principal case into a larger context. For example, while often a principal case represents the majority approach sometimes a case is chosen for inclusion in a textbook because it is a particularly thoughtful discussion of the minority approach to a key issue, a circumstance that a contextual note would ordinarily point out. Finally, some notes introduce ideas from scholarly sources in order to broaden and extend the discussion of the issue raised. A note following the Dudley and Stephens case might describe the remaining elements of the legal defense of necessity that were not raised or discussed in the case.

Where a textbook fails to properly contextualize the case discussed, the professor will often briefly describe how the case fits into the larger picture at the conclusion of the class discussion of the case. Such mini-lectures are one occasion when a law student should most definitely write down what the professor says.

Some Good News: It Gets Easier

All of this gets easier with practice. It really does. Reading cases, preparing for class, outlining a course in preparation for the exam—every single one of these tasks that you find to be difficult and time consuming will become easier and quicker to perform with time.

Think about driving a car. If you drove to school this morning you probably performed a number of complex mental operations with little conscious effort. Yet when you first started to drive you had to think consciously about every single one (brake, turn signal, look both ways, accelerate, turn the steering wheel, straighten the steering wheel, etc.). Believe it or not you will learn to read cases, think up hypotheticals and generate arguments on both sides of an issue almost unconsciously. (When that happens, please approach a first year law student at your school and tell them "it really does get easier after a while.")

Here is the thing though. It does not get easier simply with the passage of time. You won't learn how to read a case faster and better unless you work at it. But if you do keep trying, you will get better. This is not rocket science, but to succeed you do need to practice. Like baseball!

A General Piece of Advice: Don't Kid Yourself but Don't Kill Yourself Working Either

Now that you have a clearer idea of what succeeding in law school involves, allow me to offer two pieces of gratuitous "lifestyle" advice, even though they may seem somewhat contradictory.

First, don't kid yourself. You may have to work harder at law school than you have in a very long time (or ever), both in terms of how long you work and in terms of how hard you work. Mastering these new skills as you learn the law will take a lot of time. It will also take a lot of focus as you work. We are talking about quality hours of concentrated reading, thinking, and writing.

So don't kid yourself into thinking that some temporary lifestyle changes might not be required. You may have to cut back on time with friends and other recreational activities because you really need to allow yourself to spend lots and lots of time figuring things out. You will be less stressed if you accept this fact of life going in (and if you make sure that your family and friends accept it as well).

The good news is that these cutbacks will not be permanent. Second semester will be easier than the first and the second year will be easier than the first year.

So you haven't signed your life away for three years. The first year and especially the first semester is the intellectual equivalent of "boot camp" though, so expect a haircut and lots of mental pushups. Don't worry though. You regular life will grow back. When boot camp is over.

My second piece of advice seems to contradict the first, but it really doesn't. Don't "kill yourself working." Unless you are a terminator robot sent from the future to study early 21st century American law you cannot work around the clock without food, rest, and some recreation for an entire year or even an entire semester. If you pretend you can, you will just crash and burn sometime mid-semester just when you need to kick it into high gear. Humans, unlike terminator robots, need to take care of themselves to function. They don't think well if they live on junk food, and caffeine for long periods of time with little sleep and no more exercise than walking back and forth between the classroom and the library. You can and will kick it up into high gear during exams. The bottom line is that a semester of law school is a marathon with a sprint at the end.

You will figure out the balance between not kidding yourself and not killing yourself. If you used to spend two hours chatting with friends every night or playing basketball, you are probably going to have to cut that down to thirty minutes or an hour. If you go out every night, you are probably going to get along with going out on the weekends. You can dial things back up once you get the hang of things. In the meantime your friends won't forget you, and your jump shot will come back with a little practice.

A Final Piece of Good News: Law School Is Worth the Work

"If the world were perfect it wouldn't be."

Yogi Berra

It is worth it. Really. There are times in many people's lives when they work really hard at something pointless just to get by. Law school is not that. It matters. You really will learn something special and valuable. You will change how you think in a way that makes the world a more interesting place and you a more valuable contributor to it.

And if you get through the first year of law school then the odds are huge that you will graduate from law school and that you will eventually become a lawyer. Being a lawyer can be a great thing. It is a job where you get to help people while doing interesting work and earning a good living.

Don't be fooled by all of those lawyer jokes. People make jokes about lawyers because they know they can't do without us and because we remind them of all of the conflicts and disputes that do need resolving, conflicts that sometimes reflect the dark side of people and society. Tell me, do you think that our society needs more or less people who are fair enough to see both sides of an argument, patient enough to think through all the angles of a difficult problem and reasonable enough to strike a balance between competing perspectives?

We do important work. We make agreements and resolve disputes and help keep society running in an orderly, humane and fair way. None of this works perfectly, but it wouldn't work at all without us. Doing what we do requires not just knowledge of the law, but the special set of skills that you work so hard to begin learning in your very first year of law school.

Grammar experts like to say that only Superman does good, and the rest of us do well. As a lawyer you can do both. So be happy! ☺

CHAPTER 2

An Overview of Criminal Law

Criminal Law should be your favorite subject in your first year of law school. I will admit that I am biased on this question. I love criminal law. I teach criminal law, write about criminal law and practiced criminal law before I began teaching. I have loved doing all three. Let me offer you three objective reasons though why criminal law should be your favorite 1L subject.

1. *Criminal Law involves something Familiar and Interesting.* We are not talking about something unfamiliar, such as transactions involving widgets or "springing future interests." Our society is fascinated with crime and punishment, and our media saturates us with depictions and descriptions of true and fictional crime. We all intuitively understand what crime is about—hurting people or messing with their stuff.

2. *Criminal Law involves Good and Evil.* Criminal law forces us to wrestle with how we define evil, and how we differentiate between different degrees of

evil. This provides criminal law with an organizing theme that is both familiar and inherently interesting.

3. *Criminal Law enjoys a Coherent Structure.* You can sum up the basic structure of the criminal law in one sentence (which I will give you in the very next section). You can then use this sentence to organize your study of any criminal law doctrine and to analyze any criminal law problem. Not to say that the criminal law is simple. It will take you an entire semester to learn all the doctrines necessary to fully understand what this sentence means. But the structure of the criminal law brings a welcome order to its complexity. This order is particularly valuable to students in their first year of legal study.

The Structure of the Criminal Law

Here is the sentence that sums up the basic structure of the criminal law. This sentence tells you what criminal liability requires.

The Guilty Hand, moved by the Guilty Mind, under the required Circumstances that sometimes causes a bad Result in the absence of a Justification or Excuse.

Quite a mouthful I admit, but it reflects a structure that is really beautiful in its simplicity. Every word in this sentence does a lot of work, but the sentence will work for you on any criminal law case or question if you really learn what it means. Let's break it down into fundamental parts. In doing so we will preview some important concepts that we will develop more fully later.

The Guilty Hand

This phrase refers to the "doing part" of a crime. All crimes require some sort of action. There is no such thing as a "thought crime," a crime that you can commit by thinking bad thoughts. You might have the guiltiest mental state imaginable ("I so want to kill him!"), but if you do not do what the crime requires you cannot be guilty. No conduct, no criminal liability.

The Guilty Mind

This phrase refers to the mental state requirement of a crime. Oliver Wendell Holmes famously referred to the importance of mental states when he observed that "even a dog knows the difference between being tripped over and kicked." The criminal law relies heavily on the definitions of different mental states to determine whether a crime has occurred at all and to distinguish more serious from less serious crime. Even if the defendant performs the conduct required for the crime, she will not be guilty if she does not perform that conduct with the required mental state.

Moved By

This phrase refers to the concurrence requirement. With very few exceptions, the guilty mind must exist at the moment that the conduct is performed. Moreover, the guilty mind must *move* the guilty hand in the sense that the conduct must be caused or generated by the required mental state. So wishing someone dead at the moment you bump into him and knock him off a cliff would not be murder if the bump was neither intentional nor extremely reckless.

The Required Circumstances

This phrase refers to what is more formally described as the "attendant circumstances" of a crime. Some crimes—certainly not all—require certain circumstances to exist in order for the crime to take place. For example, some criminal statutes make it a special crime to do certain things on or near a school where children attend. These laws are typically passed to give special protection to children by making what is already a crime—selling illegal drugs for example—a more serious crime within some specified distance of a school. The language of the statute requiring that the sale of drugs take place within a certain number of yards of a school is an attendant circumstance.

Example: The Case of the Burgling Butt

Before we go any further, let's work through an example involving the first four elements of our sentence. We will discuss burglary at greater length later, but a simplified statement of the elements of burglary follows.

Breaking and

Entering

A Dwelling

Of Another

At Night

With the Intent to commit a Felony or Larceny therein

Assume that one Friday night when you are leaving your apartment to go out, you notice that your next door neighbor appears to have left the door to his apartment slightly ajar. He is a bit absent minded and has done this before. Usually you just pull the door closed for him. But not this night. This night you are feeling curious, dare I say snoopy. You decide that you are going to sneak into his apartment and look around. You try to slip through the opening of the door without touching it, but your butt hits the door as you go through, and it swings open a bit more. You are sitting on his couch, browsing through his magazines when you see a beautiful diamond ring on his coffee table. Deciding to steal it, you grab the ring and leave his apartment.

Have you committed the crime of burglary? Well to answer that question you would need to know a little more about how the criminal law defines some of the elements. The conduct required is breaking and entering. The attendant circumstances are that the structure entered must be a dwelling of another, and the entry must be accomplished at night. Well, we have the entry of a dwelling of another at night. Is the element of breaking present though? As we will learn, many jurisdictions define a breaking to include enlargement of any opening. So when your butt hit the door, you performed a breaking. So we have the guilty hand (or in this case the guilty butt), and we have the required circumstances. What about the mental state?

Here is where things get really interesting. Burglary requires that you break and enter with the intent to commit a felony or larceny therein. Larceny is essentially stealing, so you supplied the required guilty mind when you decided to steal the ring. Nonetheless, the crime of burglary did not occur on these facts. What is missing? The concurrence requirement. At the moment you broke and entered, you did not intend to steal anything. Your guilty butt was not moved by the required guilty mind of a felon or a thief. You only decided to steal later on after the conduct that constitutes burglary was complete.

Does this mean you committed no crime? Of course not. You committed criminal trespass and larceny, so you are a trespasser and a thief but not a burglar because of the absence of concurrence between the guilty hand and the guilty mind.

Concurrence also works in the opposite direction. Assume this time that you saw the ring through a window while walking by and decided then and there that you would enter the apartment in order to steal it. In this case your guilty butt is moved by the required guilty mind of a thief. But this time you change your mind after you have entered the apartment. You say to yourself, "hey, I am a law student; I can't go around stealing from my neighbor's apartment." Have you committed the crime of burglary? Yes! You committed the crime of burglary when your guilty butt hit the door with the concurrent larcenous intent required. The fact that you did not go through with the larceny does not "undo" the burglary you already committed.

Now, let's return to the other elements of our simple sentence.

Sometimes Causing a Bad Result

"Sometimes" does not sound very legal. However, the vast majority of crimes do not require results. For example, the crime of larceny requires the conduct of taking the property of another. Taking, in turn, requires you to move the property at least some slight distance. That movement is not thought to be a result, but part of the "doing part of the offense. What then does the criminal law consider to be a result? Homicide crimes provide easy examples.

Homicide, by definition, involves the killing of a human being. Killing is conduct causing death. If death does not result from the conduct, then no homicide takes place. If you took a shot at me with a high powered rifle intending to kill me but missed, you could not be guilty of murder. While you had the guilty hand (trigger finger in this case) and the guilty mind (an intent to kill) required for murder, you did not have the bad result (death of a human being) that murder and all other homicide crimes require. Attempted murder? Yes, but attempted murder is not considered a result crime for the very reason that the result of death is not required.

If the crime does require a result, two things must exist. First, the result must occur. In the example given, I must die. Second, the bad result must have been caused by the guilty hand. Imagine now that you did shoot me with a high powered rifle from a great distance with the intent to kill, but that during the time it took the bullet to travel towards my head I was struck by lightning and died instantaneously. You would not be guilty of murder because the bullet you launched entered the brain of a corpse. The intended result of my death occurred, but it was not caused by your conduct. Again, you would be guilty only of attempted murder. The bottom line is that causation is an issue in criminal law only in those cases where the crimes involved require results.

All first year criminal law courses spend a lot of time studying homicide, so you would be forgiven for thinking that result crimes are common. It bears emphasis that the vast majority of crimes do not require results although sometimes the distinction is not always obvious to first year law students. Assault with intent to inflict serious injury is not a result crime, for example. It requires you to assault someone with the intent to seriously injure them. The crime of assault *inflicting* serious bodily injury, on the other hand, does require the result of serious bodily injury to have been caused by the assault.

In the Absence of a Justification or an Excuse

It bears emphasis that if any one thing in our sentence up to this point is missing, that omission constitutes a defense. If you lack the guilty hand *or* the guilty mind *or* the attendant circumstances *or* causation of the required result, then you are not guilty of the crime. Certain general defenses may preclude criminal liability even if all elements of the crime are otherwise present. These general defenses are divided into two different categories: justifications and excuses.

The clearest example of a justification is self-defense. Assume you shot someone in the head with the intent to kill him and that he died as a result. Ordinarily that would be murder, but in this case the reason you shot the person was because he was charging at you with a whirring chain saw, screaming that he was going to cut you in half. You did not need to read this book to realize that intentionally killing the chain saw attacker would be justified on the grounds of self-defense. No crime occurs because you were justified in what you did.

Justifications are limited to those defenses where society either tolerates or approves of certain behavior that would otherwise be a crime. Society cheers when you kill the chain saw attacker because society is glad that you defended yourself. When you can imagine society clapping in the background, the defense involved is always a justification.

Excuses, on the other hand, involve very different types of defenses. The clearest example of an excuse defense is insanity. Let's say that you shoot someone in the head intending to kill him because you believe him to be the vanguard of an alien invasion bent on exterminating the human race. You believe this because you suffer from paranoid schizophrenia. The person you shoot is not, of course, an alien invader. You would be excused from criminal responsibility for what would otherwise be murder on the grounds that you were legally insane at the time of the killing. Excuses, unlike justifications, do not involve conduct that society approves of or tolerates. No one claps when you kill an innocent person as a result of your mental illness. Excuse defenses are essentially concessions to human frailties. Excuses relieve you from criminal responsibility even though your conduct was not justified.

Note the repeated emphasis on *criminal* responsibility. An insane killer could still be civilly responsible for his actions. In fact, people who commit serious violent acts as the result of insanity are often involuntarily committed to mental institutions under *civil* statutes. The difference between civil and criminal responsibility will be something that we talk more about when we discuss the purposes of criminal punishment later.

So once you have checked to see whether any justifications or excuses apply, you are done with your criminal law analysis. As promised, the whole of criminal law fits in one, easy to remember, sentence, but it will take the rest of this book and an entire semester of your time to really learn how to use that sentence.

Before we move into the substance of the criminal law itself, however, there are a couple of preliminary matters that we will cover in the next few chapters. These preliminary matters are often the subject of early chapters in criminal law textbooks because they provide necessary background. First, we need to learn a few things about criminal procedure. Second, we need to understand the sources of the criminal law that you will study in the course. Third, we need to explore the different philosophies of punishment that have shaped the development and interpretation of the criminal law.

CHAPTER 3

The Criminal Process

This chapter just provides background, necessary background to be sure but only background. You will not be tested in a first year criminal law class on criminal procedure. Your first year criminal law course covers the *substantive criminal law,* which concerns the definition of crimes and defenses. Still, understanding something about criminal procedure will be necessary to understanding the substantive criminal law you will be reading about in the cases that you study. This short chapter will give you the minimum you need to know to understand what you read in your textbook and what you discuss in your class.

From Investigation Through Trial

The criminal process begins with the investigation of crime by the police. That usually culminates in an arrest at some point. After a person is arrested (but occasionally before), a formal document specifying what crimes the person is accused of committing is filed in court. This document can be called different things: criminal charges, a criminal complaint, an information, an indictment.

The filing of that document initiates formal courtroom proceedings against the person charged, who is called the defendant. These proceedings adjudicate the defendant's guilt or innocence of the charges filed. The central phase of these proceedings is the trial. At the trial the prosecution must present the evidence supporting the charges against the defendant. The defendant has a right to confront the evidence against him. He can do this by making legal objections to the introduction of the evidence based on the rules of evidence (which you usually will not study until your second year of law school). He can also cross-examine the witnesses who testify against him. The defendant also has the right to present evidence in his defense. He can call witnesses to testify on his behalf, seek to introduce documents or tangible things to support his defense, or even testify himself. His evidence and witnesses, of course, are also subject to objections and cross-examination by the prosecution.

The defendant is presumed innocent until proven guilty. This means that the prosecution has the burden of proof on all elements of each charge. The defendant does not have to produce any evidence in order to be entitled to be found not guilty (which is called an acquittal.) The prosecutor must prove each element of a crime beyond a reasonable doubt. The beyond a reasonable doubt standard is the highest legal standard of proof. A preponderance of the evidence standard is the standard of proof required in a civil law suit. That requires the party with the burden of proof to prove that their case is "more probable than not," a probability of slightly over 50%. Clear and convincing evidence is higher than preponderance of the evidence and is the standard commonly used when family members wish to withdraw life support from a comatose relative. The beyond a reasonable doubt standard, although never expressed in percentage terms, is understood to be even higher than clear and convincing evidence.

The defendant also has a right against self-incrimination. This means that the prosecutor cannot call him to the stand and force him to answer questions. The prosecutor cannot even comment in any way on a defendant's decision not to testify. (Such as "don't you think he would have testified if he had a good explanation for the blood on his hands?") If the defendant does not testify the judge will instruct the jury not to consider this as evidence of either guilt or innocence.

The jury is the finder of fact in most criminal trials. The judge instructs the jury on the law, and the jury applies the law to the facts. In a criminal case this means that the judge defines the elements of the crime and the elements of any applicable defenses for the jury. The jury then decides whether the defendant has been proven guilty of the crimes charged beyond a reasonable doubt. When a jury returns a verdict of not guilty they are not declaring that they have found the defendant to be innocent. They have decided that the prosecution has not proven the defendant guilty beyond a reasonable doubt.

The Appellate Process

After a trial is concluded, either side may appeal the case to a court of appeals (known as an appellate court), but the grounds for appeal are very limited. Courts of appeals do not hear evidence or conduct trials. No witnesses are called. Rather the appellate court reviews the transcript of the trial, documents admitted into evidence at trial and other relevant court documents. The appellate court may allow the attorneys a brief opportunity to argue orally before them, but their decision is based largely on the written record of the trial and the written arguments (called "briefs") of the lawyers arguing the appeal.

Generally speaking, appellate courts do not review questions of fact; they review questions of law. For example, they generally will not second guess a jury's decision to believe or not believe a certain witness because the system places more trust in the jury's ability to evaluate the witness's live testimony than in an appellate judge's ability to assess credibility based on reading a transcript.

When an appellate court considers an appeal it does not review the entire record of the proceedings looking for any possible legal error. Rather it requires the party appealing to identify specific legal issues that the appellate court should consider. The appealing party will allege that the judge below made an error of law, and this will be the issue that the appellate court will consider.

Virtually all of the cases that you read in your textbook will be appellate decisions written by these appellate judges who read transcripts and briefs but who hear no live testimony. This is key to understanding the nature of the appellate decisions they write. They are not retrying the case based on their review of the documents. Rather they are trying to determine whether the law was followed.

Common Procedural Postures

The specific type of legal error raised in the appeal is often referred to as the "procedural posture" of the case. Understanding the most common procedural postures of criminal cases on appeal will help you better learn the substantive criminal law from these appellate cases.

Errors in Jury Instructions

This type of issue is a favorite for the textbook authors who select cases for inclusion in a textbook because jury instructions frame the issue of substantive law so clearly for the reader. Since the jury relies completely on the judge to correctly define the crime and the applicable defenses a jury instruction error poisons the entire process. Often it is only when judges wrestle with how to express a legal concept to a jury that we really learn what that legal concept means. Jury instructions are where the rubber hits the road so to speak.

Motions to Dismiss Before Trial

A motion to dismiss before the trial even begins is usually directed at the complaint or other charging document filed by the prosecutor. One reason to require the filing of such a document is to force the prosecutor to give the defendant fair notice of what he is being accused of. Prosecutors are required not just to give the defendant a list of the crimes he is accused of committing but a series of fairly specific allegations spelling out the specific things that the defendant did and the specific laws that were broken. A failure to be sufficiently specific or a failure to correctly state the law results in dismissal of the complaint. These motions to dismiss do not challenge the truth of the charge. Such a motion argues that even if every fact alleged in the complaint is true usually that the defendant is not guilty as a matter of law.

Motions to Dismiss During Trial and Challenges to Sufficiency of the Evidence

Motions to dismiss during trial are very different matters altogether. Evidence has been produced, and usually the defendant is moving to dismiss a charge on the grounds that *no reasonable juror could find this charge to have been proved beyond a reasonable doubt as a matter of law.* Sometimes these motions are made before the jury even begins to deliberate on the rationale that the jury should not even get a chance to make the mistake of returning a verdict that is not supported by the evidence. Sometimes these motions are made after a jury returns a verdict of guilty arguing in effect that the jury failed to see that the evidence of guilt was *insufficient as a matter of law*.   Such motions are a very limited form of second-guessing of the jury by the trial judge. These motions must argue that *no reasonable juror* could have found the defendant guilty even if one gave the prosecution the benefit of every reasonable inference that could be drawn in its favor.

Evidentiary Rulings

These tend to be the least common procedural postures in criminal law textbook cases because the law of evidence is itself quite complicated and the subject of an entirely different course. Sometimes though the evidentiary issue is straightforward because it flows directly from a mistaken interpretation of the substantive criminal law.   Relevance, for example, is a fundamental requirement for admissible evidence. If evidence is not relevant to an element of the criminal charge in the case then it should not be admitted. If the judge gets the definition of the legal element of the charge wrong this error will sometimes manifest itself in a decision to admit or not to admit a particular piece of evidence on relevance grounds.

Appeals by the Prosecution

The prosecution as well as the defense gets to appeal legal errors. Sometimes a jury instruction error will hurt the prosecution.   Sometimes a trial judge will grant a motion to dismiss that she should not have granted. Sometimes a trial judge will refuse to admit a piece of evidence that should have been admitted that helps the prosecution.   Prosecutors can appeal these types of error.

There is one type of error that a prosecutor cannot appeal, however. As mentioned above a defendant can challenge the sufficiency of the evidence supporting a jury's finding of guilty by arguing that no reasonable juror could have so found even if you give the prosecution the benefit of all inferences that could be reasonably drawn in their favor. A prosecutor, however, cannot challenge an *acquittal* on the grounds that no reasonable juror could have failed to return a verdict of guilty. If successful, such an appeal would give the prosecution a second chance to prove the defendant guilty. Such a second bite at the apple violates the double jeopardy clause of the Fifth Amendment to the U.S. Constitution. The double jeopardy clause prohibits a sovereign (government) from putting a person on trial twice for the same offense. It does not apply to juries that fail to reach a verdict ("hung juries") but does apply whenever a verdict is returned. This clause was written into the Constitution's bill of rights to limit government power. Without it the government could try people again and again until they found a jury that was willing to find the defendant guilty. Being subject to successive trials for the same offense was thought to be an abuse of government power.

So prosecutors cannot appeal an acquittal on the grounds that the evidence of guilt was overwhelming. The jury gets the last word against the prosecutor (but not against the defendant.)

Jury Nullification

An incident of the double jeopardy clause's prohibition on trying someone twice for the same offense is that a jury has the power—although not the right—to effectively ignore the law in returning a verdict of not guilty. If the jury votes not guilty there is nothing the prosecutor or the judge can do to challenge the jury's decision that the crime was not proved beyond a reasonable doubt *even if the prosecution has presented absolutely overwhelming and indisputable evidence.*

Does this ever happen? Yes. Why would a jury do such a thing? Usually because they disagree with the law that the defendant has been accused of breaking. For this reason this practice is called "jury nullification" because the jury is in effect nullifying the law that the prosecution seeks to enforce.

Is jury nullification a good or a bad thing? That may depend on what you think of the law being broken. Before the civil war, juries in northern states would sometimes refuse to convict people who helped escaped slaves despite overwhelming evidence of guilt. On the other hand, southern juries during the civil rights movement in the fifties sometimes refused to convict white supremacists of violent crimes against civil rights workers despite equally overwhelming evidence of guilt.

The position of the law is that jury nullification is an inevitable power of juries given the existence of the double jeopardy clause but that it is not a right of juries. For this reason, judges will not allow defense counsel to inform juries of their power to ignore the law if they wish to return a verdict of not guilty.

Note that jury nullification is a "one-way-ratchet" in that it benefits only the defense. A jury verdict which convicts despite overwhelming evidence of innocence could be challenged on sufficiency of the evidence grounds by the defense as described above.

The power of the jury to nullify the law provides an important check on the power of the legislature to declare conduct criminal. If the legislature gets too far out of touch with "the conscience of the community," then prosecutors will be unable to obtain convictions and the overall legitimacy of the criminal law will suffer as a result.

Prosecutorial Discretion and Plea Bargaining

One of the most notable aspects of our system of criminal justice is the enormous discretion exercised by prosecutors. The principal source of that power is the prosecutor's control over the criminal complaint or other charging document that begins the courtroom phase of the criminal justice process. No judge or private party can tell a prosecutor which defendants to charge and which crimes to charge the defendants with. As mentioned above, the complaint must allege acts that the legislature has declared to be criminal. Criminal statutes are very broad though, and prosecutors could theoretically charge a lot more people with a lot more crimes than they do or can, given the limited resources that exist for the prosecution of crime.

This control over the complaint continues throughout the criminal process. You are probably aware of the practice of plea bargaining. One common form of plea bargaining is when a defendant pleads guilty to a reduced charge. It is solely in the power of the prosecutor to reduce the charge stated in the complaint before trial. If the prosecutor does not wish to offer a reduced charge then the defendant must take his chances by going to trial and see if either the judge or the jury find him not guilty of some or all of the charges stated in the complaint, or of a lesser charge.

The vast majority of criminal cases are plea-bargained and relatively few go to trial. The nature of the plea bargains offered and accepted, however, turn to some degree on the parties' predictions of what would happen at trial. So an understanding of how the criminal law applies to a set of facts remains essential.

Sentencing

Sentencing, in contrast, has traditionally been the province of the judge, not the prosecutor. If a defendant is found guilty the judge will listen to argument and evidence from both the prosecutor and the defense as to what the appropriate sentence should be. The sentencing range for a criminal offense is defined by the legislature, and the judge has discretion to sentence the defendant anywhere within that range.

Legislatures in many jurisdictions have made sentencing much more determinate in the last few decades. A determinate sentencing system is one in which the charge for which you are convicted—usually in combination with any prior criminal record the defendant has—narrowly defines the range of sentences that the judge may impose. For example, under indeterminate sentencing systems it might be up to the judge to sentence a first offender to anywhere from two to ten years for a given offense. A more determinate sentencing system might allow a range of only five to seven years for the same crime.

Determinate sentencing systems essentially transfer some of the judge's sentencing power to the prosecutor. Since the charge greatly determines the sentence and since most cases are plea-bargained, the judge's discretion at sentencing is much more limited, and the prosecutor's power to shape the sentence during plea bargaining much greater.

Exam Tip: Distinguishing One Crime from Another

Because of the role that the greater role that the crime you are charged with plays in determining your sentence it is more important than ever to be able to distinguish one crime from another. For this reason many criminal law exams will contain fact patterns which raise issues about several different possible crimes. This allows the professor to assess the all-important ability of the student to understand the differences between crimes as well as to understand that a single course of action might itself violate a number of different criminal laws.

Classroom Tip: Philosophies of Punishment

The enormous amount of discretion that prosecutors, judges and juries exercise in the criminal justice system makes it extremely important for lawyers to be able to make convincing arguments about the purpose of punishment. Every day prosecutors and defense lawyers in every criminal courtroom in the country make numerous arguments about the purpose of punishment as they argue for and against various plea bargains, verdicts, and sentences. They usually don't use fancy philosophical terms such as "retribution" or "deterrence." Instead they say things like "the defendant needs to get what's coming to him," or "he does not deserve to be found guilty of this" or "we need to send people a message about this sort of crime," and so on. So when your professor tries to engage you in class discussion in figuring out how these purposes of punishment shape the criminal law she is not indulging some sort of purely intellectual interest. She is trying to help you become comfortable with wielding the rhetorical weapons with which lawyers fight every day in the trenches of the criminal justice battlefield. In the process you will also learn to relate legal rules to "big picture" social concerns that shape every area of law. If you accept her invitation and throw yourself into these discussions you may find yourself better able to make these sorts of arguments, both on the exam and in practice.

Professional Ethics

One final bit of background needs to be discussed. All lawyers, including prosecutors and criminal defense lawyers, operate under rules of professional ethics. These rules guide and constrain how lawyers do their jobs. Like criminal procedure, professional ethics is the subject of an entire course of its own. Sometimes professors like to introduce the subject by integrating an ethical discussion into a discussion of a particular case or doctrine. Two recurring issues of professional ethics particular to criminal law are worth brief mention. One concerns prosecutors and the other criminal defense lawyers.

The criminal defense issue is a simple one that most people intuitively see. How can a lawyer defend someone of a crime whom they know to be guilty? Here an important difference emerges between criminal and civil cases. If the government truly has the burden of proving the defendant guilty of all elements of the charge beyond a reasonable doubt then a guilty defendant need never take the witness stand in order to challenge that burden. In a civil case, in contrast, one side can force the other side to testify at or before trial, so a clearly guilty (or "liable" in civil terminology) defendant has nowhere to hide.

If you accept that the prosecution should bear this burden in criminal cases then you must permit lawyers to defend people they know to be guilty. Criminal lawyers cannot put such people on the witness stand because guilty defendants will either perjure themselves or admit guilt. But the criminal lawyer can and must challenge the prosecution's evidence at trial in order to guarantee that the only people being convicted really have been proved guilty beyond a reasonable doubt.

The prosecution issue is less obvious but no less important. Are prosecutors partisans in an adversary system, or are they also public officials who have an obligation to seek justice? If a prosecutor thinks someone probably committed a crime but still has a reasonable doubt as to a defendant's guilt, should she dismiss the charge, or should she submit the evidence to a jury of twelve people and let them decide? In exercising her broad discretion should a prosecutor seek to get the greatest number of convictions for the most serious crimes possible, or should she exercise personal judgment about who really deserves what type of punishment? These questions have no simple answers.

Keeping the Background Separate from the Foreground

Some students are understandably intrigued by criminal procedure and professional ethics, but the first year criminal law student needs to remember that what is being taught and tested in this course is the substantive criminal law. The matters covered in this chapter provide important background for learning the substantive criminal law, but background is not foreground. Learn what you need about these subjects in order to learn the criminal law in your first year. You can explore them in depth when you take these courses later in law school.

CHAPTER 4

Statutory Interpretation and Sources of Law

Before you jump into the doctrines that define crimes and defenses you must understand a few things about the different sources of American criminal law. Most crimes and many defenses are defined by statute, but American criminal law was heavily influenced by the common law of crimes that developed originally in England. Building on this foundation, an American common law of crimes developed on its own. Over time though more and more jurisdictions defined the criminal law through statutes passed by legislatures. Many of these statutes followed the common law. In the middle of the last century, a rival approach developed in the form of a Model Penal Code, developed by the American Law Institute. Explaining the role that the common law, the Model Penal Code, and modern criminal statues play in American criminal law is one purpose of this chapter.

The interpretation of statutes is governed by some general principles that need explanation. Judges read statutes much more literally than they read common law cases. The judiciary is bound to give effect to the plain meaning of the legislature's chosen language. If the meaning of the statutory language is not plain, judges then consider legislative intent and purpose. Each of these concepts requires brief explanation.

Finally, the U.S. Constitution also provides some modest limits on what legislatures can do when they create crimes. Criminal statutes cannot be overly vague or overbroad. The state must provide people with clear notice of what is prohibited.

Again, don't mistake background for foreground, however. Few cases in a criminal law textbook turn on questions of legislative history, and constitutional principles play a very occasional role in substantive criminal law (although it plays a large part in criminal procedure). Still, one can't fully understand what judges do when they interpret criminal statutes without understanding the limits within which they must work.

Common Law

American criminal law was heavily influenced by the English common law. Crimes and defenses in England were originally developed and defined not by a legislature, but by judges. These common law judges would decide cases on the basis of general principles and long standing customs. The rules announced in these cases would be interpreted in light of the facts of the particular case before the judge, and the judge gave reasons for arriving at his decision. Over time, the English Parliament began to play a role by passing criminal statutes. English colonists brought both types of law with them to the American colonies.

The English common law provided the foundation for American criminal law, but it was a foundation that American judges and legislatures quickly began modifying. American judges issued their own common law decisions in criminal cases. State legislatures began defining crimes and defenses by statute more often.   By the end of the nineteenth century, most states had passed comprehensive criminal codes.

Today, virtually all crimes are defined by statutes in the fifty states. You might ask why we bother studying the common law. The common law remains hugely influential in interpreting criminal statutes.   Many states essentially reduced the common law's definitions of crimes and defenses to statutory form.   Many of the terms and concepts used in these statutes were not defined by statute. Nor surprisingly judges interpreting these statutes look to the common law meaning of these terms and concepts.   For example, a modern homicide statute might simply define voluntary manslaughter as a killing committed upon "adequate provocation." Provocation in the context of voluntary manslaughter was a common law concept, so it makes sense to assume that the legislature wanted the judge to be guided by common law principles and precedents in interpreting that terms.

So the common law guides the interpretation of many criminal statutes. But common law principles do not bind a judge in the way that a constitutional principle does.   As will be discussed, a constitutional principle is one that a legislature may not violate.   Common law principles are not constitutional principles. A legislature may decide that it does not like what the common law provides and decide to do things differently. As long as the legislature makes this intent clear in plain language, a judge will follow that command.

For example, as we will learn, a conspiracy at common law simply required a conspiratorial agreement, not any further action on the parts of any of the conspirators. A majority of American states did not like that rule, so their legislatures defined criminal conspiracy as requiring an overt act in furtherance of the conspiratorial agreement.

The Model Penal Code

Not surprisingly, people eventually asked whether it would make more sense to start over from scratch, rather than modify the common law approach on a piecemeal basis. Why use as our starting point an approach to punishment that was developed hundreds of years ago? So in the middle of the last century the American Law Institute developed the Model Penal Code.

The Model Penal Code ("MPC") proved hugely influential. Slightly over thirty states adopted substantial parts of it. These jurisdictions often refer to themselves as Model Penal Code jurisdictions, and they resort to the commentaries of the MPC or to cases from other MPC jurisdictions, not to common law cases when deciding difficult issues. Even in non-MPC jurisdictions, many courts and legislatures will follow the code's approach on some issues.

U.S. Constitutional Law and Federal Criminal Law

The Constitution of the United States and the decisions of the Supreme Court interpreting the constitution play a relatively minor role in a first year criminal law course. The constitution is the supreme law of the land, a "super law" that binds all other branches of government at both the state and local level. No legislative or executive branch of federal or state government may violate the constitution, and the U.S. Supreme Court is the final authority on what the U.S. Constitution means. Constitutional law plays a small role in criminal law because the constitution grants broad powers to legislatures at both the state and national level to define crimes. The constitution provides many more limits on the procedures under which crime is investigated and adjudicated, but those are topics for second and third year courses.

Federal criminal law plays an exceedingly minor role in a first year criminal law course. The vast majority of criminal law is state law, and the vast majority of criminal cases are brought in state courts. Federal criminal law is entirely statutory, and federal courts interpret these federal criminal statutes. Occasionally a textbook includes such a federal case, but the mere fact that the case is a federal one does not grant it any sort of authority over state court decisions on related issues. U.S. Supreme Court cases interpreting federal statues sometimes influence state courts confronting similar issues in interpreting state statutes, but state courts are not bound to follow the Supreme Court's lead on criminal law matters that are not constitutional in nature.

Study Tip: MPC v. Common Law

No jurisdiction has adopted the Model Penal Code line for line, yet most professors teach the Model Penal Code in their classes alongside the common law approach. They create in essence two parallel legal universes for the purposes of study and examination: common law jurisdictions and Model Penal Code jurisdictions. The reality of course is much more complex. The two approaches overlap in many areas, and many jurisdictions mix and match. Still, this somewhat fictional construct is a useful teaching strategy because it simplifies things for students.

The distinction between the MPC and the common law often plays a key role on exam questions. Sometimes a professor will ask students to analyze a fact pattern under both approaches, which requires a keen appreciation of the differences. Other times a professor will choose one approach or the other for a particular question, which requires the student to set completely aside the approach not chosen. Either way, pay particular attention to the differences and similarities between Model Penal Code and the common law.

Study Tip: Majority v. Minority Rules

There is yet another way in which scholars, judges and professors categorize legal rules. Major variations on fundamental issues have given rise to the concept of majority and minority rules. On important issues judges and—more often—the authors of scholarly treatises and writings will identify the leading rule as the majority rule and the alternate approach as the minority rule.

Again, this distinction oversimplifies reality although in a useful way. Lots of variation exists, but sometimes two main approaches emerge, and it makes sense to learn those two. So some professors will often make a point of teaching and testing knowledge of both the majority approach and the minority approach.

Often these categories will refer to the split between the common law approach and the Model Penal Code approach, but not always. Common law jurisdictions do not take a lock step approach to the criminal law. Indeed, the variations between the different common law jurisdictions are numerous. So fundamental differences among common law jurisdictions will also sometimes be referred to in terms of a majority and minority approach.

Along these lines, one other phrase often works its way into criminal law texts. Some rules will be described as part of "an emerging trend" or a "modern approach." What this usually means is that this rule has been adopted by state legislatures or courts that have considered this issue recently.

Students are usually fine with all of this because it is relatively simple to write down a majority and minority rule. What drives some students a little nutty though is the absence of either. A case or treatise (even this guide!) will sometimes say something similar to, "many cases hold," "a few cases suggest," "some support exists for a rule that," or some other qualifying variant. Not surprisingly, a student who is focused on the need for clear rules to use on an exam finds this to be maddeningly vague.

We don't write such ambiguous phrases like this to torture students (at least I don't). We write them because sometimes there are simply not enough eggs to make an omelet. Hard as this may be to imagine, there are lots of questions that appellate courts in various states have not addressed or even resolved in reported opinions. So rather than stretch a few cases into a "trend" that might not exist, most authors will simply say it like it is.

Along these lines, don't be overly troubled if you see some conflict between treatises as to which rule is the majority and which rule is the minority. Decisions about which is which are not always clear-cut, and reasonable minds differ on some of the finer points. The only reasonable mind you don't want to ignore in this respect is the professor teaching your course. Go with the labels used by the person who is going to grade your exam!

Statutory Interpretation

A statute is a law passed by a legislature and signed into law by the executive. Unless a criminal statute violates the U.S. Constitution (or the state's constitution) a court is bound to apply the law the legislature wrote as it is written. Statutes inevitably contain gaps and ambiguities, however. Judges interpret the statutes to resolve resulting disputes about what the statute means.

In interpreting statutes, judges are supposed to do their best to honor what the legislature's purpose and intent when passing the law. A judge can't substitute her own judgment about whether the law is a good or bad idea for the legislature's judgment. Judges resort first to the exact wording of the statute.

Judges often read statutes in a very literal way. They will only look beyond the text if the plain meaning of the statute is not clear. This allegiance is referred to as *the plain meaning rule.*

If the plain meaning is not clear, judges look at legislative history to figure out what the legislature intended. Legislative history refers to the documents that were created or used by legislators and their staff as the bill was introduced, considered, and passed into law. Absent evidence of a specific legislative intent with respect to the issue at hand courts will then look to the legislature's overall purpose in passing the statute and interpret the statute accordingly.

Generally speaking, cases that turn heavily on the interpretation of legislative history don't often make it into criminal law textbooks because resolution of such a specific question—what a particular legislature was thinking at a particular time—does not illustrate much about the criminal law, generally. More to the point, legislative history is often scant or non-existent at the state level, especially with respect to statutory definitions of crimes that have been around for decades or more.

The cases that do get included in criminal law textbooks often include far-ranging discussions of policy and philosophical considerations. These opinions are chosen in part to illustrate the arguments that lawyers make to judges in the absence of clear evidence of legislature intent.

A number of general principles of statutory interpretation exists, most of which are explored in other courses with more complex statutes than a first year criminal law course. Among these "canons of statutory construction" is one that applies specially to criminal cases. According to the *rule of lenity*, ambiguities in statutes are to be resolved in favor of the criminal defendant.

First year law students need to take both the plain meaning rule and the rule of lenity with a grain of salt, however. These rules don't resolve interpretive disputes as much as they shape the language that lawyers use to make arguments and that judges use to justify decisions. A judge who does not wish to refer to legislative intent or purpose will often say, "there is no need to cloud the meaning of a text that is clear." Those wishing to consider legislative history will say that the meaning of the statutory text is cloudy to begin with.

Likewise, one would think that the rule of lenity would decide numerous cases in favor of defendants, but that is simply not the case. The reality is that those arguing for the prosecution will simply say that the rule of lenity does not apply because the meaning of the statue is plainly in their favor. Unlike baseball, a tie does not really go to the defender, the plain language of the rule of lenity to the contrary.

Constitutional Constraints

Judges will interpret statutes with an eye to certain constitutional limits. Basic to the constitutional notion of due process of law is the idea of *legality*, which means that crimes must be clearly defined in order to give people fair notice of what will be punished and to prevent arbitrary exercises of government power. Clauses of the Constitution specifically prohibit legislation which declares *past* conduct to be crimes (known as *ex post facto* laws) and legislation that declares particular people to be guilty of a crime (known as *bills of attainder*).

Bills of attainder are unheard of and ex post facto laws are usually easy to spot. More difficult to resolve, however, are issues of vagueness. The due process clauses of the fifth and fourteenth amendments to the constitution forbid vague criminal laws. *A criminal statute is constitutionally vague if it does not provide a person of ordinary intelligence with fair notice of what is prohibited.* Yet, criminal statutes are often general in nature and do not have to precisely draw the line between criminal and non-criminal conduct. Rather, they must give you a fair idea of when "you are getting warmer" in the words of the old children's game. One English jurist put it best, "Those who skate on thin ice can hardly expect to find a sign which will denote the precise spot where they may fall in."

The best way of understanding the vagueness standard is by understanding the constitutional values that clear statutes protect.

1. Clear statutes prevent the legislative branch from unconstitutionally delegating its law making function to the courts (courts are constitutionally supposed to interpret, not make law, although that becomes a pretty fine distinction).

2. Clear statutes give people fair notice of punishable conduct, giving them an opportunity to behave accordingly.

3. Clear statutes avoid giving arbitrary and potentially discriminatory powers of arrest and prosecution to the executive branch and law enforcement.

Statutes that are unconstitutionally vague often threaten all of these values at once.

Clear examples are hard to come by in this area, but a loitering statute that subjects someone to arrest for "remaining in a public place for no apparent purpose" is probably constitutionally suspect. Whether one's purpose was apparent may not necessarily be self-evident, so people arguably had little notice that they were loitering. The police could arrest almost anybody under such a standard or could use it to target those whom they wished to arrest for discriminatory reasons. Yet a similar loitering statute that prohibited "remaining in a public place for the purpose of threatening or intimidating another" would probably survive constitutional challenge. As imprecise as the words "intimidating conduct" might seem, they give the defendant some sense of when the ice beneath his feet might be thinning. They also provide some basis for evaluating the police officer's decision to arrest. The police officer would have to point to some conduct or condition that suggested that the defendant intended to intimidate or threaten others by his or her presence. Avoiding vagueness does not require precision, just some indication of where the line that should not be crossed is.

A related constitutional constraint is overbreadth. Sometimes prosecutors will seek to save a law from a vagueness challenge by giving the law a clear albeit sweeping meaning. For example, a prosecutor might argue that the loitering law described above prohibits anyone from standing in one place on a public street for more than a moment. Yet such a law would be so broad that it would effectively prohibit people from gathering together in public. Such a sweeping law would violate the First Amendment's right of assembly, and it would therefore be constitutionally overbroad.

Study/Exam Tip

Anytime you see the language of a statute defining a crime in a case or exam question highlight it. The language defining the crime at issue is often key to understanding the issues resolved by the case or raised by the fact pattern.

CHAPTER 5

Philosophies of Punishment

Law is not philosophy, yet you must understand a few things about philosophies of criminal punishment (referred to as punishment) in order to understand criminal law. Philosophies of punishment all begin with the same question: why punish? Most people see this as a rather academic question because they cannot imagine a society in which people who did bad things were not punished. Philosophers, of course, build their castles of thought from the ground up, so they require punishment to have some purpose that justifies it. This is a useful exercise for lawyers because interpreting the law often requires interpreting it in light of some imagined purpose.

Judges and lawyers have for many generations found it useful, often indispensable, to think philosophically about the criminal law in particular because criminal law has a number of purposes, and those purposes often conflict with one another. So making arguments about how the criminal law should be interpreted is easier if you can think clearly about how different interpretations serve or frustrate different purposes of punishment.

That being said, lawyers (and law students) should be careful to use philosophy and not be used by it. Law is not philosophy. Oliver Wendell Holmes once famously said that "the life of the law is experience." Purely philosophical arguments rarely triumph over arguments grounded in a society's experience. Moreover, criminal law, more than any other subject, is driven by moral intuitions about right and wrong. These moral intuitions are deeply rooted, often conflict with one another, and are sometimes not rational. So the philosopher's quest to rationalize criminal punishment is doomed from the start. Our moral intuitions are too strong to be tamed and too messy to be neatly organized.

How then do lawyers use philosophy in the criminal law? Different philosophies of punishment help us to think systematically about our moral intuitions. They organize our thinking in a way that helps us identify the most important arguments for and against interpreting the criminal law in various ways. More specifically, they provide a vocabulary for certain types of arguments that has become almost indispensable. It is impossible to read very far in a criminal law textbook without coming across the terms *deterrence* and *retribution* because these terms provide useful shorthand for referring to big ideas that are complex yet familiar.

So learn the basics of the philosophies of punishment at the beginning of your criminal law course! It will better equip you to understand and argue about the criminal law doctrines that this course covers

Retribution

Let's start with what is perhaps the most intuitive purpose of punishment. We punish people who commit crime because they deserve it. This intuition that people deserve to be punished when they do bad things is the heart of the theory of retribution. Society punishes offenders in retribution for the crimes they commit because they are morally worthy of blame.

Before going any further we should make sure that you really understand what a purely retributive system of punishment requires. Let's borrow an example from Immanuel Kant, a nineteenth century philosopher who heavily influenced retributive theories. Imagine that a jailer and a murderer were the last two people left on earth. The jailer was dying, and the murderer had not yet been punished. Should the jailer punish the murderer before the jailer dies even though there will be no one left for the murderer to harm. Pure retributivists would have the jailer punish the murderer before the jailer dies because retributivists believe that desert alone—and not preventing any future consequence—justifies punishment

A pure retributivist approach also rules out punishing people on grounds other than moral desert. Following the second version of Kant's categorical imperative, retributivists refuse to treat people as means to greater ends. Strictly speaking, this means that we should not punish people to deter others from committing the same crime or even to keep society safe. We should only punish them when—and to the extent—they morally deserve it.

But this simple intuition quickly grows complex when given further thought. There are different ways of thinking about why one "deserves" punishment that often conflict with one another. One way of thinking about desert emphasizes choice. You deserve to be punished when you steal from someone or deliberately injure them because you chose to hurt them. A different way of thinking about desert emphasizes not choice but harm. Society should punish you in response to the harm that you caused.

The tension between choice-based and harm-based versions of retributivism is easily illustrated. Return to the example of the mentally ill person who kills another because his schizophrenia leads him to believe that the victim is an alien invader bent on the destruction of all humanity. He did not "choose" to kill another human being in any sense of the word. He did not even believe that he was killing a human being, and he believed that the killing was necessary to protect himself and everyone else from destruction. Choice-based retributivism would excuse his behavior from criminal responsibility, but a purely harm-based retributivism would not. Since the person he killed was entirely innocent, he would deserve to be punished for taking innocent life.

Choice-based retributivism is not necessarily more or less lenient than harm-based retributivism. Someone deliberately tries to shoot you in the head, but he misses his shot. A purely-choice based retributivism would punish the shooter as severely as if he had killed you because the blameworthiness of his choice in both instances is exactly the same. A harm-based retributivism would justify lesser punishment on the grounds that an attempted murder inflicts less harm than a successful one. Our moral intuitions about choice and harm are both very strong, and neither consistently trumps the other when they come into conflict in the interpretation of the criminal law.

Choice-based retributivism often generates arguments for and against punishment in the very same case because our moral intuitions about choice are also very complex. Choice-based retributivism concerns itself with the blameworthiness or culpability of the choice made, yet choices have more than one dimension. Imagine that a child grows up in a home where he suffers violent abuse at the hands of his parents on a regular basis. As an adult he abuses his own children when they disobey him. He is particularly morally blameworthy because he chooses to harm children who are vulnerable and entrusted to his care. Yet his choice is heavily influenced by factors that he himself did not choose. His beatings as a child may have conditioned him to act violently, possibly on a very deep, neurological level. So retributivists could make arguments for and against offering such an offender some sort of excuse to mitigate his liability. To put it slightly differently, choice-based retributivism concerns itself both with the blameworthiness of the act—beating an innocent child—as well as the blameworthiness of the actor—a past victim of child abuse himself.

This sort of choice-retributivism—often described in terms of "culpability" or "moral blameworthiness" has greatly influenced the development of American criminal law. Culpability concerns mark the most consistent line between the civil and the criminal law. Historically we criminalize those things that we deem worthy of moral condemnation, leaving the civil law to make life more orderly, efficient and fair. The decision to punish intentional criminal acts more seriously than acts committed accidentally reflects a basic moral intuition than the person who kicks the dog is more culpable than the person who trips over the dog. As you will learn in coming chapters, we excuse or mitigate criminal liability in a number of different ways when the offender labored under some sort of condition that limited his ability to make the right choice. For example, we excuse criminal liability completely in cases of insanity; we often preclude criminal liability for many serious offenses if intoxication negated the person's ability to think; we reduce murder to manslaughter under circumstances where the offender reasonably lost control of his emotions.

Often what ultimately lies at the heart of choice-based retributivism is a concern not just with the moral blameworthiness of the act but with the character of the actor. Imagine an offender who commits a terrible crime when she was young but who escapes justice for many decades. During the intervening years she commits no further crimes, and dedicates herself to numerous good works in the community. When she is finally caught, should the prosecutor and judge consider her blameless life and many good works during the intervening years? Some would argue that the offender's subsequent good conduct informs our understanding of her blameworthiness at the time of the earlier crime. Her well lead life reveals that her earlier crime did not reflect her essential moral quality as a person. Others would argue that she had obviously changed during the intervening years. As a result she no longer deserves the same punishment because she is not the same blameworthy person that she was. Most, however, would argue against completely excusing the much-older fugitive from any criminal liability for her earlier crime because the harm she inflicted on society needs to be punished, which is an argument that appeals to our harm-based retributivist intuitions.

So retributive intuitions are influential but complex. They spring from different intuitions about desert and generate arguments both for and against criminal liability in the very same cases.

Major Utilitarian Theories of Punishment: Deterrence and Incapacitation

Utilitarianism holds that we punish crime in order to promote the greatest good for the greatest number of people. Note at the outset that this makes punishment a means to some greater end, not something that is an end onto itself because people "deserve" punishment for crimes. Such means/ends theories are caused "consequentialist" theories because they justify things in terms of the consequences they promote. Utilitarianism is the most commonly invoked consequentialist theory in punishment because the idea of promoting the greatest good for the greatest number of people has wide appeal.

The two most common utilitarian punishment theories are deterrence and incapacitation. Deterrence justifies punishment on the grounds—and to the extent that—it deters people from committing crime in the future. There are, in turn, two different types of deterrence recognized. Specific deterrence refers to the idea that punishing an offender deters that *specific offender* from committing crime in the future. General deterrence refers to the idea that punishment deters *people in general* from offending in the future. Incapacitation, on the other hand, justifies punishment on the grounds that it stops, or *incapacitates* people from committing crimes—usually by imprisoning them.

What both incapacitation and deterrence have in common is that they hold that punishment is justified by the need to reduce crime. We punish people in order to deter others from committing crime, or we incapacitate them in order to reduce crime. Reducing crime, of course, serves the greatest good of society because crime, by definition, is something that society has decided is bad. Punishment is the means to the ends of reducing or preventing crime.

A pure theory of deterrence would justify the punishment of a completely innocent person just to deter others from crime. Imagine, for example, that we decided to deter the assassination of political leaders by executing not just the assassin but all members of the assassin's immediate family. This certainly might deter some would be assassins, but it would accomplish this at the cost of punishing innocent people (assuming that the family members played no part in the assassination). As barbaric as this sounds there are places where the criminal law comes close to taking such a position. When we study mental states we will see that we sometimes punish people who did not have a blameworthy mental state in order to deter others from doing the same thing. For example, we sometimes convict violators of food safety laws of criminal offense even though they may not have a blameworthy mental state in order to deter others from compromising the safety of the food supply.

General deterrence also justifies punishing someone whom you believed would never offend again. Imagine that an elderly person commits a mercy killing of a beloved spouse who suffered in terrible agony from a terminal disease. Even though he is unlikely to kill or offend again, general deterrence requires punishing him for murder in order to deter others from committing similar killings in the future.

Deterrence, like retribution, generates arguments for differing degrees of punishment. Offenders who have completely lost control of themselves as the result of mental illness or extreme emotional states, for example, arguably cannot be deterred at the moment they commit their offenses. If the only purpose of punishment is deterrence, then their punishment should at least be reduced, if not foregone altogether.

Deterrence influences punishment in multiple ways. Generally speaking it justifies punishment for less blameworthy mental states than retribution. Deterrence justifies criminal liability for accidental harms on the grounds that punishment will teach people to be more careful. Deterrence also justifies so called "strict liability" offenses where the offender does not have a blameworthy mental state. For example, strict liability for criminal violations of food and drug laws is often justified on the grounds that strict liability deters people from endangering the public safety. Such arguments only go so far, however. Many argue that since you cannot deter people from doing things that they do not intend or are at least aware of, punishment for accidental harms should be strictly limited. Criminal violations of food and safety regulations, for example, usually carry light penalties.

Deterrence, however, can also generate a different type of argument in favor of narrowing criminal liability. The phrase over deterrence refers to the prospect of discouraging people from doing things that are not wrongful or harmful and that are often important and useful. For example, if we make food safety regulations too strict and the penalties too severe, then we will deter prudent people from going into food industries. They will fear being criminally punished some day for something that was not their fault.

Incapacitation and deterrence often operate side by side. Both justify imprisonment of people who are dangerous but not altogether blameworthy on the grounds of reducing the danger of future offenses against the public. Incapacitation, however, can justify the incarceration of people who cannot be deterred. Return to the example of our offender who was violently abused as a child. Imagine now that as a result of his past abuse he suffers from an explosive temper and commits a serious of random assaults against strangers with whom he gets into arguments. Even though both this particular offender and all other offenders who suffer from his condition might not be deterrable, many would support punishment on the grounds that he is a threat to public safety. Imprisoning him deters no one, but the act does make the public safer by keeping him away from others.

Deterrence obviously is premised on certain assumptions about human behavior. Deterrence imagines that offenders essentially engage in some of cost-benefit analysis weighing the prospects of punishment against their motivations for committing a crime. Whether offenders actually think this way in general or in certain types of cases continues to be the subject of robust debate.

Minor Utilitarian Theories

Deterrence and retribution are the two theories that influence the criminal law the most, but a few other utilitarian theories compete for a very distant third place.

Rehabilitation proponents believe that the purpose of punishment should be to rehabilitate offenders. Rehabilitation means some program of treatment or education that makes the offender less likely to offend again. Rehabilitation is not offered as an end onto itself, but as a means of making society happier and healthier by curing its most troubled members of the ills that lead them to commit crime. Ironically, rehabilitation could support broader criminal liability than deterrence or retribution since even people who don't deserve criminal liability or who are susceptible to deterrence would still be found guilty in order to facilitate their treatment. The one place where rehabilitation still exerts meaningful influence is juvenile court whose rationale for existence lies in the idea that juvenile delinquents should be helped to change their ways before they mature into adults.

Rehabilitation was briefly influential during the nineteen fifties and sixties but has been almost completely eclipsed by retribution and deterrence since then. Rehabilitation requires that offenders receive some form of meaningful treatment, an expensive proposition that rarely commands meaningful political support. Rehabilitation lost popularity because on a symbolic level it was seen as minimizing the offender's responsibility for his offense (even though many treatment programs emphasize personal responsibility). It remains an important consideration at sentencing for certain types of offenses that involve treatable conditions, such as mental illness or substance abuse. Rehabilitation also operates as a weak limiting principle on criminal liability generally. If a certain type of behavior is seen as an outgrowth of a mental health or substance abuse problem, for example, defense lawyers will argue that the person should not be prosecuted if she can avail herself of treatment. Many proponents of drug legalization or decriminalization, for example, argue that those who abuse drugs or alcohol should be treated, not convicted of drug possession or use.

Restorative justice is a philosophy that sees the purpose of punishment as repairing to the degree possible the harm done by the offense and in so doing restoring the state of affairs that existed before the crime has been committed. Restorative justice emphasizes restitution to the victim, apologies and expressions of remorse by the offender and reconciliation where possible between victim and offender. The animating premise of restorative justice is that crime constitutes a breach in the harmony of the community, and that restoration of that harmony should be punishment's paramount purpose. Restorative justice heavily favors various alternate dispute resolution mechanisms over adversarial courtroom proceedings.

Expressive punishment sees punishment's primary purpose as expressing society's denunciation of the crime. By denouncing criminal behavior, punishment acts as a safety valve of sorts for society's anger, thereby reducing the likelihood of private vengeance or vigilante justice. Stigmatizing the victim also affirms the values of the society and thereby promotes social cohesion. Finally denunciation also vindicates the victim by expressing society's collective recognition of the wrong suffered.

The Bottom Line

No one theory of punishment has ever conclusively prevailed over the others in the development of the American criminal law because the conflicting intuitions the theories appeal to remain strong. We care deeply about right and wrong, but we also care about being safe and deterring crime. We like the idea of rehabilitation, but we also feel the need to condemn certain behaviors. In practice, we mix and matches between all of the theories described, an approach that is described as a "mixed theory of punishment."

Remember that you are studying to be lawyers, not philosophers, so the lack of a single, unified theory need not trouble you. Lawyers need to be able to make and anticipate arguments. Philosophies of punishment are useful tools in that enterprise because they express and organize powerful ideas and intuitions. Using these theories to generate arguments for and against various interpretations is part of what makes the study of criminal law so interesting and enjoyable.

CHAPTER 6

The Guilty Hand

The guilty hand component of a crime is often the most straightforward aspect of the analysis. In the simplest terms, one must identify what actions the defendant must perform in order to be guilty of the crime. There are a few wrinkles that arise in atypical cases, however, and all criminal law courses spend a day or two at the very beginning of the course exploring them.

At the outset, you must come to terms with your book and your professor in this area. Different terminology exists for describing this "doing part" of criminal offenses. Some use the terms conduct or the *actus reus* to refer what actions the defendant must perform. Others include within the term conduct or *actus reus* not just the actions performed but the results caused (if any are required by the definition of the crime). Still others include attendant circumstances (such as the fact that burglaries at common law had to be performed *at night*) within these terms. You need not trouble yourself much about which way makes the most sense. You need to be alert to the fact that different judges and treatise writers may use these terms differently and learn how your professor prefers to refer to the doing part of criminal offenses. For our purposes, we will use the term "guilty hand" in this chapter to refer to the defendant's actions, not any results that he caused or any circumstances that attended his actions and certainly not the thoughts that accompanied those actions.

The Requirement of a Voluntary Act

The most fundamental point to grasp in this area is that all crimes do require some sort of voluntary act. (Except when they don't—more about this below when we talk about omission liability.) You can't think your way into criminal liability. A passage in the Catholic liturgy asks forgiveness for "thought, words, and deeds." Thoughts without deeds do not create criminal liability, although the criminal law does consider words deeds under many circumstances.

In the movie *This is the End*, Jonah Hill prays to God for the death of one of his housemates. "Dear God," he prays, "I think Jay is one of your worst creations—please kill him!" As malicious as this prayer may be, it is not a crime. Even if Jonah confessed this heartfelt prayer to the police, he could not be found guilty of attempted murder. So you must act—not just think—in order to be guilty of a crime.

Perhaps the single most important—and counterintuitive—point to remember in this area is that the word "voluntary" in the voluntary act doctrine does not mean what voluntary ordinarily means in everyday conversation. It is a term of art with a very specialized meaning. An act is voluntary for the purposes of the voluntary act doctrine if it is a willed muscular motion, a definition that includes speech, since your vocal cords do not move of their own accord.

A related way of describing voluntariness uses the concept of consciousness. A voluntary act is in these terms the product of a conscious choice. Conversely, unconscious acts are not voluntary ones. Because volition and consciousness are so fundamental to human experience most statutory definitions of voluntary in this area actually define it in negative terms. The Model Penal Code's catch all definition of involuntary, for example, is "a bodily movement that otherwise is not a product of the effort or determination of the actor, either conscious or habitual." (MPC 2.01, 3(d).

Reflexes Are Not Voluntary

The easiest example of an involuntary act is a reflex—an autonomous neurological response to external stimuli. Imagine that you go to the doctor's office for your checkup. Instead of tapping your bent knee with that little hammer to test your reflexes your doctor smashes your knee with a large rubber mallet. Reflexively your leg shoots forward with great speed and force as you cry out in pain. There is some justice in life, however, because your sadistic physician was standing right in front of you when he hit your knee. As a result your foot catches him square in the groin, and he collapses to the ground. You could not be prosecuted for battery or assault against the doctor because the required conduct—a harmful or offensive touching—was not performed voluntarily or consciously. (You would also have a mental state defense, but the analysis would not even get that far.)

Acts Done While Sleepwalking and Under Hypnosis Might Not Be Voluntary

A more controversial example of an involuntary act is an act performed while sleepwalking or under hypnosis. Some jurisdictions allow juries to find an act to be involuntary if they conclude that the defendant performed the acts in question while asleep. A few jurisdictions (including the MPC) even recognize a similar defense if the jury concludes that the defendant was acting as the result of hypnotic suggestion. Most jurisdictions, however, hold one responsible for what one does while asleep or under hypnosis on the theory that one would never do something while asleep or under hypnosis that one would not otherwise do.

Reflexive actions, sleepwalking, and hypnosis are relatively intuitive examples of conduct that might not be voluntary. Now let's consider two types of conduct that your average person on the street would think of as involuntary or unconscious but which the law considers to be voluntary and the product of a conscious choice for the purposes of this doctrine.

Acts Done Under Duress Are "Voluntary"

Imagine that your professor lost his mind and ordered you at gun point to strike the student sitting next to you in class.[1] If charged with battery or assault, could you successfully argue that there was no voluntary act? No! Actions performed under duress are considered voluntary for the purposes of the voluntary act doctrine. Your criminal liability will turn on whether you have satisfied the defense of duress, an excuse for criminal liability that we will cover later in the course (and which you should address separately if writing for the exam).

Acts Done Habitually Are Considered "Voluntary"

Now imagine a chain smoker who goes to the hospital to visit his best friend, who—not coincidentally—is also a chain smoker and who is dying of emphysema. The dying friend is in an oxygen tent, and there are signs everywhere warning "highly flammable oxygen in use," and "smoking absolutely prohibited," as well as—for the

---

[1] Maybe he was surfing the web on his laptop. That really does drive some prof's crazy.

truly dense—"smoking may result in fire and explosion." Distraught at seeing his friend laboring to breathe, our visiting chain smoker does what chain smokers often do—he unconsciously takes out a cigarette and lights it. Only after the explosion that incinerated his dear friend did our chain smoking defendant even realize what he had done as he noticed the remains of his cigarette clutched between his own charred fingers. Can he avoid criminal liability on the grounds that he did not voluntarily or consciously light his cigarette? No! Remember that "voluntary" and "conscious" are used as legal terms of art here. When we say in everyday conversation that we did something "unconsciously," we are referring to what the criminal law considers habitual behavior. Habitual behavior is considered conscious behavior for the purposes of the voluntary act doctrine. Our chain smoker's defense will turn on whether he had the mental state required for the crime, a subject for the next chapter.

Status Offenses

The voluntary act doctrine is one of the very few areas where a common law principle enjoys constitutional status. In *Robinson v. California* the U.S. Supreme Court held that criminalizing a mere status violated the Eighth Amendment to the U.S. Constitution's prohibition of cruel and unusual punishments. In *Robinson* the Court struck down a statute that made it a crime to be addicted to the use of narcotics. While the government is free to criminalize using, possessing or being under the influence of an illegal drug, it cannot criminalize the state—or *status*—of being addicted to such a substance. To do so, the Court reasoned, would be akin to prosecuting someone for being sick. In a later case, *Powell v. Texas*, the Court made clear, however, that it was not unconstitutional to criminalize behavior that resulted from sickness. The defendant in *Powell* argued that his violation of a public intoxication statute was the involuntary result of his chronic alcoholism, but the Court distinguished the case from *Robinson* on the grounds that becoming intoxicated was conduct not status. The Court rejected squarely the notion that acts committed as the result of an addiction are involuntary for the purposes of constitutional analysis.

How the Voluntary Act Doctrine Often Operates in Practice

As with many common law principles, the voluntary act requirement operates most often as a presumption of statutory interpretation. Judges presume that the legislature intended to require that the defendant must perform at least one criminal act and they will interpret criminal statutes accordingly. The difficult cases involve questions about which acts must be voluntary and when they must be committed.

Often these cases deal with defendants who were acting involuntarily at the precise moment the crime became fully completed. One leading case involved an epileptic driver who experienced a total blackout at the moment he killed some pedestrians. In such cases courts often find criminal liability by expanding the time frame of the offense to include earlier volitional behavior. In the epileptic case the court based criminal liability on the driver's earlier conscious decision to drive his car knowing that he had a history of blackouts.

These cases are difficult because expanding the time frame of the offense too much could essentially do away with the voluntary act presumption. Imagine a defendant charged with introducing illegal drugs into a county jail. What if the defendant was arrested, handcuffed and taken to jail without any opportunity to remove the drugs from his person. Few if any courts would expand the time frame of the word "introduce" to include the defendant's decision to put drugs in his pocket, not having any idea that he would be arrested later that day. Yet depending on the wording of the statutes, other courts might find that he voluntarily introduced the drugs into the jail if he was given some opportunity to disclose the presence of the drugs before being taken to jail. Different courts reach different results in these sorts of cases even where the wording of the statute involved is very similar.

The bottom line is that you should always look for at least one voluntary act in applying a criminal statute, but you can sometimes be creative in where and when you find that act.

The Philosophy Behind the Voluntary Act Requirement

The voluntary act requirement serves a number of different purposes. First, you are usually not considered morally blameworthy for acts that you did not voluntarily perform. As discussed above, choice lies at the heart of many of our intuitions about blameworthiness, and if you did not even will your muscles to move you did not choose to do anything. Second, people cannot be deterred from involuntary actions because they have never weighed the costs and benefits of acting. Finally, the requirement of a voluntary act also serves as a guarantee that we will never rely too much on mental state evidence for criminal liability. The "proof is in the pudding" as the saying goes, and requiring people to actually do something reduces the chance that we will erroneously punish someone who is not dangerous or blameworthy.

Omission Liability: The Big Exception

The philosopher John Austin once said that there are two parts to an argument: the part where you say something and the part where you take it back. The same could be said of the law. Law is filled with general rules and specific exceptions. One very important exception exists to the voluntary act requirement: one may be criminally liable for *failing to act* in the face of a legal duty.

Note at the outset that criminal liability for omissions requires not a moral duty but a legal one. If you are sitting at Starbucks and see one patron strangle another to death[2] you don't have to lift a finger to stop it. You don't even have to call 911. You can just finish your coffee and go on about your day because no general legal duty exists to aid other people or to report crime. Moral duties do not give rise to criminal liability for omissions.

What sorts of legal duties create omission liability under the criminal law? Imagine that you are drowning at a public beach. A whole crowd of people are watching you die. People are even filming your death on their phones and uploading it to YouTube, where it is instantaneously going viral (your fifteen seconds of fame!). But nobody lifts a finger to help you, despite the abundance of life saving equipment lying around. Who can be prosecuted for failing to come to your aid?

Statutory Duties

There is a police officer on the beach. She can be criminally prosecuted for failing to come to your aid because in most jurisdictions police officers have a statutory obligation to come to a person's aid in the event of an emergency. Just as she could not just walk by a person having a cardiac arrest on a public street, she can't ignore your plight.

The legislature can create legal duties for one person to aid another by statute. For example, certain categories of people have a statutory obligation to report child abuse in many states.

---

[2] Maybe they were arguing over who got to plug their laptop into the last wall socket. People get a little testy over that stuff.

Child abuse (and domestic violence) aside, such reporting statutes are rare. They usually limit the duty to certain types of people and certain types of situations.

More generally, the legislature can create a legal duty for you to do certain things. One easy example is paying taxes. Failing to file a tax return on income you earn is an omission to act in the face of a legal duty that is created by statute. Again, this sort of legal liability is the exception. The vast majority of criminal statutes criminalize things that you do, not things that you don't.

Contractual Duties

Can you believe it? The lifeguard is watching you drown, too. He has a really good view from that tall chair he sits in and is using it to good advantage as he films your death on his cell phone. He can be criminally prosecuted because his employment contract obliges him to come to the aid of people drowning. Remember that contracts may be oral or written, but all the requirements of a contract must be satisfied for a duty to arise under it.

Status Relationships

Here is the really bad news. Your mother is watching you drown, too. She is actually yelling, "I told you to stay with the swim lessons, but you had to try to become the big soccer star!" She can be prosecuted because the status relationship of parent to child creates a legal duty for her to come to your aid, and her omission to act in the face of that duty can be a crime.

The paradigm status relationships for the purposes of criminal liability are

- Parent to child

- Spouse to spouse

- Employer to employee

- Ship captain to crew and passengers

A failure to come to someone's aid in the face of a legal duty arising from such a status relationship can give rise to criminal liability.

Duties Voluntarily Assumed

While you are drowning, a swimmer who is an Olympic gold medalist decides to come to your rescue. He jumps out of his beach chair and announces loudly to the assembled crowd, "Hey, I have got this," then gestures for everyone to get out of his way. He jogs towards the shore, but as his toes touch the water he jumps back out exclaiming, "Man, that is so much colder than all of those swimming pools I have spent my life in." He goes back to his beach chair.

The Olympic swimmer can be criminally prosecuted in many jurisdictions because he would be deemed to have voluntarily undertaken a rescue that he subsequently abandoned. Voluntary assumption of a legal duty creates a legal duty for the purposes of the criminal law because such undertakings may have caused the victim to rely upon the aid or to may have dissuaded others from helping.

Creation of a Risk of Peril

Actually the reason you are drowning in the first place is that your bone-head college roommate pushed you off the edge of a pier as a joke. She, of course, had no idea that you could not swim when she pushed you. Once you are in the water, you immediately scream "I can't swim," and then begin to drown. She stands there, exclaiming "wow, she can't swim; imagine that." She then turns and walks back down the pier, stepping over the life saving equipment lying on the pier as she does so. Your college roommate can be criminally prosecuted for failing to come to your aid because she created the risk of peril in the first place. One who puts another in danger does have a legal duty to come to their aide, and failing to do so creates criminal liability.

An Important Limitation on Criminal Omission Liability

With respect to all of the above legal duties, you must only aid another to the extent of your ability to safely do so. If you are not a strong swimmer you do not have to risk your life to save theirs. That is why in the hypothetical I was careful to leave all of that lifesaving equipment lying around. On the other hand, help is often just a phone call away in our cell-phone-carrying society, so failing to at least phone for help can easily give rise to criminal liability.

The Philosophy Behind Limited Omission Liability

There are a couple of different reasons why the criminal law shies away from prosecuting people for things they did not do, even where clear moral duties exist. You can watch the Starbucks strangulation take place in legal safety because judges and legislatures have historically feared the blurriness of the lines that would define a general duty to aid people or to report or prevent crime. What if you see someone pulled over on the side of the road staring blankly into space? Are they having a heart attack? Did they just finish burying a murder victim by the side of the road? Or are they trying to remember where they put the grocery list? You hear the neighbors next door engaged in a screaming argument? If they are actually hitting one another as they scream, would you be criminally liable for failing to call the police? The blurriness of these lines also raises questions about the role of government in society. If you think your roommate is selling illegal drugs, a duty to act or report could easily turn us into a nation of informers, something that might reduce crime but that would also expand the power of the state at the expense of personal privacy and autonomy.

CHAPTER 7

The Guilty Mind

Mental states are perhaps the most important part of the criminal law. Mental states are central to our notions of blameworthiness. Deliberately doing a bad thing is universally seen as worse than accidentally doing a bad thing. Mental states are also central in a different way to our notions of dangerousness and deterrence. When people are thinking about doing bad things we want them to be deterred by the prospect of punishment. Someone who intentionally hurts people is the sort of dangerous person that we also often want to incapacitate through imprisonment. So the criminal law relies heavily on mental states to determine whether a crime took place and to distinguish more from less serious crimes.

Yet mental states are also deceptively complex things. We talk all the time in our daily lives about intent, but what does it really mean to "intend" to do something? That you have a reason to do it that you considered before acting? Or that you foresaw all the various things that might happen as a result? Or does it even include all the things that reasonably might result from your actions regardless of whether they occurred to you or not? The differences between these different mental states cover a great deal of ground, ground that matters when deciding whether and how hard to punish someone. Over time the criminal law has evolved various definitions of mental states that reflect differing levels of blameworthiness and dangerousness.

To complicate things even further, crimes often involve multiple elements, and judges often have to make difficult decisions about which mental states apply to which elements. Various rules have evolved for helping judges make these sorts of decisions, but the rules still leave substantial room for argument.

Finally, two very different approaches to mental states have developed in the United States—the common law approach and the Model Penal Code approach. While some overlap exists, the more modern Model Penal Code diverges sharply from the common law approach on many points and has proven to be very influential— even in some jurisdictions that follow the common law in many other respects.

So you have to learn to do two things to figure out what the guilty mind requires for criminal liability. First, you have to figure out what mental states a crime requires for its various elements. Second, you have to analyze whether the defendant had the required mental states. And you must learn to do this in both a common law and a Model Penal Code jurisdiction.

Both tasks can be easily mastered if broken down and taken step by step. This chapter will begin with the definitions of mental states, starting first with the more precise definitions of the Model Penal Code before tackling the vaguer terminology of the common law. Once we have covered what the various mental states mean we will then explore the more complicated rules judges follow in figuring out which mental states to require for which elements of a crime. Subsequent chapters will deal with special mental issues relating to mistakes of fact and of law as well as intoxication and certain mental health conditions.

Model Penal Code Mental State Definitions

The Model Penal Code defines four principal mental states: purpose, knowledge, recklessness and negligence. The easiest examples involve mental states concerning result elements, so that is where we will begin.

- Purposely means that it was your conscious effort to bring about the result.

- Knowingly means that you were substantially certain that the result would occur.

- Recklessly means that you consciously disregarded a substantial and unjustifiable risk that the result would occur under circumstances that constituted a gross deviation from the standard of care that a law abiding person would observe in the situation.

- Negligently means that you should have been aware of a substantial and unjustifiable risk that the result would occur under circumstances that constituted a gross deviation from the standard of care that a reasonable person would observe in the situation.

Note that the principal difference between recklessness and negligence is whether the defendant actually foresaw the risk of the prohibited result occurring or ought to have foreseen it. The Model Penal Code (and the common law for that matter) punishes recklessness more severely than negligence because someone who did a risky thing after realizing that it was risky is generally considered more blameworthy and dangerous than someone who didn't realize the risk but should have. Note also that both recklessness and negligence involve *gross* deviations from the standard care. Simple or ordinary negligence—a mere deviation from a reasonable standard of care—is left to the world of civil liability for the most part.   The common law also follows this definition of negligence, so whenever you hear *criminal negligence*, think *gross negligence*.

We can easily distinguish these four states of mind from one another with a series of hypotheticals about a mad 1L law student. Imagine that a first year law student has become unhinged and decides to blow up his most hated law professor. He brings a bomb wrapped as a gift to the professor during office hours. He sets it down on the professor's desk after asking that it not be opened in front of him. He notices, however, that sitting across from his most hated law professor is the student's most loved law school professor. The student leaves and walks down the hall a safe distance before taking the remote detonator switch out of his pocket. He hesitates for a moment, torn between his desire to kill his most hated professor and his deep regret at losing his most loved professor. Then he pushes the detonator button, sending them both to the law classroom in the sky.

In this first hypothetical, our mad bomber is *purposeful* as to the death of the hated law professor but only *knowing* with respect to the death of the loved law professor because it was his conscious object to kill only the former although he was substantially certain that the latter would die in the blast as well.

Now imagine a variation where after he leaves the office, he closes the door only to see his first year study group clustered outside the office waiting for office hours to begin. He walks down the hall and looks back at them standing there. He loves his study group and pauses to consider whether there is enough explosive in the bomb to harm them even though the door is closed. He says "Nah" to himself and pushes the button. The blast, contrary to his expectations, blows through the door and kills the study group.

In this second hypothetical, our mad bomber is not knowing but *reckless* as to the deaths of his study group. Even though as a matter of physics it might have been substantially certain that they would be killed in the blast, *he* was not substantially that they would die therefore he was not knowing. He was conscious of the risk though—as exemplified by the "nah" moment—which makes him *reckless* with respect to their deaths.

In our last variation, there is a study group of 2Ls sitting in a courtyard below the window of the law professor's office. (Since they are 2Ls they do their "studying" in the sun.) The blast blows the external wall of the office off, and it falls into the courtyard killing all of them. Our unhinged bomber is arguably only criminally *negligent* with respect to their deaths. He was not reckless with respect to their deaths because it never occurred to him that people in the courtyard below could have been harmed. He should have been aware of such a risk, and setting off a bomb is such unjustifiable and substantially risky behavior that his neglect of that risk would easily be considered a gross deviation by any finder of fact.[3]

What does the MPC provide if a defendant has a more blameworthy mental state than the law requires? For example, what if a statute defines as vandalism recklessly damaging the property of another? Is it a defense if the person claims that he damaged the property not recklessly but purposely? Obviously not. The basic rule is that a more culpable mental state satisfies a

---

[3] These result-oriented examples gets the main idea of the differences between these mental states across. The definition of purpose and knowledge apply differently to conduct elements or to attendant circumstances, however. For conduct elements and attendant circumstances, a person need only be aware of the nature of the conduct or the existence of an attendant circumstance in order to be either knowing or purposeful.

requirement for a less culpable mental state. So knowledge is satisfied by purpose, reckless is satisfied by knowledge or purpose, and negligence satisfied by any of the above.

Common Law Mental States

Here we must begin not with a list but with a story because understanding how common law mental states evolved is important to understanding how they are applied. Faulkner once said, "the past is not dead; it is not even the past." Nowhere is this more true in the criminal law than in the area of common law mental states. The moral intuitions that animated the common law's early approach to mental states are powerful and persistent. They continue to influence the criminal law even after the doctrinal definitions they gave birth to have been discarded. For this reason, many criminal law casebooks use some old common law cases to introduce common law mental states.

The common law term for mental state was *mens rea*, a Latin phrase that means "guilty mind." Initially no mental state at all was required for criminal liability, but this gave way to the idea that you had to have some sort of guilty mind to be guilty of a crime. The earliest definition meant some sort of morally blameworthy mental state. Simply put, it meant that the person was "up to no good." Over time this evolved into a definition that required your guilty mind to relate in some way to the crime that you were accused of committing.

One wonderfully illustrative common law case involved a sailor who accidentally burned down his ship when he ignited the rum he was stealing by dropping the candle he was holding. The prosecutor argued that the *mens rea* requirement for the crime of arson was satisfied by his intention to steal. The rum thief argued that he intended to steal rum, not burn a ship down. The court of appeals reversed on the ground that the generally guilty mind of a rum thief was a very different thing from the guilty mind of an arsonist.

If being "up to no good" would not necessarily give you the mental state required for any crime, what would be enough? What did it mean for the offender to criminally intend the offense at hand? The common law moved to a general notion of criminal intent that essentially included purpose, knowledge, recklessness or negligence with respect to the elements of the offense. So the rum thief discussed above would be found guilty of arson if he either knew that the burning of the ship would be the necessary or even the natural and probable consequence of his handling of the candle around the rum or that he foresaw the risk of the ship burning or that he even ought to have foreseen it. He would not be guilty of arson, however, just because he was bent on stealing rum when the burned the ship down.

Specific Versus General Intent

The common law has almost always distinguished between a general intent and a specific intent to commit a crime. This distinction has confused generations of judges, lawyers, and law students because it has meant different things at different times in different places. While it is not necessary to discuss all the different meanings of the two terms, a few basic definitions remain important. General intent has been defined in the following three different ways.

1. *A generally blameworthy state of mind.*

2. *A general awareness of the nature of what you are doing.*

3. *Recklessness or even negligence as to the existence of the elements of the element in question.*

Specific intent essentially means something more than all of the above. Specifically, it has been defined as follows.

1. *A further intent beyond what is otherwise required to establish the crime.*

2. *An intent to achieve a specific result or condition.*

3. *A purposeful or knowing state of mind as to the existence of the element in question.*

Assaultive crimes allow us to illustrate both concepts at once. Battery is an unlawful and offensive touching of another, and it is a general intent crime. Imagine that a man in a crowded elevator begins enthusiastically reenacting a mixed martial arts match that he just watched on pay-per-view in his hotel room. He swings his fists right and left, reenacting a flurry of blows. People next to him edge away, but eventually he accidentally clocks one of them in the face. Is he guilty of criminal battery? Yes, under any of the definitions given above, he has the requisite general intent. He was generally aware of swinging his arms around and doing so in such a crowded space would be considered by most to be both generally blameworthy and reckless or negligent.

But what if he is charged with assault with intent to inflict serious injury. (He hit the guy really, really hard.) The further intent would be the intent to inflict serious injury, and arguably it would not be satisfied on these facts. Such a further intent contemplates that there was something "specific" that you had in mind, and such a specific intent fits most easily with our notions of purpose or at the very least knowing behavior with respect to this further result to be achieved. While aware of his actions and reckless and negligent with respect to the danger of an injury he did not specifically intend to injure under in any sense of the word and would not therefore be guilty of assault with intent to inflict serious injury.

Having made this distinction as simple as possible, I know must make it more complicated. First, specific intent is not infrequently interpreted to require not just a knowing but a purposeful state of mind. Second, sometimes whether a specific intent requires purpose or knowledge depends on the nature of the element in question. As with the Model Penal Code, a specific intent with respect to an attendant circumstance or with respect to conduct—not results—is often interpreted to require knowledge or awareness.

The good news is that the distinction between general and specific intent means less than it used to. Subsequent chapters flag where it matters most.

Strict Liability

Strict liability is the "non-mental-state, mental state" in the sense that to be held strictly liable is to be held liable in the absence of a mental state. There are no "pure" strict liability offenses because some mental state is always required for at least one element of an offense. An offense is considered to be a strict liability offense if no mental state at all is required for at least one material element.

A relatively familiar crime involving strict liability is statutory rape. Having sex with a person under age of consent constitutes statutory rape. Statutory rape is considered a strict liability offense in most jurisdictions because no mental state is required as to the age of the minor. This means that even if a person appeared to be well over the age of consent, and even if you examined their passport to verify that they were above the age of consent, you would still be guilty of statutory rape if it turned out that their passport contained a typo for the date of birth entry and that she was in fact a minor. Wait, you might complain, there was no reasonable way for you to know that she was below the age of consent. That would be a defense, of course, if even simple negligence were required as to the age of consent. Strict liability, however, means that even an entirely reasonable (and thereby non-negligent) belief is no defense because no state of mind of any sort is required for the element to be satisfied. Strict liability means that you act at the peril of being wrong, no matter how reasonable your belief.

Analyzing Mental State Requirements

Having figured out what various mental states mean, we turn to the more vexing question of how one figures out which mental states are required for a crime to occur. This question takes different forms. Sometimes a statutory definition of a crime will not contain any mental state language. The question then is whether to read in a mental state requirement and which mental states to read in. More often, the statutory language will contain some mental state terms but it will be unclear which elements the term modifies.

Imagine, for example, interpreting the following statute.

"A person who purposely transports into the United States animals not indigenous to the United States which he knows to be endangered is guilty of a felony."

Two mental states appear on this statute, purpose and knowledge, but which elements do they modify? Must one purposely transport the animals into the United States or must one only purposely transport them and is some lesser mental state—if any at all—require for the element of their entering the United States? Must one know the animals to be nonindigenous or must one know them to be endangered as well? If knowledge is not required, must one be reckless or negligent as to their endangered status? Or is one strictly liable with respect to whether the goods are endangered or not without regard to what one believed, reasonably or otherwise? In answering such a question you must first consider whether you are in a Model Penal Code or common law jurisdiction.

Model Penal Code Default Rules

In this area the Model Penal Code provides a series of default rules that help judges decide when and where to read various mental states into criminal statutes. First, if no mental state appears at all on the face of the statute, then the MPC requires at least a reckless mental state as to all material elements. Second, if only one mental state appears in connection with one material element then the MPC assumes that the legislature intended that term to apply to all material elements absent clear language to the contrary. Third, the MPC precludes strict liability with respect to any material element of a criminal offense and provides that at least negligence will apply to material elements for which no clear legislative intent applies. For example, in the statute described above, if the court did not require that the defendant know that the artifacts were stolen she would at least require that the defendant have been grossly negligent with respect to their stolen status. These rules do not resolve all interpretive ambiguities, but they cut them down significantly.

Common Law Default Rules

Mental state ambiguities are much more difficult to resolve in common law jurisdictions, unless those jurisdictions have adopted some default rules along the line of the Model Penal Code's as described above.

Absent some clear evidence of legislative intent or purpose, modification questions regarding mental states are resolved primarily based on the text of the statute. Generally speaking a mental state usually does not modify elements that appear before and does modify the element that appears immediately after it. Looking once again at the sentence "A person who purposely transports into the United States items which he knows to be archaeological artifacts which are stolen is guilty of a felony," a common law court would clearly require the transport to purposeful and knowledge that the item was an archaeological artifact. Beyond that, however, no clear rules exist to resolve the remaining issues. One must anticipate arguments for and against different interpretations of the statute based on the legislative intent and purpose and the philosophies of punishment described above.

Some principles do exist to guide courts in common law jurisdictions in determining when to presume that the legislature intended a defendant to be strictly liable with respect to a particular element. First, the common law was said to generally abhor strict liability. Few strict liability offenses existed at common law with the exception of offenses such as statutory rape. Second, statutes that define crimes that are similar to old common law offenses are presumed to require at least general criminal intent with respect to all material elements. Third, even if a statute defines a non-common law criminal offense, a court will only presume that strict liability was intended if the court deems the crime a *public welfare offense*. Public welfare offenses are generally regulatory offenses. While no iron-clad definition exists, courts have over the years identified a number of factors that guide their decisions.

1. *The more severe the penalty the less likely the court will find strict liability.*

2. *The greater the stigma of the offense the less likely the court will find strict liability.*

3. *The more innocent the nature of the activity the less likely the court will find strict liability.*

4. *The greater the danger to the public the more likely the court will find strict liability.*

5. *The more regulated the activity generally the more likely the court will find strict liability.*

6. *The easier it is for defendants to determine whether the offense element exists through the exercise of ordinary diligence the more likely the court will find strict liability.*

7. *The harder it will be for the prosecutor to prove a culpable mental state with respect to the element the more likely the court will find strict liability.*

With respect to the innocence of the activity in question, two related doctrines sometimes come into play: legal wrong and moral wrong. If the activity in question is either illegal—even if not necessarily criminal—or immoral, courts are sometimes more likely to presume that the legislature intended strict liability on the theory that individuals engage in such behavior at their own legal peril that their activities might subject them to criminal liability.

CHAPTER 8

Mistakes and the Guilty Mind

What if the defendant was mistaken about one of the elements of the crime? Is that a defense? The concept of mistake seems simple enough, but the legal doctrines dealing with mistake in the criminal law do not always make sense to people. One can iron out these wrinkles easily enough if one remembers and truly understands a few related principles.

1. Mistake of Fact doctrine makes no real difference with respect to whether a crime took place.

2. Mistakes of Fact generally do not have to be reasonable.

3. Mistakes of Law usually only excuse criminal liability only when the legislature clearly wants them to.

Mistake of Fact Doctrine Makes No Real Difference with Respect to Whether a Crime Took Place

This strikes many people as counter intuitive because people who are mistaken seem less blameworthy, less dangerous, and not as easy to deter as people who know what they are doing. Yet we decide when we do and don't want mistakes to matter when we decide what mental state is required for the crime. Sometimes the absence of the required mental state can be described as a "mistake," but whether you call it a mistake or not does not change whether the mental state exists or not.

Theft provides an easy example. At common law and under all modern statutes theft—or larceny as it is known—requires you to intend to permanently deprive someone of their property. That means that if as you leave a party you walk off with some else's umbrella thinking that it is your own you are not guilty of theft. This comports with our common sense understanding of what it means to "steal" something.

Most people would say that you made a mistake. The law would regard this as a mistake of fact because you were mistaken about who owned the umbrella you took. So at your trial for the theft of the umbrella (it belonged to the chief prosecutor for your county), your lawyer might well ask for a jury instruction that says something like the following. "It is a defense to the crime of larceny if the defendant was mistaken as to whose umbrella he took." Now imagine that the judge refuses to give this mistake of fact jury instruction. Furthermore, the judges tells your lawyer that she may not use the word mistake in her closing argument. Do you still have a defense? Well, the standard jury instruction for theft explains to the jury that they must find beyond a reasonable doubt that you intended to deprive another of their property.

Your lawyer argues to the jury that since you thought the umbrella was yours that you did not intend to take the property of another.

The result is the same either way because either you have the mental state required for the crime or you don't—here the belief that the umbrella belonged to someone else. Whether you call the absence of that mental state a mistake or not makes no real difference.

At the end of the day, the question is this: does your mistake mean that you did not have the required mental state? The law's somewhat awkward way putting this is whether your mistake "negated" the required mental state, but it means the same thing.

What purpose does mistake of fact doctrine serve? In modern courtrooms a mistake instruction will sometimes help a jury better understand what the mental state required means. Without the mistake instruction a jury in our umbrella case might scratch their head and wonder about whether it makes a difference that you "made a mistake" although hopefully they would figure out that if you thought it belonged to someone else then you could not intend to take the property of another.

Mistakes of Fact Do Not Have to Be Reasonable

This principle also throws a lot of people for a loop because intuitively it seems that a mistake should be reasonable for it to matter to criminal liability. In fact a few jurisdictions tried this approach. When you think it through however, you realize that requiring all mistakes to be reasonable would reduce the mental state for all crimes to simple negligence, something that obviously we don't want to do.

The most dramatic examples involve murder. Imagine that a jurisdiction defines murder as intentionally killing someone and involuntary manslaughter as negligently killing someone.

Remember that intentionally generally requires that a person acts purposely or knowingly with respect to results. So intentionally killing someone requires that you act at least knowing that another human being is substantially certain to die as a result of what you do. Now imagine that a deer hunter accidentally shot and killed another hunter. The defendant shot at what he thought was a deer moving in the underbrush, but it turned out to be another hunter. He intended to kill what he was shooting at but he was mistaken about what he was killing. He would not seem to have the mental state required for murder because he did not intentionally (knowingly) kill a human being.

Now further assume that it was not reasonable for him to shoot into the underbrush without being sure that it was a deer—not another hunter—that was moving. This means that his mistake was not reasonable. If mistakes of fact have to be reasonable in order to constitute his defense, then his unreasonable mistake about what he was killing cannot be a defense to the charge of murder. Yet the legislature had provided that negligent or even reckless killings are not murder but manslaughter. Requiring mistakes to be reasonable would change the mental state required for murder in these sorts of cases from intentional killing to negligent killing. For this reasons most jurisdictions have come around to recognizing that mistakes of fact generally do not have to be reasonable.

The Common Law Distinction Between Specific and General Intent

At common law, a mistake of fact did not have to be reasonable to be a defense to a specific intent crime but did have to be reasonable to be a defense to a general intent crime. Since, specific intent crimes require that a person act with knowledge or purpose, it makes sense that a genuine but unreasonable mistake would mean that you did not have specific intent. In the hunting example given above the hunter's unreasonable mistake did not mean that he specifically intended to kill a human being. Since general intent crimes only require recklessness or negligence, however, it does make sense that these mistakes be reasonable ones. For this reason our unreasonable deer hunter would be guilty of involuntary manslaughter because that crime requires only negligence.

Mistakes of Law Are a Defense Only When the Legislature Clearly Intends Them to Be

One must start with a principle that is easy to say but surprisingly hard to fully accept: ignorance of the law does not excuse. In general you do not need to prove that a person knew he or she was breaking the law. We are all presumed to know what the law prohibits. We are, in fact, presumed to know not just what is written in criminal statutes, but every word of every judicial decision interpreting those statutes. It does not matter how complex the law is. It does not even matter that judges themselves might disagree about what the law means. Whatever the highest court determines the law to mean, that is what we are presumed to know. This presumption applies to every single one of us. Whether you be a law professor of a street sweeper, ignorance of even the most arcane, convoluted and difficult to understand law does not excuse violating it.[4]

There are a couple of related rationales for this rule, but they all basically boil down to choosing utilitarian concerns over blameworthy concerns. The blameworthiness concern is relatively straightforward. Someone who does not realize that what they are doing is illegal is not as blameworthy as someone who knowingly

---

[4] A law is not unconstitutionally vague if it is complex or difficult to understand. Vagueness and complexity are different things.

breaks the law. The utilitarian concerns in favor of the rule are numerous. First, if ignorance of the law excused, then there would be an incentive to know as little about the law as possible because only the knowledgeable could be successfully convicted. Second, it would be arguably a lot more difficult to convict people of many types of crime. Presumably juries would be easily convinced that defendants knew it was against the law to commit murder and theft and all of the various crimes that have always been crimes, but it would be much harder to convict people of the various regulatory crimes that modern criminal codes include, things that are not necessarily obviously criminal in and of themselves. The third argument in favor of not allowing ignorance of the law to excuse is actually a blameworthiness argument. It is blameworthy of you not to know the law, so we will hold you strictly liable for your ignorance of it.

Malum Prohibitum Crimes

Crimes that are considered to be wrong in and of themselves are often referred to by judges as *malum en se*, which means bad or evil in itself. Crimes that are considered to be wrong only because the state has decided to prohibit them are often referred to by judges as *malum prohibitum*, which means prohibited wrong. An easy example of a *malum prohibitum* crime is the law making it a crime to drive on the left side of the road. There is nothing inherently wrong about driving on the left side of the road (unless you think there is something evil about being left handed), but we need to pick one side or the other to keep driving safe, so we prohibit driving on the left side.

As the number of *malum prohibitum* offenses has increased in our increasingly complex modern society, some have argued that judges should take a second look at the idea that ignorance of the law does not excuse because many people might not have an idea that they are breaking the law. Those people have largely lost this argument, however, because judges have concluded that society needs people to learn about and obey these *malum prohibitum* offenses and presuming knowledge of the law in criminal cases is a good way to make sure that they do so.

When Mistakes of Law Do Excuse

There are three exceptions to the rule that ignorance of the law does not excuse.

1. Where knowledge of the law being broken is expressly required by the words of the statute.

Sometimes the wording of a statute explicitly requires proof of knowledge on the part of the defendant of the law being broken. For example, use of the word "willful" in a criminal statute, especially a complex regulatory statute, is often interpreted by courts as requiring knowledge of the law being broken. Since legislatures know that courts interpret "willful" in this way it has become over time a reasonable presumption. For example, the Supreme Court interprets the word "willful" in federal criminal tax evasion statutes as requiring proof that the person knew that they were obliged to pay taxes. This turns out to be not terribly difficult to prove, but proved it must be.

2. Where the legislature creates by statute a limited "reliance" defense on some legal authority other than the statute itself.

Both the Model Penal Code and many common law jurisdictions have created by statute—or sometimes by common law presumption—a limited defense of reasonable reliance on some official interpretation of the criminal statute in question. Such provisions usually recognize three types of legal authority upon which the defendant may reasonably rely.

- *A statute later found to be invalid or unconstitutional.* Imagine that the legislature exempts certain types of behavior from the reach of a criminal statute, but the legislation is subsequently struck down as unconstitutional. A defendant who relies upon this legislative exemption during the period of time between its passage but before it being declared unconstitutional is legally excused from liability by virtue of his reasonable belief that his conduct was lawful.

- *A judicial interpretation of a statute later found to be erroneous.* In a similar vein, a judge might interpret a statute in an officially published opinion as not prohibiting the type of conduct in which the defendant engaged, but that interpretation might later be overruled by a higher court. If the defendant is prosecuted for that same conduct during the period of time between the publication of the judicial opinion and the overruling of that opinion he again has a defense based on his reasonable reliance on the overturned decision.

At first glance it might strike you as odd that you can only reasonably rely on statutes or judicial decisions that later turn out to be invalid or erroneous. If the statute or judicial decision that you relied on was not erroneous, however, you would not need a mistake of law defense at all. You would simply be not guilty because your understanding of the law was the correct one!

- *An official interpretation by an agency or official charged with enforcing the law.* Sometimes law enforcement or regulatory agencies will issue official interpretations of a criminal statute, regulation or ordinance. If a defendant who relies on such an interpretation is nonetheless arrested and prosecuted he too may claim reasonable reliance.

This last exception is an easy one to misinterpret. You cannot rely on an oral or even written statement by a police officer on the street for example, because the interpretation of any one officer is not considered to be an official one. An interpretation by the local district attorney would not even be sufficient. Otherwise, police and prosecutors would essentially be able to usurp the role of the legislature in defining crimes and the role of the courts in interpreting them. Usually the interpretation must come from the state's Attorney General's office in an official opinion.

It must be stressed also that the official statement must be an interpretation of the law, not simply a promise not to enforce it. One who relies on the promise of a law enforcement officer or a prosecutor that they will not be prosecuted for violating the criminal law simply does so at their own peril in all but a very few cases.

It probably goes without saying that one cannot simply rely on the opinion of one's own attorney as part of this defense. Otherwise private attorneys could effectively insulate their clients from criminal prosecution by giving "bad" legal advice, a perverse incentive if ever was one because unscrupulous clients might beat a path to such an attorney's door to collect their "get out of jail free" cards.

3.   Where the crime contains a mental state element that itself requires knowledge of some law other than the law defining the offense itself.

This last exception is by far the most perplexing to students. The best example comes from an English case that is often described in passing in a note in the textbooks. A tenant who was evicted by his landlord was prosecuted for vandalism when he removed some acoustic ceiling tiles from his apartment before he moved out. He believed that the ceiling tiles belonged to him, since he had bought and installed them himself. Under English real property law, however, once one attaches such a tile to a wall or ceiling, it becomes part of the structure. So legally the tiles belonged to the landlord. The vandalism statute required, however, that the defendant knowingly damage the property of another. Since the defendant did not know that the ceiling tiles were the property of the landlord the court found that he did not have the mental state required for the crime.

Note that the law of which the defendant was ignorant was a law *other than the law defining the offense itself*. If the defendant had simply argued that he did not know that it was against the law for a tenant to damage the property of the landlord he would have had no defense. Note, too, that the crime he was charged with by its very terms required knowledge of the circumstance that was defined by this *other law*. If the statute had prohibited damaging the property of another regardless of whether you knew it was not your property then again the defendant would have had no defense.

It is the rare case in which a crime's mental state requires knowledge of some other law, but when it does ignorance of that *other law* will excuse.

Model Penal Code

The Model Penal Code largely tracks the common law's approach to mistake of fact and mistake of law. With respect to mistake of facts though, the MPC provides that if one's mistake belief would make one guilty of another offense if circumstances had been as the defendant believed them to be, then the defendant can be punished for that other offense if it is a lesser offense. So if a defendant burglarized a store not realizing that it was also a residence for the storeowner then the defendant would be punished for the lesser crime of commercial burglary. If, on the other hand, he broke into a store believing it to be a home, he would not be prosecuted for the greater crime of residential burglary under the MPC. Some common law jurisdictions apply a "legal-wrong" doctrine that would find the defendant guilty of whatever offense he thought he was committing, whether it is greater or lesser.

CHAPTER 9

Intoxication

I always begin teaching the doctrine of intoxication in my criminal law class by offering someone in the front row a drink. I plop down a cup and a bottle of tequila in front of a student and ask, "would you like to take a series of shots over the course of the class hour." I quickly take the bottle back (more students have reached for the bottle over the years) and instead pose a hypothetical to the class. Assume that the student took me up on the offer, grew increasingly intoxicated and belligerent and, as a result, struck a student after class after bumping into her. Should the intoxicated student be punished more harshly, less harshly, or just the same as if completely sober? The vast majority of students vote that intoxication should not make any difference to the punishment.

This intuition that intoxication should not matter to criminal liability is honored for the most part in the criminal law. Intoxication is an issue that has a large role in crime but only a tiny role in the substantive criminal law. It plays a large role in crime because many people commit many crimes in some state of intoxication. Perhaps because intoxicating drugs and alcohol play such a big role in crime, society wants to deter people from becoming intoxicated enough to commit crimes and considers them blameworthy for getting so intoxicated that they broke the law.

Since the criminal law generally treats intoxicated people as if they were sober, learning the doctrine of intoxication means learning a series of exceptions to this general rule.

Overview

Intoxication can pop up all over the place: voluntary act doctrine, insanity, premeditation and deliberation for first degree murder, provocation under voluntary manslaughter and mental states generally. Among these topics the most important rule to learn is when and how intoxication is relevant to whether a person had the mental state required for a crime.

The general rule on this point can be stated two different ways, although each essentially means the same thing.

- *Voluntary intoxication may negate a mental state of purpose or knowledge but not a mental state of criminal recklessness or negligence.*

- *Voluntary intoxication may negate a specific intent but not a general intent to commit a crime.*

There are three important things to note about these two simple rules.

First, they mean essentially the same thing because generally speaking, specific intent crimes require a purposeful or knowing mental state, whereas general intent crimes usually require a reckless or negligent mental state. So saying that voluntary intoxication may only negate a specific intent and that it may only negate a purposeful or knowing mental state is basically saying the same thing.

Second, notice that I slipped in the word *voluntary* before the word intoxication when I stated the rules. We will discuss the difference between voluntary and involuntary intoxication in more detail below, but the basic idea is that if you get intoxicated against your will or through no fault of your own then you have more possible defenses than these more limited rules describe.

Third, the use of the awkward phrase "negate the capacity" further limits the role that intoxication plays in criminal liability. Alcohol and many other intoxicating drugs loosens one's inhibitions in a way that leads to various crimes. This sort of inhibition-loosening effect does not come within the mental state defense these rules describe. Rather, you must be so intoxicated that you are no longer able to form the intent or other mental state required for the crime. Think "really drunk," not just "tipsy." You don't actually have to be falling down drunk, but you have to be way beyond "feeling a buzz."

Let's apply these rules to our tequila-drinking student in the front row of my criminal law classroom. Assume that she was really, really intoxicated and that she punched someone in the face breaking their nose. She is completely out of luck with respect to the general intent offense of simple battery. Her intoxication could be a defense to the more serious charge of assault with intent to inflict serious injury, however. That specific intent crime requires that one act with the purpose to seriously injure someone. Her lawyer could argue that she was so intoxicated that she was unable to think clearly enough to form that sort of intent. If the jury had a reasonable doubt as to whether she intended to seriously injure, they should find her not guilty of that more serious charge.

Intoxication as a General Mental State Defense

Let's explore in more depth the majority rule that voluntary intoxication may only negate a purposeful or knowing (specific intent) state of mind. As discussed, this effectively means that the defendant is held to the standard of a sober person when evaluating his mental state. That sounds reasonable from society's point of view because society considers it blameworthy and dangerous to get so intoxicated that you commit crimes. From the defendant's perspective though it is completely unreasonable because it often forces the jury to *pretend* that the defendant was sober when he was not.

Let's assume that our tequila-drinking student did not punch her classmate. Rather, imagine that frustrated by the slowness with which her classmate was moving out of her way (and feeling a rather sudden and uncomfortable need to get to the nearest bathroom) the tequila-drinking student started angrily flailing her arms around and yelling, "Move, move, move." When her puzzled classmate turned around to see what all the fuss was about, she was struck square in the nose by one of the flailing arms.

If this jurisdiction defines battery as including a harmful or offensive touching committed with criminal negligence, then a guilty verdict seems fair. Arguably, it was grossly negligent of the tequila-drinker to flail her arms so forcefully and so carelessly in such close proximity to another person. More to the point, it seems intuitively right to most people that being intoxicated should not be a defense to crimes of criminal negligence. Do we want to hold our tequila-drinking student to the standard of care of a reasonable *sober* person or a reasonable *intoxicated* person? Putting aside the contradictions implicit in the idea of a "reasonable intoxicated" person, most people accept the idea that part of being reasonable is not getting so intoxicated that you act unreasonably. To put it in more analytical terms, since negligence involves measuring the person's mental state against an *objective* standard of reasonableness, then it makes sense that we don't allow the jury to take into consideration the defendant's *subjective* condition of intoxication.

Things change when it comes to recklessness, however. Recklessness is a more culpable mental state usually reserved for more serious crimes. Imagine now that the more serious assault or battery crime with which the tequila-drinking student is charged requires a reckless state of mind. Recklessness requires both a subjective and an objective component. The objective component is that you must disregard a substantial and unjustifiable risk under circumstances that constitute a gross deviation from a reasonable standard of care. The subjective component is that you must *consciously* disregard this risk. That means that you must have been *actually aware* of the risk for at least a moment.

So to be found guilty of this reckless assault/battery charge the tequila-drinking law student must have been consciously aware for at least a moment as she flailed her arms about that she might strike someone inadvertently. This mental state definition requires us to peer inside the brain of the defendant and ask subjectively what she was actually thinking at the moment she committed the prohibited conduct. Once you peer inside the defendant's brain, it is impossible not to notice her intoxication. She might have been too intoxicated to be aware of the risks of her flailing arms. Yet the **majority rule does not allow evidence of voluntary intoxication to negate a reckless mental state.**

So the majority rule in effect requires juries to pretend that the defendant is sober when asking whether the defendant was *subjectively* aware of the risk involved. Most scholars use a fancier word than pretend, of course. They say that the majority rule *imputes* to the intoxicated defendant a capacity to be conscious of the required risk. It is important to note that on this point **the Model Penal Code follows the majority rule.**

Many people criticize the majority rule on the grounds that it is not fair to hold a defendant criminally responsible for a mental state that they are not capable of forming. The rationale behind the majority rule, however, is that the dangers of intoxication are well enough known that it is fair to hold such a defendant criminally responsible under such circumstances because he most probably was conscious of a substantial risk that he might do something wrong at the time he voluntarily and soberly decided to get intoxicated in the first place.

Fairness aside, most people see the majority rule as utilitarian and grounded in deterrence concerns. We don't want to encourage people to become intoxicated. If intoxication was a defense to reckless or negligent crimes, then intoxicated defendants would have an advantage over sober ones in court. While you might conclude that someone who soberly commits the same crime is more blameworthy in a purely retributive sense (they *really* knew what they were doing), we want to deter people from becoming intoxicated enough to commit crimes in the first place, so we pretend that people accused of reckless crimes are sober when they are not.

Minority Rules

There are not one but two minority positions that need to be mentioned: one takes a more generous approach to intoxication than the majority approach, and one takes a less generous approach than the majority.

1. A small number of jurisdictions allow evidence of intoxication to negate recklessness.

2. A few jurisdictions do not allow evidence of voluntary intoxication to negate *any mental state including purpose or knowledge* Under this second position, the jury could not consider the tequila-drinking student's intoxication in deciding whether she was guilty of assault with intent to inflict serious injury.

Intoxication as a Conduct Defense

It is important to note at this point that intoxication is not always offered as a mental state defense. Sometimes evidence of intoxication is used to argue that the defendant did not perform the conduct required for the crime. For example, in one noted case a heavily intoxicated defendant was found in a car with a dead body and another heavily intoxicated man. The dead man had been shot in the head with a handgun that it was in the car. The defendant had no memory of the time in question but argued that he was too intoxicated to hold the gun and pull the trigger. So remember to distinguish intoxication as a mental state from intoxication as an "it wasn't me" defense.

On a related note, it is conceptually possible that an extremely intoxicated person could have performed the prohibited act in a state of "automatism" akin to sleepwalking. A memory "blackout" does not necessarily mean that you were not conscious, however, just that you don't remember. In any event, the few cases that discuss this defense seem to reject an automatism defense based on intoxication. So make sure you sleepwalk sober if you think you might be committing crimes!

Intoxication and Murder

As will be discussed in the homicide chapter, evidence of intoxication may be used to argue that the defendant did not premeditate and deliberate in killing someone.   This would ordinarily have the effect of reducing the murder from first to second degree.   Remember though that the defendant must be so intoxicated as to not have the *capacity* to premeditate and deliberate.   Simply realizing after a few drinks that you really do hate this guy and want to kill him does not count.

In contrast, one may not use evidence of intoxication to argue for a voluntary manslaughter verdict on the grounds of provocation.   Legally adequate provocation requires at a minimum circumstances under which a reasonable person would lose control of his or her emotions.   This means a *reasonable sober* person, not a "reasonable intoxicated" one.

Intoxication and Timing

Not surprisingly, the courts take a rather dim view of people who drink in order to commit crimes.   One who knows that he gets violent when drunk and drinks himself drunk for that purpose will not have a defense.   A person who decides to kill someone and then intoxicates himself before killing, would probably be found to have premeditated and deliberated about the killing before he became intoxicated.   You may find your courage to commit a crime in a bottle, but you won't find your defense there.

Intoxication and Defensive Force

The legal use of defensive force generally requires a reasonable fear of an imminent harm.   This fear must be that of a *reasonable sober* person.   So a person who becomes paranoid on LSD and shoots a pizza delivery person accidentally as a result would not be found to have such a reasonable fear.

Intoxication and Insanity

There are three different relationships between intoxication and a mental impairment so profound as to constitute insanity, and each of the three has different legal consequences.

Temporary Insanity

What if you drink so much that you don't know the difference between right and wrong, or don't know the nature of what you are doing or can't control your actions? **Temporary insanity resulting from voluntary intoxication is not a defense to a crime.** Temporary insanity resulting from involuntary intoxication, however, is a different matter, as will be discussed below.

Settled Insanity Resulting from Intoxicating Substances

Sometimes people drink or drug themselves into mental illness. Organic brain damage resulting from chronic abuse of alcohol, for example, can produce various mental health impairments that meet the test for insanity. Most—but not all— jurisdictions accept such a "settled" or "fixed" (as opposed to temporary) insanity as a defense, even if it had been created by long term abuse of alcohol or other drugs. Such settled or non-temporary insanity would be treated like any other form of insanity. It would provide a complete defense to all crimes but would ordinarily result in the involuntary commitment of the defendant to a mental health facility until they were cured.

Intoxicated While Insane

Sometimes mentally ill people intoxicate themselves. If someone meets the definition of insanity independent of their use of an intoxicating substance, the fact that they were intoxicated at the time they committed a crime will not deprive them of their insanity defense.

Involuntary Intoxication

The defense of involuntary intoxication is harder to establish, but it provides a much broader defense than voluntary intoxication. A few cases suggest that involuntary intoxication could negate one's capacity to form a general intent (recklessness or negligence). This would mean that our intoxicated front row student would have a defense to the misdemeanor charge of simple battery if I had slipped tasteless, pure alcohol into her open can of coca cola, and she had lost her capacity to be non-negligent or non-reckless as a result.

The law recognizes three types of involuntary intoxication. Courts have generally been very strict about applying these definitions, and examples of successful defenses are rare.

The defendant does not know the intoxicating qualities of the substance consumed. "So that is what Vodka tastes like! I thought it was a strong mouthwash." Someone who unknowingly consumed a tasteless intoxicating substance would have the strongest case for a defense. Think marijuana brownies disguised as regular brownies, LSD laced peanuts, PCP powdered donuts and other similar goodies. This type of involuntary intoxication also includes people taking prescription medication without knowing or having any reason to know about its intoxicating effects. (That is why they put those warning labels on the pill bottles!)

Coerced Intoxication. Someone really needs to hold you down and pour the alcohol down your throat or hold a gun to your head. (Not exactly your friendly neighborhood bar.) Simple peer pressure from a fraternity or sorority hazing ritual won't cut it.

Pathological Intoxication. Some people have truly excessive reactions to intoxicating substances. One drink and they are off to the races, so to speak. Don't over interpret this defense though. First, the reaction has to be truly excessive. Claiming a "bad trip" on a hallucinogen like LSD won't cut it because hallucinations are understood to be one of the risks of taking even one hit of the drug LSD. If our tequila-drinking student became extremely belligerent and uncoordinated after a single shot, that might count as involuntary intoxication. Second, the person must have had *no way* of knowing that they would have this excessive reaction. Think of this as the "one shot" rule. *The first time* you learn that tequila turns you into a raving maniac *is the last time* that you can use this reaction to support a defense of involuntary intoxication.

Involuntary Intoxication and Temporary Insanity

The case law is very sparse here, so it is not really meaningful to identify majority and minority positions. That said, a consensus seems to exist among the few cases that exist and the scholars who write about them that involuntary intoxication could be a complete defense to *any* crime if it impaired one's mental state sufficiently to meet the definition of insanity. The advantage of such *temporary insanity* is that one will not be involuntarily committed to a mental hospital (as discussed in the insanity chapter) because one is not mentally ill.

Homicide: An Overview

Lots of people die in criminal law classes each year because homicide is the favorite topic of most criminal law professors. Many professors essentially teach the most important parts of the criminal law through the law of homicide. Because the taking of human life has long been considered the gravest crime, homicide law has played a key role in the evolution of criminal law. Judges wrestle hard with difficult questions in homicide cases because so much is at stake and often write detailed opinions explaining their reasoning. These opinions engage student attention because they deal with fundamental issues of criminal law in the context of compelling facts. For all of these reasons, criminal professors spend far more time in class—and on the exam—on homicide than any other single crime.

There are lots of different ways to slice up the homicide pie, and different professors and textbook authors do it different ways. So it is worth taking a quick look at each so that you can follow whatever path your teacher chooses to take.

Homicide is killing a human being. Note that the word "killing" actually does a lot of work. To kill someone is to engage conduct that causes a person's death. So "killing" actually incorporates three different types of element: conduct, causation, and a result required by the offense to occur. To put it in quasi mathematical terms:

Homicide = Conduct Causing Death of a Human Being

Now not all homicides are crime. Whether a homicide crime has been committed usually turns on the mental state that accompanied the conduct that caused the death. So our homicide crime equation looks like this:

Homicide Crime = Conduct Causing Death + Accompanying Mental State

The accompanying mental state, of course, determines not just whether a homicide crime occurred but also *which* homicide crime occurred. This is a very important distinction because there are almost as many different homicide crimes as there are different mental states.

The simplest and most common way of dividing up the homicide pie is to divide it between intentional and unintentional killings. This sort of division creates the following pieces in most jurisdictions.

Intentional Killings

Premeditated and Deliberate killings

Killing someone intentionally but without premeditation and deliberation

Killing someone intentionally but in the heat of passion

Some killings committed during felonies

Unintentional Killings

Extremely Reckless, extremely indifferent killings

Reckless killings

Grossly Negligent killings

Negligent killings (only in a few jurisdictions)

Some killings committed during Felonies

Now a different way of slicing up the pie is distinguish between murder and manslaughter. Manslaughter is a less serious category of homicide crime that is punished less severely.

Murder

Premeditated and Deliberate killings

Intentional killings

Extremely reckless, extremely indifferent killings

Felony Murder

Manslaughter

Voluntary Manslaughter: intentionally killing someone in the heat of passion

Involuntary Manslaughter: killing someone recklessly, with gross negligence, or (in few jurisdictions) with simple negligence.

Note that not all intentional killings are murder, and not all unintentional killings are manslaughter. You can kill someone intentionally in the heat of passion and get convicted of voluntary manslaughter, whereas someone who kills another in an extremely reckless fashion could get murder instead of involuntary manslaughter. (The division between voluntary and involuntary manslaughter reflects the distinction between an intentional and unintentional killing.) So don't be confused as you march through the law of homicide when you see murder crop up in both intentional and unintentional killings, or when you realize that unintentional killings can include murder as well as manslaughter. Just make sure you understand what each piece requires.

You may wonder at this point about degrees of murder. TV shows love first degree murder, so you have probably heard that term a lot. Most jurisdictions do divide murder up into degrees of murder, but there is a lot of variation in how these divisions are made. The most important thing in practice or on an exam is to read the statute that applies and make sure you understand how that jurisdiction slices up the homicide pie. In the absence of clear statutory definitions, you can rely on the following rough rules of thumb that describe the most common approach.

1.   First degree murder is usually reserved for premeditated and deliberate killings and other particularly heinous types of murder.

2.   Second degree murder usually includes intentional and extremely reckless killings.

3.   Felony murder is a bit of a tossup. Some jurisdictions treat it as first degree, others as second degree, and some split up felony murder between both degrees based on the type of felony committed.

In the chapters that follow I split up homicide up into four chapters. The chapter on common law murder covers three of the four types of homicide recognized as murder at common law: intent to kill murder, intent to grievously injure murder and extremely reckless murder. The next chapter deals with premeditated and deliberate murder, a crime that many states have created to punish more severely the worst type of intentional killings. Felony murder, the fourth type of common law murder gets its own chapter because of its complexity. The chapter on manslaughter covers both intentional killings (voluntary manslaughter) and unintentional killings (involuntary manslaughter) that fall short of murder.

CHAPTER 11

Common Law Murder

Understanding the common law definition of murder remains important because a number of common law jurisdictions—though not all—do not define the term "murder" in their statutes. These statutes often define different degrees of murder, but the word murder itself is never defined. Jurisdictions taking a more modern approach define the different degrees of murder by specifying what mental state must accompany the conduct that caused the death.

You may have heard the colorful phase "killing with malice aforethought." Malice was the common law's definition of murder. If you killed someone with malice, then that was murder. If you killed with some lesser mental state then it was manslaughter (assuming it was not completely justified or excused in which case it was not any crime). What you will quickly figure out is that malice just refers to a bunch of different mental states. Most modern homicide codes specify these mental states instead of relying upon the concept of malice. Many cases in common law jurisdictions still discuss malice, and a few codes in common law jurisdictions don't specify the mental states required for murder.

In these jurisdictions—and on the Multistate Bar Exam (a multiple choice test that many jurisdictions use as part of their bar exam) you need to know the common law definition of murder.

Malice is divided up into two types: express and implied. Express malice refers to an intent to kill. Implied malice refers to everything else.

Express Malice: Intent to Kill

Implied Malice:

> *Intent to commit Grievous Bodily Injury*
>
> *Abandoned and Malignant Heart/Depraved heart*
>
> *Intent to commit a dangerous Felony*

The common law implied the malice required for murder in these sorts of cases because it judged the offender to be just as evil or just as dangerous as someone who intended to kill. A bank robber who killed accidentally, or an assailant who just wanted to maim you, or a person who was so careless that he just didn't care where you lived or died were considered to murderers if someone died as a result of their conduct.

We will go through each of the different types of common law murder below in more detail. Indeed, what you will eventually see is that these categories greatly shaped how modern codes draw the line between murder and manslaughter. Those codes just don't often use the word malice anymore.

Intent to Kill Murder

Think of intent to kill murder as the baseline of murder. An easy case would be someone who purposely shoots some else in the head. If you consciously desire that someone die—or are substantially certain that they will die—by your conduct then you intend to kill them. Note that intent to kill includes both purposeful and knowing conduct with respect to death. So if I blow up a plane to kill you specifically, I will still be found guilty of the murder of all the other passengers since I clearly knew that they would die, as well.

People are generally presumed to intend the natural and probable consequences of what they do. If I push you off the roof of a ten story building, the natural and probable result of that would be your death. More specifically, juries are often told that they may infer intent to kill from the use of a deadly weapon directed at a vital part of the human anatomy. So a baseball bat to the head would do nicely for intent to kill as long as the prosecutor could prove that the defendant did intend to hit the victim in the head with the baseball bat.

Obviously one can intend to kill another in any number of ways. Not only are weapons not required, you don't even have to touch the other person. Telling someone to turn left instead of right with the intent that he walk off a cliff could be murder. Omissions to act in the face of a legal duty can also be murder although it is often not easy to prove an intent to kill based on something that a person failed to do. Returning to our drowning hypothetical from chapter 5 if you push me off an ocean pier not knowing that I can't swim, you did not intend to kill me. But failing to throw me a life preserver could be intent-to-kill murder if you hear me screaming, "I am drowning."

Intentional killings can also be entirely impulsive. Despite the fact that the mental state for murder at common was termed "malice aforethought," intent to kill murder does not require that you have thought about it in advance.

Intent to Grievously Injure Murder

The idea here is that the killer only meant to seriously or grievously injure the victim, not kill them. At common law this was murder, but today only a minority of jurisdictions recognize intent-to-grievously-injure killings as murder. Imagine that Joey the Loan Shark decides to cut off your pinky finger because you owe him money and have been late paying. You unexpectedly bleed to death. Joey would be guilty of murder at common law. He clearly did not intend for you to die (if you die, he will never get his money). He just wanted to send a message to you and all of his other deadbeat customers about the importance of timely payment. He may not even have been reckless with respect to the risk of your death (he handed you a sterile compress bandage as soon as he finished amputating the finger). But the amputation of even a pinky finger is a grievous injury, and the common law considered people who would intentionally hurt someone grievously to be just as bad as an intentional killer.

The point of the example is that the loan shark clearly does not want the victim to die because if he dies, the debt will never be repaid. Nonetheless, if the maimed deadbeat dies unexpectedly, that would be murder at common law and under the minority rule.

The more common scenario for this type of murder is a fight or a beating that "gets out of hand." Beating someone to a bloody pulp with your fists or using a deadly weapon against a non-vital part of the human anatomy would suffice. But the mere fact that a grievous injury occurred—which must have happened since the person ended up dying from it—does not necessarily mean that the killer intended the grievous injury. Intent, of course, requires a knowing and state of mind, not just a reckless one, with respect to the injury. So the assailant must at some point intend that the fight "get out of hand."

How bad does the injury intended have to be? Definitions vary, but generally something that makes your seriously worry about "life, health or limb." Despite the risk of puncturing a lung, a broken rib might not do it even though such an injury would easily suffice for felonious assault in most jurisdictions. Something that is going to seriously impair you in a permanent or semi-permanent way would be enough.

Does this mean that our violent loan shark is safe from a murder charge in the majority of jurisdictions? Not necessarily. Intentionally maiming someone who ends up dying might count as murder under the following category.

Depraved Heart Murder

Imagine someone so utterly careless that they seem just as evil and just as dangerous to you as someone who actually intended to kill. You need to imagine the sort of carelessness that makes you yell, "Oh my God," or "Damn," or worse. A bank robber who uses a child as a human shield during a gunfight. A dentist who killed not one, not two, but three patients in a row by being mind-bogglingly careless about infection procedures. A driver who drove ninety miles an hour down the sidewalk of a busy street. Someone who adopted a pit bull that had been trained to fight and who left the gate on his pen open, despite the fact that preschool children lived next door. An airline captain and copilot who show up drunk to fly a 747. You now have the main idea behind depraved heart murder.

Common law had all sorts of colorful labels for this sort of extreme carelessness.

- Depraved Heart
- Abandoned and Malignant Heart
- Wicked Disposition

- Wanton, Cruel, Callous

- Hard Hearted

All of these phrases tried to get at the same thing: the idea that this was as bad a person as someone who actually intended to kill and thereby deserved the label and corresponding penalty of murderer. Notice how many of the phrases use the word "heart," and how much they allude to not just mental state but character as well.

More modern jurisdictions, especially those who follow the Model Penal Code in whole or in part, use slightly more analytical and slightly less emotional language. These jurisdictions often speak in terms of "extreme recklessness." The MPC includes within its definition of murder an "extreme indifference to human life.

The bad news is that once one gets beyond the easy-because-they-are-so-extreme cases there is not a very clear line between the sort of carelessness that constitutes murder as opposed to involuntary manslaughter (discussed below). How reckless or indifferent do you have to be? What about your garden-variety drunk driver who has too much to drink and misses a stop sign? Or your garden-variety idiot who plays Russian Roulette with his friends? Should murder or manslaughter be the crime if death results? Cases go both ways although the recent trend has been decidedly in favor of prosecuting aggravated drunk driving cases as murder.

Exam Tip: Reckless Murder

Reckless murder issues are common exam issues because they test the student's ability to argue both sides of an issue since no clear line exists between murder and manslaughter. The best way to sort your way through this confusion on an exam is by working your way through the elements of recklessness.

- Conscious Disregard of a

- Substantial (magnitude of the harm times probability of harm) and

- Unjustifiable Risk that constitutes a

- Gross Deviation from the standard of care of a reasonable person

What almost always distinguishes murder from manslaughter is that the evidence supporting one or more of the elements will be overwhelming to the point that it is disturbing. Risks about food poisoning in a restaurant or fire exits in a crowded building are very substantial because many people will die even if they might not be all that probable. Driving a car down a busy sidewalk is murderous because of the high probability that someone will die, even if you are racing to take a sick child to the hospital. Playing Russian roulette is murderous because even though the possibility of the gun going off is only one in six, the risk is completely unjustifiable since the participants do it "just for kicks."

The easiest cases for extreme recklessness murder are often ones that involve risks that are not just unjustifiable but involve what some jurisdictions quaintly call "base or anti-social purposes." Think of someone training a dangerous animal for fighting competitions or a drug dealer who is cutting his illegal drugs with toxic substances. What is considered base or anti-social (fancy words for evil or super dangerous) changes over time. Drunk driving, for example, has gone from being considered mischievous, to criminal, to potentially murderous in many jurisdictions over the last thirty or forty years. Harder cases involve business people engaged in legal enterprises but whose carelessness creates a high risk of death for the public. Such business people are "trying to make a living," not "make a killing." On the other hand, cutting corners on safety standards to "make a quick buck" can seem murderous if a great risk of death is created for many people.

CHAPTER 12

Premeditated and Deliberate Murder

Premeditated and murder is what you almost always see on TV. Someone has a reason to kill someone, and they think about it before hand. Most jurisdictions today define premeditated and deliberate killings as first degree murder. A killing that one thinks about beforehand is thought to be more blameworthy, and a person who commits such a killing is thought to be more dangerous.

A "hit man" who kills for money is perhaps the clearest example of such a killer. Many textbooks, however, contain at least one example of a mercy killing where a grief stricken spouse or child reluctantly takes the life of a loved one in order to spare them pointless suffering. Such examples make the point that the people who think before killing are not always more evil than those who do not. The criminal law punishes more harshly killers who reason their way into killing more harshly, but it does not attempt to distinguish between good and bad reasons.

You can, of course, intend to kill someone without premeditating and deliberating about it. Imagine a very thin skinned sports fan who works at a shooting range. His arch rival taunts the sports fan about his team's recent abysmal performance. The sports fan impulsively picks up his gun and shots his rival in the head. That killing would be considered intentional in all jurisdictions but not premeditated and deliberate because most jurisdictions require something more than mere intent for this type of murder.

Premeditation and Deliberation Defined

Premeditation and deliberation require both quantity of thought and quality of thought. Quantity of thought refers to the time one spends thinking about killing. Quality of thought refers to how clearly you were able to think about it. Some jurisdictions use premeditation to refer to both requirements, and others use deliberation to refer to the quality of the killer's thinking. Either way, all jurisdictions require you to have both.

There is a broad and a narrow definition of premeditation and deliberation. The broad definition treats premeditation and deliberation as virtually the same thing as intending to kill. Jurisdictions using this broad definition require "no appreciable time" for premeditation reasoning that "no time is too short for a wicked man" to decide to kill someone. One such court said that one can premeditate and deliberate in the time that it takes to pull a trigger. Most jurisdictions, however, require something more. Their narrower definition requires a period of "brief reflection" although no jurisdiction identifies a minimum period of time. Under the majority approach you must have enough time to change your mind, to give your decision "a second look."

Time to think about killing is not by itself enough. The jury must conclude that the killer actually thought about the decision in some meaningful way. Imagine a rage filled killer who, after discovering that his best friend had betrayed him, chanted over and over again "I am going to kill him, I am going to kill him, I am going to kill him" before killing. Such a killer may have been too caught up in his rage to actually deliberate the passage of time notwithstanding.

Deliberation (or the "meditation" part of "premeditation") requires that the killer actually reflect on what he is about to do. Some jurisdictions talk about deliberation as a process where you think of the reasons for and against. Others emphasize the need for a "cool purpose," free from the influence of passion or excitement. "Cold-blooded killers" such as hit men are easy examples of deliberation.

Failed Excuses

Many conditions that do not excuse killing may be enough to prevent a jury from finding that a killer premeditated and deliberated. Voluntary intoxication not sufficient to completely negate an intent to kill, mental defects short of insanity, or provocation that excites hot blood but fails to meet the strict tests for manslaughter described in later chapters might be sufficient to establish that the killer was not capable of the quality of thought required for premeditated and deliberate murder.

Earmarks of Premeditation and Deliberation

One of the most useful things courts have given us in this area is a list of three "earmarks" of premeditation and deliberation. While not required, the presence of one or more of these earmarks makes the argument for premeditation and deliberation a lot easier.

1.   Planning activity

2.   Motive

3.   Manner of killing suggests passage of time or advance thinking

Planning activity speaks for itself because you can't plan something that you do on the spur of the moment. Motive means that that the killer had a reason that he could have thought about in advance. A husband with a multi-million dollar insurance policy on his dead wife is easier to convict of premeditated murder because he has millions of reasons that he could have weighed against her life. The manner of killing earmark refers to things such as lying in wait for someone, or acquiring a weapon in advance which also suggests some advance thinking.

Remember though that premeditation and deliberation does not require good planning or good thinking. Unlike the crafty TV killers that capture everyone's imagination, many of the killers who inhabit the pages of criminal law textbooks are pathetic figures who kill for stupid reasons and in stupid ways. Killing thoughtfully but stupidly can still be first degree murder.

Also, don't imagine that courts or juries find the line between premeditation and deliberate murder and merely intentional murder to be clear. One court refused to find that strangulation was proof of premeditation because of the time and effort it takes to strangle someone. Another court found proof of premeditation in thirty stab wounds, reasoning that while the first stab may have been impulsive, the 30th could not have been. Both courts were from the same jurisdiction!

Model Penal Code

Some jurisdictions, most notably the Model Penal Code, abandoned or never adopted the distinction between premeditated and deliberate murder and intentional murder. The Model Penal Code, for example, does not divide murder up into degrees. A purposeful killing is murder, whether you thought about it for a second or a year.

Exam Tip: Premeditation and Deliberation

Ask three questions of a fact pattern raising this issue. First, when could the killer have begun thinking about killing? When he found out that his roommate had stolen his life savings? When his roommate admitted it but taunted him that no proof existed? When the killer picked up a baseball bat and followed the former roommate out to his car? The prosecution will generally try to move the time of decision as far back in time as possible to create more time for thought, and the defense will try to move it as close to the killing as possible to make the killing seem impulsive and unpremeditated. Second, what reasons existed to kill? Monetary gain is probably the easiest because it conjures up an image of a cool, calculating killer. The clearer the reason the easier it is to argue that the killer deliberated about that reason. Third, what conditions existed that might have made it hard for the killer to think straight about those reasons. In addition to intoxication and mental illness don't forget to think about strong emotions. Revenge is a common reason for violence, but it raises the possibility that the killer was too emotional to deliberate. When the reason to kill is an emotional one, the more time the prosecutor can put between the decision to kill and the act the easier it is to argue that the decision was a deliberate one, not the result of impulse or emotion.

CHAPTER 13

Felony Murder

Felony murder is a very important area of practice because it is widely used by prosecutors, and it is a common subject of law school exams because it requires students to work through a complex set of interlocking rules and definitions. Think of it is as a "sweeping homicide crime" with lots of exceptions and limits.

Before dealing with the limits and exceptions, let's get our heads around the basic rule in its classic form. **One is guilty of felony murder if a death results from a felony one commits or attempts to commit.**

Felony murder is a sweeping homicide crime because this definition covers so much ground. For starters, it involves both intentional and unintentional killings. Think of the butterfingered bank robber who drops his gun during the robbery. The gun goes off and kills a bank teller. What is the bank robber guilty of? Negligent handling of a firearm during a bank robbery? Involuntary manslaughter because he was careless with the gun and someone died? No, the butterfingered bank robber is guilty of murder under the felony murder doctrine, and in many jurisdictions, he is guilty of first degree murder.

Let's take it a step further. Assume that the butterfingered bank robber was not actually careless with the gun. He wore special sticky gloves, and practiced drawing the gun over and over again to avoid mishaps. He still is guilty of felony murder in most jurisdictions. (And as we will learn when we deal with complicity, so is his hapless driver who is waiting outside the bank in the getaway car when the gun goes off.) Wait, you might ask, don't we care whether or not he was careful in handling the gun? More broadly, doesn't homicide liability always depend on what mental state accompanied the conduct causing the death? Yes, that is the case *except for felony murder!*

What sets felony murder apart from all other homicide crimes is that strictly speaking the law does not care what your mental state was with respect to the conduct causing the death. Whether the bank robber was careful or careless with the gun does not matter under a classic felony murder rule. What matters is whether the killer had the mental state required for the felony! If he committed (or was attempting to commit) a felony covered by the rule and death resulted then he is guilty of felony murder.

For this reason, many describe felony murder as a form of strict liability because felons are held strictly liable for resulting deaths regardless of their culpability with respect to how the person actually died.

Policies Behind the Felony Murder Doctrine

Why do we allow such strict liability for murder when the common law is generally so hostile to strict liability? The short answer is because we really don't like felons. The longer answer consists of the following three policy arguments in favor of felony murder liability.

1. To deter felonies.

2. To deter accidental deaths during felonies.

3. To ease proof of homicide during felonies.

Obviously, the fact that you will be executed or go to prison for life if someone dies during your felony might discourage you from committing the felony in the first place. Less obvious, but equally important, is the idea that the felony murder rule creates an additional incentive to avoid *accidental* deaths during your felony. Felony murder applies to both intentional killings as well as accidental ones, but an intentional killing will already be prosecuted as murder. Accidental killings might otherwise be prosecuted as involuntary manslaughter if they involved only grossly negligent conduct. They might not be prosecuted as homicide crimes at all if they involved only simple negligence. Imagine that your kidnapping victim suffocates in the trunk of your car while you are driving to your hideout. Was that negligent? Grossly negligent? Reckless? Extremely reckless? Who cares? Under most versions of the felony murder you will be guilty of first degree murder, not "negligent transport of a kidnapping victim."

Finally, the felony murder rule also sometimes eliminates proof problems when dealing with multiple felons. Imagine that a hostage gets executed during a botched bank robbery. There are three bank robbers. Which one killed the hostage? What if the bank robber who killed the hostage did so without consulting with his colleagues? Who cares! Under felony murder, the prosecutor need only prove that each defendant participated in the bank robbery, and the death resulted from that felony. All three robbers are guilty of felony murder.

Limitations on Felony Murder Liability

Now that you see how sweeping felony murder can potentially be in its scope, you are in a better position to understand the need for ways to limit the resulting murder liability. There are lots of limits on felony murder liability (although none would spare the butterfingered bank robber or his hapless driver from first degree murder liability in most jurisdictions). What makes this area particularly tricky for first year law students is that some of these limitations will be written in the statute, and other limitations will be read into a statute by a judge who interprets the law against the background of the common law. Here is a quick preview of these limitations and exceptions.

1. Limits on the types of felonies that trigger the felony murder rule.

2. Exceptions for felonies that are not independent from the homicide itself.

3. Limits on the causal relationship between the felony and the resulting death.

4. Limits on the time during which the felony occurs.

One important point needs to be made about these limitations: they are creatures of the common law that have been incorporated into modern homicide schemes by judges or legislatures. These limitations often operate as presumptions by judges who assume that the legislature intended to incorporate the common law's limits on felony murder into the jurisdiction's statutory scheme. They are not constitutional principles though. This means that where the legislature clearly intends to ignore one of these limits, a judge will abandon a contrary common law presumption and apply the statue as the legislature wrote it. This idea will become clearer after we discuss the first two limitations on felony murder liability.

Limitations on Types of Felonies

In the song "Alice's Restaurant," the narrator commits "felony littering" by dumping a truckload of garbage where he shouldn't. Imagine that a homeless person was sleeping where the trash was dumped and suffocated as a result. (You might want to further imagine that the dumper reasonably had no way of anticipating that a person would have been sleeping in that spot to rule out murder or manslaughter on the grounds of recklessness or negligence just to make things more interesting.) Could the dumper be convicted of felony murder for his felony littering? The answer is almost always no because very few jurisdictions would allow this type of felony to support felony murder

Enumeration

There are two ways that jurisdictions limit the type of felonies that create felony murder liability. The first way is "enumeration." Enumeration means that the statute lists the felonies that suffice for felony murder and limits felony murder liability to that list. The following felonies all created felony murder liability at common law and are also the most commonly enumerated felonies in those jurisdictions that list them in their statute.

- Rape
- Robbery
- Burglary
- Arson
- Kidnapping

Note that enumeration can work in a couple of different ways. Some statutes enumerate felonies but do not limit felony murder liability to that list. Others create first degree felony murder liability for enumerated felonies and second degree murder liability for non-enumerated felonies. Read your statute with care on this point!

The Inherently Dangerous Felony Rule

The second type of common limitation on the type of felony required is the *inherently dangerous felony* rule. At common law only felonies that were inherently dangerous to human life supported felony murder. This would seem to rule out felony murder for our felony litterer, but his liability would in turn depend on which of two very different interpretations of "inherently dangerous" his jurisdiction followed.

Many jurisdictions interpret inherently dangerous in an *abstract* or *per se* way. This means that a felony is inherently dangerous only if there is no way the felony can be committed without creating a substantial risk that someone will die. Note that this means that you forget about the facts of the case before you (in which someone obviously did die), and you ask yourself is there some possible way that the felony could have been committed safely. Since there are million ways to litter without endangering anyone the answer would probably be yes in our example, so our felony litterer could easily escape felony murder liability. Even felonies that are often dangerous fail to satisfy the abstract version of the inherently dangerous limitation because there is often a safe way to commit the offence. For example, a person who commits the felony offense of evading a police officer by reckless speeding away in a car could escape felony murder liability if the statute also applied to someone who ran away from a police officer on foot since foot chases ordinarily don't endanger human life.

Many other jurisdictions (treatise writers refuse to say which is the majority and which is the minority camp) interpret inherently dangerous *by manner of commission*. This means that a felony is inherently dangerous if it was committed in a dangerous manner in the case before the court. The high speed car chase described above would easily satisfy this definition of inherently dangerous. In the felony littering example a judge in such a jurisdiction would ask whether the dumping of the litter created a substantial risk of death. Now just because someone died, that does not necessarily mean that the risk was substantial. The defense would argue in such a case that it was a freak accident that someone happened to be asleep in that exact spot at that exact time. But that argument can be a hard one to make. A judge might see even a slight risk as a substantial one with the benefit of hindsight since someone did end up dying.

Finally, note that the inherently dangerous rule is not applied to felonies that are enumerated in the statute. The fact that the legislature listed the felony precludes the need for further analysis on this point.

Limiting Felony Murder to Independent Felonies

While death must result from a felony in order to have felony murder, the felony must be independent from the murder. This confuses many students initially, but most understand why when they think about it a little bit.

Imagine that one person has badly beaten another, and the victim dies. Ordinarily the prosecutor would have to prove an intent to kill in order to obtain a murder conviction. If the evidence suggested that he intended to hurt, not kill, the victim, then the jury would return a not guilty verdict on the murder charge if they harbored a reasonable doubt as to whether he in fact intended to kill. Now imagine what would happen if a clever prosecutor could charge felony murder, based on the felonious assault. (An assault committed with the intent to seriously injure another is usually a felony assault.) Even if the prosecutor could not prove intent to kill, he could use the felony murder rule to "bootstrap" what was really just a felonious assault that up into a murder conviction. For that matter, why would a prosecutor ever try to prove intent to kill if he could rely instead on an intent to seriously injure under the felony murder rule? Murder liability would quickly expand to cover many deaths that were unintended. The same paradox results if the law allows criminally negligent or reckless conduct to satisfy felony murder requirements on the grounds that such conduct constitutes the felony of involuntary manslaughter.

To avoid this result, judges limited felony murder to felonies that were *independent* of the resulting homicide. Assaultive crimes and crimes such as drunk driving causing death where the assault was unintentional but criminally negligent were said to "merge" into the resulting homicide and did not constitute felony murder.

At this point many students scratch their heads and wonder how can a felony that is independent of the homicide result in the homicide? A felony is considered independent if it has an *independent felonious purpose*. The easiest examples of felonies that can easily result in death but that have such an independent purpose are the felonies most commonly enumerated: rape, robbery, burglary, arson and kidnapping. You don't rape, or rob, or kidnap someone in order to kill them ordinarily. Each of these crimes are committed for their own reasons. So they do not merge into any homicides that result from their commission, and they create felony murder liability. An intent to seriously injure someone on the other hand is not considered to have a purpose independent of any resulting homicide.

Once again, it bears pointing out that the legislature can enumerate any felony it wants to, including felonies that are not independent of their resulting homicides. A number of jurisdictions, for example, have enumerated felony child abuse as a basis for felony murder. Such a clear expression of legislative intent overcomes the presumption that common law judges would ordinarily apply against felony murder for assaultive crimes under the merger doctrine.

Limits on the Causal Relationship Between the Felony and the Resulting Death

There are a couple of different types of rules that define the relationship that must exist between the death and the underlying felony for felony murder to occur. Don't feel confused if they seem to overlap in a couple of places because they do overlap, and even judges and scholars don't always keep them straight.

The simplest way to organize your thinking in this area is to divide these rules up into the following three groups.

1.   Time and Place Rules

2.   Logical Relationship Rules

3.   Causal Rules

All three types of rules have been referred to by the Latin phrase *res gestae*, which is simply Latin for the words "thing done." (Not exactly a phrase that one uses all the time in casual conversation.) The idea was that felony murder required that the killing be within the "thing done" by the felony.

Time and Place Rules

Central to *res gestae* was the idea that the death must have been related in time and place to the underlying felony. Time is the more important of these two factors. Many courts describe common law felony murder rule as applying to *deaths occurring during the commission or attempted commission of the felony* and this language has been incorporated into many modern statutes.

Courts have generally held that the felony begins with conduct sufficient to constitute an attempt and ends when a defendant reaches a place of temporary safety. Beginning felony murder liability with the attempt is logical given the deterrent purposes of the rule. Deciding when to end felony murder liability is more difficult. Many felons flee the scene of the crime, and some remain "in flight" for days, months, or even years. Extending felony murder liability to any death they cause during their flight seemed to be too open-ended to many courts, and the temporary safety rule seemed a reasonable place to end liability.

Imagine that a bank robber runs over and kills a pedestrian as he pulls his car into the bank parking lot and then runs over and kills a second pedestrian several miles away as he is fleeing the robbery. Having safely eluded the police he stops at a motel to check into a room and take a nap. (All that stress has him worn out.) When he wakes up he turns on the TV and learns that there is a manhunt under way for him using a perfect description of him and his car. As he is hurriedly pulling his car out of the parking lot he hits and kills a third pedestrian. Under conventional *res gestae* rules he would be guilty of felony murder of the first pedestrian (his attempt began when he became dangerously proximate to committing the offense) and the second pedestrian (distance from the scene notwithstanding he was still fleeing the crime) but not the third pedestrian (he may not have been completely safe in the motel room but he was temporarily and relatively safe). So two counts of felony murder and one count of involuntary manslaughter for our bad-driving-bank-robber.

One unusual twist that courts sometimes see in this area is the homicide that precedes a felony. Imagine that you see your hated college roommate from freshman year, and you immediately shoot him dead over some trivial past slight that bubbles up into your consciousness (you are a bit of a grudge-holder). After you shoot him you decide to go through his pockets for spare change. You find a wallet stuffed full of hundred dollar bills (he may have been a jerk, but he did pretty well for himself), and you take the money. On these facts, you are guilty of second degree murder for an unpremeditated intentional killing, but not first degree felony murder because the killing preceded and was not "within the thing done." If you shot him hoping to get the money back that you lent him freshman year that, of course, would be an easy case of felony murder because the killing was simply the first step in the felony robbery.

Logical Relationship Rules

Duration rules only take us so far though. What if you see your hated freshman roommate while you are robbing a bank and shoot him? One might argue that you killed him out of fear that he recognized you and could identify you to the police. Let's put a ski mask on you though to rule that possibility out and assume that you just killed him out of spite. That would not be felony murder because the killing was not logically related in any way to the felony. (Something that means a lot to your accomplices who would otherwise be on the hook for a murder that truly had nothing to do with the felony they committed.)

At common law it was sometimes said that felony murder liability applied to *acts committed in furtherance of the felony*, language that many jurisdictions have adopted by statute or by court decision. The mere fact that a killing coincided in time and place with a felony does not mean that the act causing the death was necessarily committed in furtherance of the felony. Similarly many courts have found that the language *in the commission or attempted commission of a felony* also implies a logical or causal relationship to the felony.

Note that the death itself need not further the felony, just the act that caused the death. In the case of the buttered-fingered bank robber the accidental death of the teller does not necessarily further the felony of robbery in any way but the carrying of the gun did.

Some courts have gone beyond requiring a logical relationship between the death and the felony and have replaced the time and place rules discussed above with a "logical nexus" test. Such courts say that time and place are only factors to be considered when assessing whether a killing was logically related to the felony.

Returning to the freshman roommate scenario, imagine now that you did not wear the ski mask, and your former roommate recognized you, but you did not shoot him in the bank. A year later, while you are still on the run, your former roommate recognizes you in the parking lot of a local supermarket (maybe you should have moved somewhere else). If you shoot him, then that probably would be felony murder in a jurisdiction using a logical nexus test. Under traditional *res gestae* rules, your felony murder liability would have ended long ago when you reached a place of temporary safety from arrest. A court applying the logical nexus test would probably infer that you killed him to stop him from reporting your whereabouts to the police, which is obviously logically related to the bank robbery.

Don't be confused if *res gestae* and logical relation seem to be closely related to ideas of causation. They are! The cases, however, often speak of them separately, so it is important to be able to do the same in arguing to a judge or writing for an exam.

Remember that your job as a student—and as a lawyer—is often not to make the law simpler or more logical than it is, but to learn to make arguments using the concepts and rules as they have been developed.

Causation Rules

As has been discussed, requiring a logical relationship between the death and the felony implies causation. Two types of causal rules come into play with felony murder: general causal requirements applicable to all deaths and special rules dealing with killings committed by non-felons.

The general causal rules are critically important to the scope of felony murder liability. Two approaches exist. One requires only actual causation, also known as factual or but for causation. But for causation means that but for the felony the death would not have occurred. The second requires not just actual causation but proximate causation. Proximate causation for felony murder essentially means that the death was a foreseeable or natural result of the felonious act. (Both of these types of causation will be discussed in much greater detail in the chapter on causation that follows, but these rough definitions will do for now.)

Requiring only actual causation greatly expands the scope of felony murder liability. In one widely noted case, an armed robber was found guilty of felony murder when one of the people in the store he robbed had a heart attack and died after the robber left. Instead of straining to call the death foreseeable, the court said that the deaths need only be actually caused—not proximately caused—in order to come within felony murder. Had proximate cause been required, most courts would not have found felony murder on these facts because while it is conceivable that someone might have a heart attack as a result of an armed robbery it is sufficiently improbable to be considered abnormal as opposed to a natural result.

While some jurisdictions require only actual causation for felony murder, most also require proximate causation. That said, those jurisdictions that do require proximate causation define it very broadly. Our butter-fingered bank robber would probably be found guilty of felony murder under either approach because dropping a gun and having it fire and kill someone would be probably be considered a natural and foreseeable result of waiving a gun around during an armed robbery.

Don't be too troubled if you find both of these examples to be equally foreseeable or equally unforeseeable. First, these rules of causation don't always produce predictable results. Courts from different jurisdictions and even within a jurisdiction often differ in how they apply them to similar cases. Second, further nuances about the rules of causation will be discussed in the chapter on causation. (I put the causation chapter after the homicide chapters because that is where it appears in many textbooks and because homicide crimes provide the best illustrations of causation principles.)

For example, one important difference between the two examples given is that death by gunshot is the same general type of harm contemplated by one who engages in an armed robbery whereas death by heart attack is not. Some courts might also see the heart attack as the sort of intervening cause that "breaks the chain of causation" between the defendant's acts and the resulting death where the butter-fingered bank robber's dropping of his gun more directly caused the death of the teller. Each of these principles will be discussed in more detail later.

Killings Committed by Non-Felons

Does felony murder liability include killings by people reacting to the felony? The classic examples involve a police officer, crime victim, or bystander who kills someone in the process of trying to foil an armed robbery.

The majority of jurisdictions, however, refuse to extend felony murder liability to killings by non-felons. They employ what is sometimes called an *agency theory* of felony murder reasoning that the act causing death must be performed by an "agent" of the felony, not someone resisting it.

A minority of jurisdictions, however, hold the felons liable for felony murder for such deaths under a *proximate causation theory*. So if the store owner shoots at one of the robbers and accidentally kills an innocent customer the robber gets convicted of felony murder for the death of the customer on the theory that it is foreseeable that people might resist an armed robbery with deadly force and that a bystander might get killed.

Within the minority of jurisdictions that extend felony murder liability to killings by non-felons most of those states do not include within felony murder *killings of a co-felon by a non-felon*. So if the store owner kills your accomplice to the robbery, you will not be found guilty of felony murder for his death even though you would be found guilty in such a jurisdiction if the bullet had hit and killed a customer standing next to him. (So as an armed robber you actually want straight shooting store owners in such a jurisdiction as long as you are not the felon being shot!)

A minority of jurisdictions within the minority of jurisdictions that extend felony murder liability to killings by non-felons include killings of co-felons by non-felons within felony murder. So not only do you lose your accomplice to the straight-shooting storeowner, but you get convicted of murder for his death. Talk about adding insult to injury!

Other Types of Felony Murder Liability

Up to this point we have been discussing the felony murder rule in its "classic form" which is largely based on its common law form. Many jurisdictions, however, have modified the rule to make it less harsh. They do so generally by writing into the rule a requirement that the defendant have some sort of culpable mental state of with respect to the conduct that caused the death. You might think of this as "felony-murder-lite." Some jurisdictions require that the felon perform an act "inherently dangerous" or "clearly dangerous" to human life. Other jurisdictions use felony murder only as a "grading provision. These statues require proof of some form of express or implied malice but then provide that such murders shall be first degree murders if committed in the course of certain types of felonies.

The Model Penal Code, for example, contains a felony murder provision that "felony murder purists" would not even consider to be felony murder at all. MPC section 210 includes within murder, killings committed "recklessly, under circumstances manifesting extreme indifference to the value of human life." The MPC tells the jury that it can presume such recklessness and indifference exists if the defendant is engaged in rape, robbery, arson, kidnapping, burglary, or felonious escape, although this presumption can be rebutted by the defense. So our butterfingered bank robber could potentially escape liability for murder by showing that he was not extremely careless in handling his gun.

Some jurisdictions that do not have true felony murder treat an underlying factor as a factor aggravating the degree of murder committed. Such a jurisdiction might require for example, an intent to kill or extreme recklessness for the act causing the death but would then raise the resulting liability from second to first degree murder because the murderous act was committed in the course of a felony. So our butter-fingered bank robber would be in luck in such a jurisdiction because simply firing a single warning shot in the air might not be reckless enough to satisfy the standard for extremely reckless murder. If he fired multiple shots over the heads of the tellers, however, and inadvertently shot one extremely tall teller then his extreme recklessness would result in not a second but a first degree murder conviction because his extremely reckless act was committed in the course of a bank robbery. Such statutory provisions essentially treat the commission of felonies as a grading factor for murder. A careful reading of the statute at hand usually distinguishes such grading provisions from true felony murder rules.

Misdemeanor or Unlawful Act Manslaughter

Many jurisdictions specifically provide for involuntary manslaughter liability when death results from an unlawful act that does not satisfy the jurisdiction's felony murder rule. These provisions often include both felonies that are not enumerated or not inherently dangerous as well as misdemeanors. Our felony litterer described above could be found guilty of misdemeanor manslaughter as could a driver who kills someone not recklessly or even negligently but through some minor traffic infraction.

Exam Tips: Felony Murder

Felony murder fact patterns are favorite exam topics for many criminal law professors because they test a student's ability to apply a complex set of interlocking rules and doctrines. Even the most complex fact pattern can be broken up into the following simple steps, however.

- Figure out who is guilty of the felony

- Figure out whether the felony resulted in a death

- Figure out whether the felony satisfies that jurisdiction's felony murder

Depending on the call of the question you might want to switch around the order of these questions. Are you being asked to analyze liability for all crimes? Then start with the analysis of whether the person is guilty of the felony and then work your way up to felony murder. Are you being asked to analyze liability for only homicide crimes? Then you might want to figure out whether that felony would satisfy the felony murder rule first before spending time analyzing whether the felony was committed or not.

If you are being asked to analyze liability for all crimes in a fact pattern that raises felony murder issues, don't forget to include reckless murder and involuntary manslaughter in your analysis. Many a "failed felony murder" fact pattern will support a reckless murder theory. For example, imagine that you conclude that an "evading the police" felony does not satisfy felony murder in a jurisdiction because the felony is not inherently dangerous in the abstract. The actual driving involved in the case at hand might be so reckless and indifferent to human life that it might constitute reckless murder in its own right. You would get points on the exam for discussing both theories for murder liability, so make sure you discuss both!

CHAPTER 14

Manslaughter

Manslaughter is the homicide crime below murder. It is punished less harshly than murder in all jurisdictions. The first and simplest thing to get clear is the distinction between voluntary and involuntary manslaughter. Involuntary manslaughter involves an accidental killing, and voluntary manslaughter involves an intentional killing. So group "voluntary" with "intentional" and "involuntary" with "unintentional," and you will be able to keep this distinction straight.

Voluntary manslaughter should be one of the most interesting parts of your criminal law course because it raises fundamental issues that go to the heart of the criminal law. Think of voluntary manslaughter as "discounted murder." You intended to kill someone, which ordinarily is murder, but the crime and your sentence gets "discounted" down to voluntary manslaughter. Put this way, you can see the grounds for controversy. Why should we give discounts to any murderer? To make things even more interesting, voluntary manslaughter is not some newfangled product of modern sensitivities. It is an old common law doctrine.

The main idea behind voluntary manslaughter is that not all intentional killings are equally blameworthy. Some intentional killers are worse than others, and we should reserve murder for particularly evil intentional killers. The old common law word for this sort of evil was malice. The common law discounts murder down to manslaughter when—in the awkward phrasing of the common law—something "negates the malice" required for murder. What could negate the express malice of an intentional killer? Adequate provocation!

Voluntary Manslaughter

Voluntary manslaughter doctrine is a concession to human frailty, a recognition that we sometimes do things we wish we hadn't in the heat of the moment. So at common law an intentional killing committed in a "sudden heat of passion" sometimes constituted voluntary manslaughter instead of murder. Heat of passion would only mitigate murder down to manslaughter if it was a response to "adequate provocation," however, and adequate provocation was very strictly defined.

The main idea behind provocation doctrine is not that a reasonable person would kill under the same circumstances. (If that were the case then the appropriate verdict would be not guilty of any crime.) Rather the idea is that under these circumstances a reasonable person might get caught up in their emotions and lose control of themselves. Colloquially, we might say that such a person "was not in their right mind," or "not themselves." As a result, their actions don't fully reflect blameworthiness but rather the sort of average human weakness that we want to partially (but not completely) forgive.

Note that the idea has never been to reward the hotheaded. Adequate provocation is limited to those things that would make an *ordinary* person of *average* disposition "liable to act rashly" or "incapable of cool reflection." Adequate provocation is for the reasonable person, not for the reasonable drunken or short-tempered or vengeful person because being drunk or short-tempered or vengeful is not considered reasonable.

Over time many common law jurisdictions have loosened up and expanded their definitions of provocation, and this is the big story that many criminal law textbooks tell. The Model Penal Code actually replaces provocation with an even more forgiving doctrine called Extreme Mental or Emotional Disturbance, but that will be discussed a bit later.

Elements of Provocation

Both the strict and looser versions of provocation doctrine follow the same basic structure. Four elements must be satisfied.

1. The killer must have been actually provoked.

2. A reasonable person would have been provoked.

3. The killer must not have cooled off before killing.

4. A reasonable killer would not have cooled off before killing.

Each of these elements deserves further discussion, but let's do a quick overview.

1. *You must, of course, be actually provoked.* Someone discovers his spouse engaged in an act of adultery but does not actually care. He kills her anyway to collect on her life insurance policy, however. This is not voluntary manslaughter because he was not actually provoked. He was not in the heat of passion but coolly killing to collect the insurance money. So this would be murder, not manslaughter.

2. *The grounds for provocation must be reasonable.* Our killer becomes enraged and kills after he discovers his wife engaged in a game of "paddy cake" with another man. This would also be murder, not manslaughter because while witnessing your spouse engaged in an act of adultery has always been considered a reasonable grounds for provocation, discovering your spouse engaged in an act of patty cake has not.

3. *You can't have cooled off.* The spouse is initially enraged by the adultery but then laughs about it before killing the cheating spouse for the insurance money. This would be murder, not manslaughter because the killer was no longer in the heat of passion when he killed.

4. *The time between the provocation and the killing must also be reasonable.* The killer stays enraged about a single act of adultery by his spouse for a year, then kills her on the anniversary of the adulterous act. This, also, would be murder, not manslaughter because a reasonable person would have cooled off after a year even if he did not.

Note that two of the four elements are what your professor might describe as "objective factors" and two are "subjective factors." The subjective factors are that you must *actually* have been provoked and that you cannot have *actually* cooled off. The objective factors—so called because they hold you to an objective standard as opposed to one tailor made to your own personal, subjective qualities—are that a *reasonable* person would have been provoked and that a *reasonable* person would not have cooled off in time.

Now that we have the basics in mind, let's go through the legal definitions of the two objective factors noting the differences between the strict and looser approaches in common law jurisdictions. These two approaches go by different names in different textbooks and treatises: traditional v contemporary and common law v. modern are two of the more common dichotomies. I prefer strict v. loose because it is more descriptively accurate, but make sure that you adopt the terminology of your professor and course.

Adequacy of Provocation

Early common law took what many aptly describe as a strict categorical approach. There were five categories of provoking events.

1. Witnessing your spouse in the act of adultery.

2. Witnessing a violent assault on a member of your immediate family.

3. Being violently attacked.

4. Being illegally arrested.

5. Being engaged in mutual combat.

If you were provoked by something not on the list then you were guilty of murder. Also, these categories were very strictly construed at common law and still are in some common law jurisdictions. For example, with respect to adultery, some courts do not give manslaughter instructions to the jury if the killer didn't actually see the adultery, or if he witnessed oral sex instead of vaginal intercourse, or if it was his girlfriend or boyfriend as opposed to his husband or wife.

Note that the category of illegal arrest has been abandoned in most if not all jurisdictions. If you get illegally arrested, you are supposed to hire a lawyer, not get mad and start fighting with the police. So this no longer seems like a reasonable ground for provocation to most courts.

The looser approach to provocation expands how these categories are interpreted and sometimes adds brand new ones. The basic idea is to give the jury the option of returning a manslaughter instead of a murder verdict any time that a reasonable person might lose control. That said, most common law jurisdictions stay close to the two basic types of provoking events that the common law recognized: violent acts and sexual betrayal. Looser jurisdictions might give your jury a manslaughter instruction if you learned that your live-in boyfriend or girlfriend was cheating on you, or if you learned that a cousin or close friend was raped, for example.

One early common law rule that has survived largely intact in most common law jurisdictions is that "mere words" cannot adequately provoke. Sticks and stones may break your bones but calling you names won't earn you a manslaughter instruction if you kill the name caller. Some jurisdictions, however, make an exception for "informational words." For example, if you kill someone who just told you that they killed a member of your close family, your jury would be given a manslaughter instruction in such a jurisdiction even though you did not witness the act yourself (and possibly even if the act was not actually carried out at all).

Jurisdictions that have abandoned the strict categorical approach for the looser "reasonableness" standard have had to further define the "reasonable person" for the purposes of provocation doctrine. What sorts of characteristics do you take into account in deciding whether someone was not just provoked but reasonably provoked? Many jurisdictions will instruct juries to take the age and sex of the defendant into account, recognizing that a "reasonable seventeen year old" might be provoked differently than a "reasonable eighty year old woman." Beyond age and gender things get murky, however. One leading scholar has observed that things that affect the gravity of the provocation are more likely to be taken into account than things that affect the degree of self-control one might have. So a blind person who was pushed and taunted from different directions would be judged under the standard of a reasonable blind person rather than a reasonable sighted person. A person with an anger management disorder would be held to the standard of self control of an average person though. In a similar vein, morally idiosyncratic views are completely out of bounds. There is no such thing as a "reasonable racist person" standard, for example.

Reasonableness of Cooling Off Period

How long would it take a "reasonable person" to cool off and to regain their ordinary level of self-control after having witnessed an act of sexual betrayal or after having been beaten? Ten minutes, an hour, a day, a week? Courts have been reluctant to put an exact time on such things. Generally speaking someone might be expected to cool off after an hour and virtually always after a day depending on the gravity of the provocation. Historically, the common law was very strict about this, and judges often refused to give manslaughter instructions to juries if too much time had passed. The modern trend is to leave the issue of how long it should take a reasonable person to cool off to the jury.

As a practical matter, the more important issue with respect to the cooling off issue is not how much time has passed but when you start the clock running. For example, in one widely noted case a man was raped by one of his co-workers and routinely taunted about it for weeks. When he finally "snapped" and shot his assailant to death the judge denied him a manslaughter instruction because too much time had passed between the rape and the killing. Some courts today would count the time differently, using a "slow burn" or "last straw" approach. The taunts "reignited" a passion that had been burning slowly since the time of the rape, and the last taunt was the straw that broke the camel's back given the cumulative nature of the taunts and the rape taken together. Note that this does not mean that taunting someone about a past act of abuse or violation alone would constitute adequate provocation. Rather the taunt or other recent provoking event taken *in combination with* the earlier, more traditional act of violence or betrayal provides the basis for the manslaughter instruction.

Model Penal Code and EMED

The Model Penal Code dispensed with the notion of provocation altogether. Instead it mitigates murder down to voluntary manslaughter when a person kills purposely or knowingly or extremely recklessly but does so while suffering from an "extreme mental or emotional disturbance," otherwise known by the acronym of EMED. A "reasonable explanation or excuse" must exist for this disturbance, but the reasonableness must be "determined from the viewpoint of a person in the actor's situation under the circumstances as he believes them to be."

Note first the absence of the word "provocation" in this standard. Instead the standard asks whether the killer was extremely disturbed for a reason that that the jury can understand in a rational way. Furthermore, by defining reasonable from the perspective of the disturbed person, the MPC creates a hybrid standard that many scholars describe as "objective/subjective." Despite the medical sound of the words "mental or emotional" this condition does not need to rise to the level of a mental disease or defect but requires only an extreme "disturbance." Instead of a cooling off requirement, the MPC requires that he person still be "under the influence" of the disturbance at the time of the killing.

The general effect of the MPC's EMED doctrine is to open up voluntary manslaughter to include even more excusing conditions than the looser version of the common law provocation doctrine. Medical conditions which might not satisfy the test for insanity such as postpartum depression or severe personality disorders that make people react impulsively or aggressively fit more easily into EMED than into provocation. At the outer boundaries of EMED lie people who get into profound "funks" or "rages" about something that people can understand. Getting unjustly fired from a job, dumped by a longtime boyfriend or girlfriend, or just abused or humiliated by someone on an ongoing basis by someone could trigger a jury instruction on this issue.

Dispensing with the provocation element also means that the person killed does not have to have done anything to create the killer's disturbance. EMED makes it easier to find manslaughter when the person killed is blameless because it clearly operates more as an excuse than as a justification.

Consider a mother who killed her infant while in the throes of postpartum depression. Postpartum depression falls well short of insanity, and a helpless baby is not likely thought of as "provoking" when it cries. A jury that might never be able to find "provocation" might be able to find that the mother was disturbed for a reason that they can excuse and return a verdict of manslaughter as a result.

EMED generally throws more questions to the jury than provocation and often with less guidance than provocation instructions provide. Remember though that the fact that the jury gets to hear the issue does not mean that they must or will accept the "reasonable explanation or excuse" offered.

Philosophical Issues

Voluntary manslaughter is a great opportunity to explore some of the deeper, philosophical issues in a criminal law course. One of the biggest questions is whether we "discount" murder to voluntary manslaughter because we think the conduct is partially excused or partially justified. To put it more bluntly, do we feel that victim had it coming? If so, then manslaughter is a partial justification. If we feel that the person was understandably "out of their mind" because of some strong emotion, then we see manslaughter as a partial excuse. What if, for example, a righteously enraged defendant kills the wrong person? Imagine a father who sees his child run over by a drunk driver but who in his range kills a passerby who tries to intervene. If you treat provocation as a partial justification then you do not give the jury a manslaughter instruction because there is no justification for killing someone who did not harm the child. If you treat provocation as a partial excuse, then you might give the manslaughter instruction anyway because the father lost control due to his grief and anger.

Some textbooks and professors pause at this point in the course to consider whether some or all of the grounds for voluntary manslaughter should be abolished. Should sexual infidelity even partially excuse or justify a violent reaction? Should people who willingly engage in fights get the benefit of a manslaughter instruction if they lose their temper and kill as a result? Should we discount murder to manslaughter because people lose control, under circumstances that are not as blameworthy as those who kill without provocation or disturbance, or should we use the full weight of a murder conviction to deter and condemn any intentional killing that is not otherwise fully justified? The point of debating such philosophical questions is to help you see more clearly the connections between why we punish and how we define different levels of criminal liability.

Involuntary Manslaughter

Involuntary manslaughter is the baseline offense for very wrongful but unintentional killings. As discussed above, it is the extraordinary unintentional killing that constitutes extremely reckless murder. Not all unintentional killings even constitute manslaughter, however. Virtually all jurisdictions require at least criminal or gross negligence. Some jurisdictions require reckless as opposed to criminal negligence. Recklessness involves a higher level of culpability because it requires that the actor consciously disregard the substantial and unjustifiable risk of death whereas you are criminally negligent if you fail to recognize such a risk.

Modern statutes often specify what state of mind is required for involuntary manslaughter. In the absence of a statutory definition on an exam question one would ordinarily fall back on majority and minority rules as a default standard. The leading treatises disagree however, on which whether recklessness or criminal negligence is required for involuntary manslaughter in the majority of jurisdictions. (Unless your professor or textbook specifies one or the other you should analyze the fact pattern under both standards in the absence of a statutory definition.) Some jurisdictions, following the Model Penal Code, require recklessness for involuntary manslaughter but create a lesser crime of negligent homicide which only requires criminal negligence. Just a very few jurisdictions allow for some form of reduced homicide liability on the basis of simple or ordinary negligence, but many casebooks include such a case in order to illustrate the distinction between simple and gross negligence.

What both recklessness and criminal negligence have in common however is that the actor was *really* careless in some aspect.   Drunk driving, mishandling firearms, gross violations of safety regulations are some of the favorite textbook examples. Remember to pay particular attention to crimes of omission in this area.   For example, a gross failure to take care of a child or elderly person entrusted to your care is a common manslaughter scenario.

Finally, many jurisdictions recognize a form of involuntary manslaughter called unlawful act manslaughter.   Unlawful act manslaughter was discussed in detail at the end of the chapter on felony murder.

CHAPTER 15

Causation

Most crimes don't require results, just a guilty hand moved by a guilty mind. Result crimes require both the result to occur and that the result be *caused* by the conduct defined by the crime. So result crimes require the application of legal principles that define causation. Causation in criminal law is usually pretty straightforward, so you will spend much less time talking about causation in criminal law than you will in torts. The reason for this is that tort liability is not as closely tied to fault as criminal liability. A tighter connection between the act and the result is required in criminal law because of the central role that moral condemnation plays in criminal punishment.

Overview of the Elements

Two types of causation are required: actual causation also known as cause in fact, and proximate causation, sometimes referred to as legal causation. Never forget that you need both for criminal liability.

Most people think of cause in fact as "but for" causation in the sense that "but for" the act the result would not have taken place. You shoot a bullet at my head, but the bullet misses. I die at that moment from an unrelated brain aneurysm. You cannot be guilty of murder because you did not "actually" cause my death. I would have been dead anyway even if you hadn't fired your shot. (Although we would have you dead to rights for attempted murder, which by definition means that the required result for the complete crime did not occur.) If your bullet strikes me and kills me, however, then we have an easy case of actual causation because but for your shot I would not have died when I did.

Proximate causation is more complex because ultimately it reflects the criminal law's judgment about who can be held responsible for harm. The central principle of proximate cause is foreseeability. We limit criminal liability to foreseeable harms. If you shoot me in the head because I happened to be parachuting down on top of your duck blind just as you are firing at a flock of ducks, then you are probably not going to be found to have proximately caused my death because that we don't ordinarily foresee people falling down out of the sky on top of us.

The distinction between mental states and causation deserves mention here. In response to the parachutist/duck blind hypo described above you might rightfully think that the duck hunter would not be reckless or grossly negligent or even negligent. Probably not, but the foreseeability requirement of proximate causation would not even let things get that far with respect to homicide liability. If you did not proximately (foreseeably) cause the result then it does not matter what mental state you had with respect to your conduct.

What complicates both types of causation is the reality that all results have multiple causes. How do we pick out the ones that count for the purposes of criminal liability? The problem is trickier for proximate causation because proximate causation "does more work" as the philosophers like to say. Actual causation *rules out* possible causes. If you were not a but for cause then you can't be a cause. Proximate causation *rules in* a much smaller set of but for causes. That is where most of the work gets done and where most of the rules need to be learned.

Actual Causation Generally

Actual causation seems simpler than it is. Any result has lots and lots of causes. Imagine that an unbalanced individual goes on a shooting rampage at work and kills me in my office. I was still in my office that day because one of my colleagues delayed my departure from work by chatting with me about a particularly exciting college basketball game that had been played the night before. You could say that but for my colleague's actions I would still be alive. That would make my colleague a but for cause of my death. So are the people who made the gun and the bullets. You could even say that the basketball players who played the exciting game the night before actually caused my death. For that matter, if my mother had never given birth to me then I could not have ever been killed!

Ultimately actual causation relies on our sense of the ordinary for its meaning. No ordinary person would ever say that my mother caused my death by giving birth to me because that is what mothers do in the regular course of things. Likewise there is nothing out of the ordinary about chatting with a colleague or playing in an exciting basketball game. People who see guns and bullets as inherently evil might be tempted to look there for the cause of my death, but unless there was something unusual about the gun or the bullets it would be hard to argue that the manufacturer caused my death either. Scholars refer to these ordinary events that form part of the background of daily life as "conditions," not causes. Walking up to someone and shooting them, however, is anything but ordinary, so your doing so will be seen as an actual cause of my death.

Multiple Actual Causes and Substantial Factors

Often criminal results do have multiple concurrent causes. A group of people might attack someone, for example, and the victim dies. These people are almost always working together, however. As you will see when you learn the doctrine of complicity any one accomplice can be held liable for the acts of another. So if two of you work together to attack me with baseball bats and I die the criminal law does not have to worry whether either or both of you actually caused my death. Under complicity each of you is responsible for the acts of the other, and together you killed me. So usually complicity liability fills in any gaps in causation that occur when more than one person causes the bad result.

The tricky questions arise (usually in treatises and law review articles, not in actual cases) when you have *multiple, independent* causes of the bad result. Sometimes these are successive acts where one accelerates the required results; other times they are concurrent acts where each contributes to it. Actual court decisions confronting such issues are so rare that the law is sketchy here. The important general principal to keep firmly in mind, however, is that **an actual cause does not have to be an exclusive cause but can be a substantial factor.**

1. *Accelerating Causes.* An accelerating cause is an actual cause. Someone stabs me and leaves me along the road dying. Before I actually die a "Bad Samaritan" finds me in the road and shoots me, the Bad Samaritan actually caused my death by *accelerating* it. Courts have gone both ways on whether the stabber can be found to have caused

my death under these circumstances, with some courts finding that the shooting was an "obstructing cause" that stopped the initial cause from being realized.

2. *Concurrent Sufficient Causes.* What if two people acting independently stab and shoot me at the same time, with either wound being enough to kill me. (Boy, am I having a bad day.) One could say that neither was a but for cause of my death since the other concurrent cause would have killed me anyway. In such cases courts often fudge by saying that each act was a "substantial factor" in bringing about my death. (I say "fudge" because these courts usually don't define substantial factor or explain the principle behind the test clearly.)

3. *Concurrent Insufficient Causes.* What if neither wound would have been fatal in and of itself but that cumulatively both wounds resulted in my death. Paradoxically, this is an easier case for the law because now each act clearly satisfies the but for test. But for the stabbing, I would not have died. But for the shooting I would not have died. Both attackers are actual causes of my death.

The Year and a Day Rule

At common law one could not be guilty of a homicide crime unless the victim died within a year and a die of the homicidal act. The period of time has been increased or the rule has been abolished altogether in a majority of jurisdictions.

Proximate Cause Generally

They say that variety is the spice of life. Well, variety is the source of the more difficult issues of proximate cause in the criminal law. Specifically, variety in how a required result occurs creates the need for principles that deal with 1) results that involve unintended or unexpected victims and 2) results that occur in unintended or unexpected ways.

Harms often result in unintended or unexpected ways due to causes that "intervene" between the defendant's actions and the required result. Whether such intervening causes "break the chain" of causation between the defendant's act and the required result generally depends on the foreseeability of the intervening cause although the causal chain between the defendant and the criminal result is less likely to be broken if the intervening cause was a response to—and not independent of—something the defendant did.

Unexpected Victims and Transferred Intent

Harming the wrong person ordinarily does not break the chain of causation between the defendant and the result. This principle is called transferred intent when the crime requires that the harm be intended. Imagine I try to shoot a student in my class who is never prepared, but the unprepared student ducks quickly, and the bullet kills the unfortunate student sitting behind him. The law transfers my intent to kill from the intended to the actual victim for the purposes of causation (and also for purposes of intent as discussed earlier).

It is less clear whether recklessness or negligence can be transferred in the same way although it may be more of a theoretical issue than a real one. Imagine that instead of shooting the unprepared student I decide to terrorize and humiliate him by forcing him to dance in front of the whole class while I shoot at his feet. (And you thought cold calling was bad.) Obviously if he were to stumble and get shot in the head I would be guilty of extremely reckless murder (or involuntary manslaughter at the least). What if he does not fall but one of the bullets ricochets and kills one of the many students raptly watching and filming this very unusual teaching method on their cell phones? It is not clear according to the treatises whether one could transfer recklessness of shooting at the intended victim's feet to the unintended victim for the purposes of causation although some have observed that the case for transferring recklessness is stronger than negligence. Transferring the mental state might not be necessary in any event because most courts would probably find me directly liable for extremely reckless murder for the death of any student in the room on the theory that I consciously disregard a risk to all students when I began firing the gun in the enclosed space of the classroom.

Intervening Causes

Sometimes the intended or expected victim of a person's criminal conduct suffers harm in an unexpected way. Figuring out whether to hold the actor causally responsible in such cases gets a little complicated. Let's introduce the legal terms used, and then we will illustrate how the rules work.

- *Intervening Cause.* The force or event that causes the harm to occur in the unexpected way.

- *Chain of Causation.* A metaphorical term that refers to a sequence of causally related actions or events. When we say that the chain of causation is broken we mean that we no longer consider the defendant's acts earlier in the chain to be responsible for the results after the break.

- *Dependent Intervening Cause.* An intervening cause that was a response to something that the defendant did. (Usually does not break the chain of causation.)

- *Independent Intervening Cause.* An intervening cause that operated completely independently of the defendant's actions. (Often breaks the chain of causation.)

- *Superseding Cause.* An intervening cause that is not just unexpected but sufficiently unforeseeable that the law finds the chain of causation between the defendant's act and the criminal result to be broken.

Now let's use a hypo to illustrate these concepts in action. Assume that while you are robbing a bank you decide to fire a warning shot in the air, but the bullet ricochets off the ceiling and kills a bank teller. This would be a straightforward case of proximate causation. Wait, you might complain, you were not purposeful, knowing, reckless, or even grossly negligent? Putting aside whether in fact you were not at least grossly negligent, proximate causation does not require any of the above. Causation cases don't use the language of mental states, of course, but of foreseeability. For a result to be a foreseeable does not require that it be foreseen by you; foreseeability just requires that it be foreseeable b a reasonable person. If you do translate foreseeability into mental state terms, foreseeability comes much closer to a simple negligence standard than anything else.

What this first example nicely illustrates is that *a direct cause is usually a proximate cause.* Here you directly caused the death when you pulled the trigger of the gun, so it should not be a big surprise that the resulting death was considered foreseeable.

Dependent Intervening Causes

While all direct causes are proximate causes not all proximate causes are direct causes, however. What if the bullet struck the bank teller in the arm, and the teller died in surgery when the doctor nicked an artery while trying to remove the bullet? Here the direct cause of the death was the nicking of the artery. You obviously still have actual/but for causation, but do you also have proximate causation? Or has the intervening cause of the surgical error broken the chain of causation between the shot you fired and the resulting death? Probably not.

The surgical error is a dependent intervening cause because the surgery itself was a reaction or response to your wrongful act of firing the shot. *Generally a responsive/dependent intervening cause will only break the chain of causation if it is not just unforeseeable but highly unusual.* Surgical errors are neither unforeseeable nor highly unusual. Even medical negligence is considered foreseeable. For the surgical error to become a *superseding intervening cause* that would break the chain of causation it would need to be gross negligence. If the bullet only nicked the arm of the teller, and an extremely drunk surgeon picked up the wrong surgical instrument and sliced through the arm's major artery and then failed to stop the bleeding in time to prevent death, that would be not just unforeseeable but highly unusual and would relieve you of liability for the teller's death by breaking the chain of causation.

Responsive/dependent intervening causes also include actions by the victim. Now imagine that the bank teller runs screaming out of the bank after getting nicked in the arm and gets run over by a car when he dashes across the street. Once again the negligence of the teller in not looking both ways would not break the chain of causation because it is foreseeable that victims might panic and act unreasonably under such circumstances. *Negligent acts by the victim that respond to the defendant's acts generally do not break the chain of causation.* To relieve the defendant of causal responsibility the victim's actions must be unusual enough to be bizarre. (e.g. The teller decides to kill himself when he sees you pull out the gun.)

Pre-Existing Weakness of the Victim

What if the bullet wound kills the bank teller only because he has a rare clotting disorder that makes it unusually easy for him to bleed to death? The rule for the criminal law here is the same as in torts. *A victim's pre-existing weakness or particular vulnerability does not break the chain of causation between the defendant's act and the resulting harm.* In criminal law, as in torts, a wrongful actor "takes the victim as he finds him."

Torts has a catchy albeit gruesome metaphor that makes this idea easy to remember. The "eggshell plaintiff" is someone whose skull is as thin as an eggshell. Knocking down such a person might well kill them, so the surviving family members of the eggshell plaintiff in such a case could sue the tortfeasor who wrongfully knocked the plaintiff down for damages resulting from the death. Criminal law does not have plaintiffs—we have victims—so remember this as the eggshell victim rule in criminal law.

Before you protest against murder liability for knocking someone down, remember that the eggshell victim rule only establishes causation, not mental state. Even if you deliberately knocked the person down it would be impossible to prove an intent to kill or even a reckless or criminally negligent state of mind with respect to the risk of death. You might be guilty of misdemeanor manslaughter, however, since all that is required is guilt of a misdemeanor or unlawful that causes death. Just your bad luck to have shoved someone with an eggshell skull!

Independent (or Coincidental) Intervening Causes

Let's go back to the bank. Now imagine that he bullet only nicked the arm of the teller but that while he was in the waiting area of the emergency room an enraged patient goes on a shooting rampage, killing everyone in the waiting room. (That is one way to get to the front of the line.) *Forces that do not respond to or depend on the defendant's acts usually do break the chain of causation unless they are foreseeable.* The enraged patient is not responding to what you did in the bank in any way. His actions do not depend on what you did in the bank. It is true that the bank teller would not be in the emergency room but for being shot by you, but this establishes only cause in fact. So you would not be criminally liable for the death of the teller because the enraged patient is a *superseding intervening cause.*

Foreseeable independent intervening causes are rare but not unheard of. Imagine now that you take the teller hostage, and leave him wandering the road on the outskirts of town near a dangerous neighborhood in the middle of the night. He is then robbed and killed by someone who sees him wandering down the street. On these facts, the force that killed him was truly independent but not unforeseeable, and you could be found to have caused his death for the purposes of homicidal liability. (Whether you could be found to be grossly negligent or reckless with respect to the risk of death would be another matter, of course: finding proximate causation does not mean that the person necessarily has the mental state required for the crime.)

Pulling the Plug on Life Support

Not infrequently victims of homicidal acts who have lapsed into coma's or other vegetative states are taken off life support by doctors acting in accordance with established principles and procedures. In such cases defendants often argue that the doctor caused the death, not the defendant. Usually such arguments fail because courts find that the termination of life support in such a state is a foreseeable consequence of the injuries inflicted.

Model Penal Code

Not surprisingly, the Model Penal Code simplifies causation by relying on its more carefully defined mental states. Only actual causation is required, and actual causation is defined as but for causation. The MPC treats proximate causation as a mental states issue and substitutes a simpler albeit vaguer standard for the common law's more complicated rules of proximate causation. Section 2.03 provides that no culpable mental state exists if the injury or harm was **"too remote or accidental in its occurrence to have a [just] bearing on the actor's liability or on the gravity of his offense.** For good and for bad, this language frees up the finder of fact to do what they think is fair when more complicated issues of causation arise.

Exam Tip: Look for the Strange

The good news in this area is that difficult causation issues are hard to miss in an exam fact pattern. Causal chains usually jump out at the reader because they are so unusual. Instead of dying from the gunshot wound the victim staggers to a window and jumps out of it, or is run over by a speeding motorist, or is hit by a meteorite . . . you get the idea. When you see a result crime such as homicide and a crazy story about one thing leading to another, remember to consider proximate causation. Alternately, when you see multiple actors and multiple causes hammering the same poor victim ("the really bad day scenario" where you are being shot, stabbed and bit by a rabid dog all at once), analyze cause in fact issues. Finally, remember always to keep your eye out for complicity theories that simplify many potentially difficult causation issues. If the actors are working together as accomplices then each can be held criminally responsible for harms caused by the group as a whole.

Rape

Rape law is a fascinating, important, and difficult subject, both to teach and to learn. Many professors choose not to teach it at all, but those who do often consider it is one of the most rewarding subjects of their course for both teacher and student. The special challenges of rape law shape how casebook authors and classroom teachers approach it, so this chapter begins with a discussion of those challenges before proceeding with an overview of the elements of rape.

The Challenges and Rewards of Rape Law

Rape is not an easy topic to talk about. Statistically, it is very likely that someone in your class has been raped. It is much less likely but not inconceivable that someone in your class may have been falsely accused of rape. That obviously makes the topic a sensitive one to discuss. These same facts, however, make rape law an important and potentially rewarding topic to discuss.

Rape law also raises profoundly difficult issues of gender, autonomy, and the role of the criminal law in the most intimate areas of our lives. The law of rape was formed during an openly patriarchal time when woman were subjugated by law in numerous ways. At common law men were legally incapable of being guilty of the rape of their wives because the consent of the wife to intercourse with her husband was conclusively presumed as a matter of law. Since adultery and sex outside of marriage were each crimes in their own right, common law judges worried that a woman would "cry rape" to avoid criminal liability herself. This skepticism towards rape complainants continued into modern times, often in the form of procedural requirements such as corroboration of the woman's claims, a prompt complaint, and admission of evidence of the rape complainant's past sexual history to rebut the claim of non-consent. In sum, rape law often protected men too much and women too little, and it still does in some jurisdictions.

Race also complicates discussion of rape in a different way. Historically rape allegations played a large role in the oppression of racial and ethnic minorities. Rape allegations against men of color often were the pretext for lynchings and other racial violence. Rape carried the death penalty in some southern states, and rape charges were often brought against African American men for raping white women. Rape and sexual violence against African American women by white men in contrast often went unreported and unprosecuted. Rape prosecutions also played a role in enforcing prohibitions against sexual relations between races. A white woman discovered to have had sexual intercourse with a man of color faced ostracism and possible criminal prosecution if the intercourse was consensual. If she alleged rape, however, all-white juries often returned convictions on the basis of an assumption that a white woman would not willingly engage in sex with a man of color.

Recent reform efforts have made some headway, but ongoing attempts to redefine rape remain deeply controversial. Even putting issues of patriarchy and gender discrimination aside, the definition of rape requires the law to essentially take a stand on how people should and should not speak to and touch one another when engaged in intimate sexual activity. Deciding how much or how little the criminal law should regulate sexual activity would not be easy for any society, much less one with the gendered baggage that our own and most other societies carry. Figuring out where and how to draw this line is both interesting and important though.

Finally, rape is very complex legally. Most serious crimes place great importance on mental state requirements. Rape law historically did not. This confuses many students because what separates rape from perfectly lawful sexual activity is the absence of freely formed consent, a circumstance that obviously is mental in nature. To make matters even worse, rape law is incredibly varied. The rape law reform movement did not generate a consensus approach. While all jurisdictions have reformed their rape laws, they have done so in many different ways.

So professors teaching rape law face multiple challenges. They must untangle a complicated legal doctrine and lead discussions that are both respectful of the various sensitivities involved as well as robust in engaging the deeper, truly difficult issues that demand resolution. These challenges shape how professors and casebook authors teach rape law in ways that students should understand in order to learn what is being taught.

First, the sensitive nature of the topic leads many professors to abandon or limit use of hypotheticals because such hypotheticals often require a student to put themselves in the position of someone who is being raped (a particularly disturbing experience for someone who has actually been raped). Instead, professors will often substitute policy questions that ask students to approach the legal issues as legislators with an eye to deciding what the law of rape should be.

Second, most professors find themselves giving students more latitude during classroom discussion.   Discussing rape law is difficult enough for many students without having the professor question them closely about what they have just said.   Students can also learn much from hearing what their classmates say in these more free flowing discussions, although the conversation is not always a comfortable one.

Third, the incredible variety of rape law statutes means that any selection of cases or statutes will provide at best a partial and selective view of how rape law operates.   Professors who emphasize black letter rules will usually settle on a few examples of different approaches.   Professors who emphasize statutory interpretation might expose students to a wider variety of rape definitions to develop their ability to read statutes carefully. With this in mind, this chapter tries to give you a feel for the major issues of rape law without any pretense of describing a consensus approach that simply does not exist.

Overview of Elements

The traditional elements of rape are easy to list but hard to define.

- Sexual Intercourse
- Accomplished by
    - Force or
    - Threat of Force or
    - When the Victim is Unconscious or Lacks Capacity
- Without the Victim's Consent

Rape then can be usefully divided into three different conduct elements: a sexual act, force, and non-consent. The definition of the sexual act that lies at the heart of rape has been expanded to include more than just sexual intercourse, as will be discussed below. The greatest difficulty in rape law comes from defining force and non-consent.

Rape is a general intent crime, which means that the defendant must be generally aware of his or her conduct. More specifically, many jurisdictions hold that the only mental state required is that one be generally aware that one is having intercourse. This means that *even a reasonable mistake as to whether the victim consents to the intercourse would not create a mental state defense to rape under the traditional view.*

The absence of an explicit requirement of a more blameworthy mental state for such a serious felony is both very confusing to most students and the key to understanding the elements of rape. *Rape did not traditionally require a more blameworthy mental state because the conduct elements were defined in such a way that only a wrongful actor could satisfy them.*

Consent in rape law is defined objectively, not subjectively. Whether consent exists or not does not depends not on what the victim thinks or what the defendant thinks, but on what the victim and defendant say and do (or fail to say or do). Since consent is determined from the observable circumstances, a victim's purely private or "secret" lack of consent will not satisfy the lack of consent element. A defendant who had intercourse under circumstances where consent reasonably seemed to exist would not be found guilty of rape because consent would be found to have existed *regardless of the subjective beliefs or thoughts of the victim.*

Similarly, force has often been defined in such a way that it would be impossible for a person to reasonably believe that the victim consented to the intercourse. Often it meant the use of violent force or the threat of violent force. It would not have been possible for a defendant to use such force and reasonably believe that the victim consented to the intercourse.

So despite the absence of a culpable mental state requirement, the traditional definition of rape did not involve a risk that men who reasonably believed that the woman consented to the intercourse would be wrongfully convicted. In fact, the elements of force and non-consent were defined in a way that made it far too easy for a man who forced intercourse upon a woman against her will to escape conviction. When jurisdictions reformed their rape definitions to make it less difficult to prosecute blameworthy men for rape, most did not add mental state requirements. Instead, they strove to redefine the force and non-consent elements in ways that made it easier to prosecute the blameworthy while still protecting the blameless. Drawing that line in a clear way has been difficult, however, and remains deeply controversial.

One further point needs to be made before each element is discussed in turn. Force and non-consent operate in what might be described as a symbiotic relationship: each must be defined in light of the other. The more you require of one, the less you need of the other.

For example, assume for the sake of argument that you defined consent in purely subjective terms. This would mean that even a victim's private or "secret" lack of consent would satisfy the element. Such a definition would not endanger blameless defendants if force were defined to require actual violence or the threat of violence because blameless defendants do not ordinarily threaten or commit violence against their sexual partners.

Alternately, imagine that force is defined in such a way that simply the physical force required to achieve sexual intercourse were sufficient for that element. Again, the risk of convicting blameless defendants would not exist if non-consent were defined to require observable acts of resistance, even if only verbal.

This symbiotic relationship between force and consent obviously affects the victim's interest just as directly. For example, a definition of force that required not threatened but actual violence would leave unprotected many victims who do not wish to engage in intercourse but who feared physical injury too much to resist, regardless of how consent were defined. Similarly, a definition of non-consent that required victims to physically resist the defendant would force victims to choose between the physical and mental violation that rape entails and the physical injury that resisting rape might precipitate, regardless of how force was defined.

So the division of labor between the elements of force and non-consent in ensuring that the blameworthy, but only the blameworthy, are convicted is key to the definition of rape. Unfortunately for the student of criminal law, jurisdictions varied widely in how they reformed rape law. Some leaned on the force requirement to do the hard work; others use the non-consent element to do the heavy lifting.

A few observations can be made on a very general level about current state of rape law. Traditionally force was required for rape, and the victim had to resist to establish non-consent. Today force is not always required, and verbal resistance (or in some jurisdictions the absence of affirmative consent) is sufficient to establish non-consent.

The Predicate Sexual Act

All definitions of rape or serious sexual offense have as their predicate some form of sexual act. At common law the only sexual act that could constitute rape was sexual intercourse defined as the penetration of a female's vagina by a male's penis. Many modern statutes have broadened this definition in a number of different ways. The predicate sexual act for rape has been variously defined as including the penetration of the anus with a penis, the penetration of any bodily orifice with the penis or any body part or even mechanical objects, and various forms of oral sex. In some jurisdictions these acts are considered rape when performed forcibly or without the victim's consent; in other jurisdictions the term rape is reserved for some subset of these acts with the other acts being called a felonious sex offense of a degree that is often equivalent to rape for sentencing purposes.

The early definition of the required sexual act as the penetration of a vagina by a penis essentially limited rape to a crime committed by a man against a woman. Many modern statutes with broader definitions of the required sex act are written in gender neutral language and allow any gender to be capable of raping any other gender or the same gender.

Force

At common law rape often required the use or threatened use of force that was likely to cause great bodily harm. In the presence of such extreme force or an explicit threat of the same, no resistance was required. Lesser force—which could easily include punching, hitting and holding a woman down—required some resistance which the man's force overcame. Such "resistance to the utmost," required a woman to fight until she was too exhausted, injured or frightened to continue.

No jurisdictions require such "resistance to the utmost" anymore. Some have abolished the resistance requirement altogether. "Earnest resistance" or resistance that is "reasonable under the circumstances" is required by others. Verbal resistance is often sufficient. Some critics argue that the force and resistance requirements should be abolished altogether.

Even in the absence of an explicit resistance requirement, difficult questions remain as to how much force should be required for a rape to occur. One line of cases requires no more force than is necessary to accomplish the act of penetration. Other cases require some greater degree of force, although usually not force likely to cause great bodily harm. So choking someone while one penetrates them (or threatening to do so) is no longer required. Holding someone down while one penetrates them would likely be sufficient, but simply holding onto someone while one penetrates them would not be. A factfinder might find the difference between holding someone down and holding onto someone to lie in whether the person being held physically resists.

Finally, jurisdictions that eliminate or reduce the force requirement often shift the hard questions over to the non-consent requirement. Alternately, jurisdictions that retain the force requirement tend to require more force than is necessary to accomplish penetration when a genuine issue exists as to whether the intercourse was without consent.

Lack of Capacity

Even at common law certain individuals were presumed to lack the capacity to consent to sexual intercourse, and this category of individuals has been expanded over time. Intercourse with individuals under the age of 18 is defined as statutory rape in many jurisdictions. As previously discussed, statutory rape is a strict liability offense with respect to the age of the victim, although a minority of jurisdictions recognize a defense of reasonable mistake as to this element. Intercourse with people who are unconscious is also presumed to be nonconsensual. Likewise, intercourse or equivalent sexual acts with individuals who otherwise lack mental capacity to consent as a result of mental disabilities is also defined as rape or an equivalent sex offense in some jurisdictions. Intercourse with a person too intoxicated to consent is considered rape in a minority of jurisdictions. If the defendant administered the intoxicants without the victim's knowledge and consent, however, all jurisdictions find rape to have occurred.

Non-Consent

At common law, intercourse had to be without the victim's consent in order to be rape. At common law and in a majority of jurisdictions, until relatively recently, non-consent had to be demonstrated by the victim's active physical resistance. While resistance to the utmost is generally not required anymore, defining non-consent remains a difficult issue. Doing away with resistance requirements does not resolve the issue of what conduct and circumstances are necessary to establish a lack of consent.

Rape is unique among crimes against the person in being founded on a physical act that is ordinarily consensual. People don't ordinarily consent to being punched in the face. If someone punches you in the face, people generally don't presume you consented to the punch, unless you are wearing boxing gloves and standing in the middle of a boxing ring. Sexual activity between people is ordinarily consensual though. So the definition of the non-consent element in rape is uniquely important and uniquely difficult.

The fact that intercourse is ordinarily consensual, however, does not necessarily mean that consent should be considered the default position. Some rape reform advocates argue for a "yes means yes" standard that requires the giving of explicit affirmative permission for the sexually regulated act, although some take the position that explicit affirmative permission could be physical, not verbal. Others argue that a "no means no" rule would be sufficient to guarantee the autonomy of would be victims of rape. Still others argue for the elimination of the non-consent element altogether and would define rape solely in terms of the amount and nature of the force used to accomplish the sexual act in order to keep the jury's focus on what the defendant did, not what the victim failed to do.

The policy questions that lie at the heart of defining non-consent in rape are not easy to resolve. Feminist scholars disagree about whether consent must be affirmative and verbal, with some arguing that such a requirement is the only way to effectively protect rape victims, and others arguing that such a requirement is paternalistic and treats woman as incapable of expressing their unwillingness to engage in sexual intercourse.

Gender concerns aside, the definition of non-consent in rape also raises questions of privacy and autonomy and about the government's role in regulating sexual relations.

Some strongly believe that requiring such explicit communication during sexual activity robs sexual intimacy of a natural and spontaneous quality that is important. These critics believe that an affirmative consent requirement imposes by fiat one particular way of relating to one another sexually. Some argue further the criminal law is too blunt and powerful an instrument with which to regulate our most private moments with such particularity.

Others argue equally strongly that requiring a verbal or physical indication of affirmative consent is a small price to pay to both reduce the possibility of misunderstandings and to make easier the prosecution of individuals who would violate the sexual autonomy of their partners. They argue that nothing would be lost by requiring affirmative consent because sexual intimacy is at its best when grounded in mutual sexual autonomy realized through clear communication.

No easy answers are to be found here.

Acquaintance Rape and Rape Among the Married

In an earlier era, consent would often be presumed in cases where the defendant and the victim were acquainted with one another. With the growing recognition that "acquaintance rape" was both prevalent and a serious problem this presumption no longer seemed reasonable. While few rape statutes make explicit distinctions between acquaintance and stranger rape, the existence of a prior relationship of some sort between the defendant and the victim continues to play an important role in the thinking of prosecutors, judges, and juries in deciding whether non-consent existed in any particular case. While it no longer seems reasonable to presume that you consented to sexual intercourse with someone just because you were dating him or her, it continues to seem reasonable to presume that you did not consent to sex with a complete stranger in a deserted parking lot in the middle of the night. So while prior acquaintance does not rule out rape as it once often did, it is usually not irrelevant to determining non-consent either.

That said, all jurisdictions have abolished the common law's marital exemption for rape liability. Consent to acts of intercourse between people who are married is no longer conclusively presumed. To be sure, marital status, like prior acquaintance, is not irrelevant to a fact-finder's deliberations about whether consent existed as to any particular sexual act, but it is no longer the basis for a conclusive presumption.

Mental State as to Consent

Contrary to the strong trend described earlier, a few states recognize a reasonable mistake of fact as to whether the victim consented as a defense to rape, although some states will only give such an instruction in the face of substantial evidence of equivocal conduct on the victim's part.

Degrees of Rape

Many jurisdictions recognized degrees of rape to distinguish more serious from less serious violations. First degree rape in many jurisdictions is reserved for defendants who commit rape with weapons, or with accomplices, or who inflict serious bodily injury on their victims.

The MPC

Discussion of the Model Penal Code has been noticeably absent up to this point because the Model Penal Code has had a negligible influence on how jurisdictions define rape and related sexual offenses. Even huge fans of the MPC usually acknowledge that the MPC got rape wrong. Most notably the MPC failed to abolish the marital exemption for rape and retained the early common law's requirement that claims of rape be corroborated.

Exam Tip: Think Through Both Sides of a Rape Policy Question

As mentioned earlier, exam questions dealing with rape are often framed as policy questions. As is always the case, the most important thing to demonstrate on a policy question is your ability to think deeply through both sides of a question. This does not mean that you cannot ultimately reach a strong conclusion one way or the other. It does mean that you should only arrive there after dealing with the opposite's side's very best arguments. Because rape law involves so many difficult and deeply controversial questions it is a great vehicle for assessing your ability to do so.

CHAPTER 17

Miscellaneous Crimes Against the Person

Assault and battery offenses truly are the wrongly neglected children of the criminal law family in terms of course coverage. Most textbooks deal with them only in passing, yet assault and battery is covered on the Multi-state Bar Exam and a staple of any criminal law practice. For every one homicide there are many thousands of assaults and batteries in any given year. Also covered on the bar exams and playing only a supporting role in most criminal law textbooks are the related crimes of false imprisonment and kidnapping

What first year law students and third year law students both need is a quick overview of the elements of these miscellaneous crimes against the person. Understanding the elements of each is all that is necessary to understand the background role they play in some cases in the first year criminal law textbook, and coverage on the bar exam rarely goes beyond the fundamental points..

Assault and Battery Distinguished

Strictly speaking a battery is very distinct from an assault. As originally understood a battery required a touching whereas an assault did not. This distinction has broken down in some jurisdictions that include battery within assault. Generally assault statutes are much more numerous and include much more serious crimes than battery statutes. This puzzles some because assaults by definition typically don't require even a touching or contact much less an injury. What you will soon realize, however, is that assaultive crimes focus more on the culpable intent of the assailant and make important distinctions about the level of harm intended. The absence of an injury or contact requirement also makes them easier to prove.

Battery

- A Harmful or Offensive

- Application of Force against the Person of Another

- Committed either Intentionally or with at Least Criminal Negligence

- That is Unlawful

When I was a child, commercials for toys often carried the warning, "Batteries not included." If you see a fact pattern that contains some violence but not actual *contact* against the victim, then you should think "battery not included" among the possible crimes.

The application of force required for battery requires contact with the victim. A simple shove is enough because most would be offended by being shoved even if they were not harmed. The defendant need not actually touch the victim, however. You could batter someone by throwing a rock or a paper clip at them. For that matter you can batter someone by spitting at them, (definitely offensive), but the spit must actually hit them. I can also commit a battery by setting a force in motion, like releasing an angry dog to attack someone or even taking the parking brake off a car that will roll downhill towards a crowd of people.

Note that battery is a general intent crime, which means that criminal/gross negligence is all that is required. So if I am swinging my fists around in a crowded space while watching a prize fight on TV and end up hitting you, then I could be guilty of battery, although gross negligence would require me to be taking really big swings in a really crowded space.

The application of force must, of course, be unlawful. People consent to be tackled when they play football; security guards are legally authorized to grab running shoplifters; everyone is legally justified in using force in self defense. All of these applications of force would be lawful, and none of them would constitute battery.

Aggravated batteries are usually defined by statute, often classified as felonies, and typically involve one of three aggravating factors.

1. An especially vulnerable type of victim such as a child, or elderly person, or police officer.

2. Use of a deadly weapon.

3. The actual infliction of serious bodily harm or worse.

Note that the third aggravating factor creates a result crime. The prosecution must prove the occurrence of the harm as well as causation.

Assault

Assault is a bit trickier because there are generally two types of assaults: an attempted battery and an intentional attempt to frighten.

Attempted Battery Assault

Assault as an attempted battery is more straightforward. Think if it as "a swing and a miss." Imagine that I see former NBA basketball star, Shaquille O'Neal walking down the street and decide that I am going to punch him in the face. Shaq is, of course, over 7 feet tall, whereas I am just under six feet and have a two inch vertical leap. I miss Shaq completely. I am guilty of assault, not battery.

Like all crimes of attempt, an attempted battery requires intent to commit the crime. So even though a battery is a general intent crime requiring only criminal negligence, the attempted battery type of assault requires me to intend to apply force against his person, which is, of course, a specific intent. If I was not trying to hit O'Neal but was jumping up to waive my autograph book in his face and came inches from hitting him, I would not be guilty of an assault. (If I hit him with the book, though, I would be guilty of an actual battery because it was arguably grossly negligent of me to do so.)

A minority of jurisdictions require for this type of assault that the defendant have the present ability to commit the attempted act. Assume instead that I was trying to hit former NBA star Yao Ming in the nose. Yao is 7'6" tall. If I can't reach his nose with my fist, then I would not be guilty of assault for taking a swing at him on a theory of attempted battery in such a jurisdiction (although they will get me under the next type of assault). Most jurisdictions don't care whether the defendant has the present ability to succeed in the attempted battery.

Finally, assault as an attempted battery does not require any sort of mental state on the part of the victim. The victim does not need to be afraid and does not even need to be aware of the attempted battery. So assume again that I was trying to hit O'Neal, but he did not even see or otherwise notice the swing. I am nonetheless still guilty of the attempted battery version of assault.

Intent to Frighten Assault

This more sweeping and more common type assault could be thought of as a "scare crime," although actual fear as we will see is not required.

- Intentionally

- Causing the Victim to Reasonably Expect

- An Imminent Battery

- By More than Mere Words

This type of assault covers much more ground. Pointing a gun or a knife at someone would obviously do. Angrily shaking my (comparatively small) fist in O'Neal's face would also be enough. My simply yelling angrily at O'Neal that I am going to punch him in the nose would not be enough. If my "mere words" were accompanied by the clenching of one of my fists, however, that would be enough to satisfy the elements of an intent to frighten assault.

One important point of difference between this "scare crime" assault and an attempted battery assault is the subjective awareness of the victim. For the attempted battery the victim need not be aware of "the swing and the miss." The scare crime assault requires the defendant to cause the victim to expect an imminent battery. So if I jump up and shake my fist at Neal yelling that I am going to punch him, but he neither sees nor hears me, then I would not be guilty of an assault under the intent to frighten theory. (I would also not be guilty of assault under the attempted battery theory since I arguably had not begun the attempt.)

Note that fear is not actually required for this type of assault, merely the reasonable expectation of an imminent battery. Can you imagine Shaquille O'Neal being actually afraid of me? Did I mention that he weighs over 300 lbs. and that his arms are probably thicker than my legs? The only way that he could get hurt by me would be if he fell down laughing. Actual fear of bodily harm is not required, however. He need merely reasonably expect an imminent battery, which includes of course not just a harmful touching but an offensive one.

Finally, the fear must be of an imminent battery. Telling him that I going to punch him in the nose tomorrow as I shake my fist will not cut it.

Aggravated Assaults

Once again, these are often defined by statute and usually classified as felonies. The list of aggravating factors is slightly longer than for aggravated batteries.

1. An especially vulnerable type of victim such as a child, or elderly person, or police officer.

2. Use of a deadly weapon.

3. The actual infliction of serious bodily harm or worse.

4. The intent to inflict serious injury.

Note in particular the fourth type of aggravated assault. Any assault committed with the intent to seriously injure someone suffices. Definitions of serious injury vary, but broken bones, injuries requiring stitches or knocked out teeth suffice.

False Imprisonment

- Unlawful

- Intentional

- Confinement of Another Person

- Without His or Her Consent

Assume you decide to lock your roommate in her room until she finally catches up to you in binge-watching your favorite Netflix show. (You really hate to watch those episodes alone.) Unless she agrees to be locked in, you have committed the crime of false imprisonment, even though she is being locked in her own room.

Kidnapping

All the elements of false imprisonment are contained within the crime of kidnapping (making it a lesser included offense), but an additional element is required.

- False Imprisonment AND

- Movement of Victim OR

- Concealment of the Victim

If you drag your roommate out of her bedroom and lock her in your room you have graduated from false imprisonment (often just a misdemeanor) up to kidnapping (usually a felony). That is it! No ransom notes or guns or secret hideouts required. Also, note that you only have to forcibly move the victim a short distance for false imprisonment to morph into kidnapping. Shame that they won't let you watch Netflix in prison.

Aggravated Kidnapping

Many statutes provide increased penalties for kidnappings accompanied by ransom demands or committed for the purpose of some other crime (like a hostage in a robbery).

Exam Tip: Felony Murder

Remember that kidnapping is one of the felonies that support felony murder liability. It is considered inherently dangerous, does not merge, and is often enumerated in any event. So if your roommate bumps her (eggshell) head and dies as you drag her to her Netflix session you may just have committed felony murder!

Remember though that felonious assaults or batteries generally do not support felony murder because they "merge" into the homicide and involve no independent felonious purpose.

CHAPTER 18

Property   Crimes

Property crimes, too, are little taught in first year criminal law courses but often tested on the bar exam and are a staple of criminal law practice.   People like to mess with other people's stuff, but there are more ways of messing with other people's stuff than you might think.   The result is a series of different types of crime against property, and the trick on both the exam and in real life is to distinguish one from the other.

Most property crimes orbit around behavior that the common person would simply consider to be different forms of "stealing." These are the different crimes that constitute "stealing."

- Larceny

- Embezzlement

- Obtaining Property by False Pretenses

- Forgery

- Robbery

Sometimes the difference lies in the nature of the thing taken, sometimes in the nature of the taking.   In the case of robbery, the difference is the combination of assault and larceny. We all know stealing when we see it; we just need to learn the different labels for it that the law uses.

In an attempt to simply things, a number of jurisdictions (including the Model Penal Code) have passed into law a consolidated theft statute which covers all of this ground. Such statutes can be somewhat unwieldy, however, and this is one reform that has not really caught on.

The two other important crimes in this area are crimes *against* property as opposed to crimes *of* property.

- Burglary

- Arson

Burglary, as we have discussed earlier is basically the combination of trespassing with a felonious or larcenous intent. Arson is a particularly serious and dangerous form of destruction of property.

As is always the case, each of these crimes can be understood in terms of the elements of a guilty hand moved by a guilty mind. Keeping an eye on the finer points of the definitions of conduct and mental state is particularly important.

Larceny

- Wrongful Taking and

- Carrying Away of

- Personal Property of

- Another with the

- Intent to Permanently Deprive the Owner of It.

Larceny is simply the heart of what most people think of as stealing or theft. Shoplifters commit larceny. So did that kid in the fifth grade who used to steal the cookies out of your lunch when you were not looking.

That said, each of the elements listed above does important work, so you don't want to take larceny for granted.

Taking

Larceny first requires that you take something. Picking it up could be taking it, but destroying something would not be taking it. Taking also means that you take it from someone else's lawful possession. The person possessing the thing need not be the owner, but it can't of course be you. If you already have possession of something you may end up being guilty of a property crime, but it won't be larceny. (See embezzlement below.) Property that is abandoned is in no one's possession and cannot be "taken," but property that is merely lost can be taken because the law considers it to be in the "constructive possession" of the owner

The taking must be wrongful or "trespassory". If your roommate told you that you could borrow her dress anytime you wanted to, then you can't be guilty of larceny when you remove it from her closet.

Larceny by Trick

You can't "trick" your way out of larceny liability. Say you deceive someone at a party that the last umbrella left in the umbrella stand is yours, not theirs. They hand you the umbrella, and you run outside laughing about how gullible they are. Don't laugh too hard because in addition to being quite a jerk you have just committed the crime of "larceny by trick," a crime created by law to deal with people who do not "take" things but lie their way into being given them.

Asportation

Let's go back to you and your roommate's dress. If she did not give you permission to take the dress but happened upon you just as you picked it up you are not yet guilty of larceny. While you have taken it you have not yet carried it away. The fancy legal term for the carrying away requirement is "asportation." (Try throwing that one around at the next party you go to.) "Where did you "asport" my coat when I came in.) Asportation requires some slight movement, but it does require movement from one place to another. If she caught you walking out of the door to her room with it you would now have taken *and* "asported" it.

Personal Property

One cannot commit larceny against land or its fixtures. One also cannot commit larceny of intangible things. If you sneak into the next big (fill in your favorite band's name here) concert without paying you are not guilty of larceny because the experience of the performance is not tangible property. You better take off running if you see security coming after you though because you are guilty of other crimes (just not ones you are likely to study or be tested on in law school).

Another's Property

This trips people up because you actually can be guilty under some circumstances of stealing stuff you own. Imagine that your property is in the lawful *possession* of another. Let's say that you left your suit at the dry cleaner's to get a stain removed before a big interview. After you inspect the suit you decide to run out the door without paying. Well, I am sure you looked great at your interview, but if hired you may have to explain a larceny conviction to your new employer because you just committed larceny. Even though the dry cleaner does not own your suit state law in many jurisdictions gives him the right to retain *custody* and *possession* until you pay. That confers upon you the dubious distinction of having stolen your own stuff!

Intent to Permanently Deprive

There are a number of ways this intent might be satisfied and a few ways that it can't. Remember that each of the following assumes that the thing was wrongfully taken to begin with.

Equals Intent to Permanently Deprive

- Keeping something

- Giving or Selling it to someone else

- Destroying it

- Exposing it to Substantial Risk

Does Not Equal an Intent to Permanently Deprive

- Borrowing it

- Slightly using it

Let's play around with these distinctions a bit. A teenager borrows his Mom's car against his Mom's wishes. That would not be larceny since the teenager is only borrowing it. (Many states have a separate offense for "joyriding" when someone uses another's automobile without permission.) The teenager would be guilty of larceny, however, if at the time of the taking she plans to drag race the car because this would be a substantial risk. Now assume that the teenager borrows her Mom's dress without permission and plans to dance the night away in it. That also would not be larceny since such slight and non-risky use is not the equivalent of permanent deprivation.

Good Faith Mistakes

You cannot intend to permanently deprive another of their property if you believe that what you take is rightfully yours. Assume that as I leave a party I grab the wrong umbrella from the umbrella stand. If I honestly believe that the umbrella is mine then I am not guilty of larceny. What if my umbrella is black and the umbrellas I grab is pink? That would be an unreasonable mistake, but I am still not guilty as long as I *believed in good faith* that the umbrella was mine. In common law terminology, larceny is a *specific intent* crime that requires you to specifically intend to take something that does not belong to you. That means that people who are unreasonably stupid have a complete defense. There is no such thing as recklessly or negligently stealing something. We all understand intuitively that one who steals *knows* that they are taking something that does not belong to them.

Remember though that the more unreasonable your belief the less likely that a jury would believe that you did really believe that you were entitled to possession of the thing. A pink umbrella is pretty far from a black one. Hopefully the jury will believe that I am the stereotypical absent-minded professor.

Doctrine of Continuing Trespass

The requirement that a crime's mental state exist concurrently with a crime's conduct would seem to create a loophole for a certain type of thief. Imagine that you borrow your roommate's dress without her permission but fully intending to return it after you wear it once or twice. It looks so darn good on you though that you decide to keep it after receiving just one compliment too many on how it matches your eyes. You would seem to be guilty only of a trespass, not larceny, since you did not intend to permanently deprive your roommate of the dress at the time you took it. Only later did you form the intent required for larceny. Well, the law contains what is really a legal fiction to close that loophole. The law bridges the gap in time between your initial wrongful taking and your subsequent larcenous mental state by finding that the trespass continued until you decided to steal the dress at which point your crime changed from trespass to larceny. Under the doctrine of continuing trespass you would be guilty of larceny.

Embezzlement

Embezzlement is a trust offense. Basically, it means that you are messing with stuff that other people have entrusted to you. The law calls "messing with stuff" *conversion*. There is no taking involved because the owner entrusted the thing to you.

- Conversion of the
- Personal Property of Another
- By One in Lawful Possession
- With the Intent to Defraud

Conversion means any significant interference with the owner's rights in the property and includes selling, consuming, discarding, or badly damaging it. Slight use is not enough. One need not personally gain by the conversion. Donating someone else's property to charity could constitute conversion. Once again property means something tangible, so letting your friends in free into the movie theatre where you work would be some crime other than embezzlement.

Finally, the reason why embezzlement is truly a trust offense is that the element of lawful possession means more than just lawful custody. The owner must have given you some sort of authority over the property. The fraudulent intent requirement is satisfied when you intentionally violate the terms under which the property was entrusted to you.

Say that I park my Ferrari (yeah right!) on a public street and leave the keys in it. If someone jumps in and drives off then that would be larceny. If I park it in a paid parking lot and the valet parking attendant drives takes it for a hundred mile spin around the outskirts of Chicago (shades of "Ferris Bueller's Day Off") then that would be embezzlement. When I handed the valet parking attendant the keys I invested him with the authority to drive the car to a parking space. When he abused that trust by heavily using and thereby converting the car to his own use he committed the crime of embezzlement.

Obtaining Property by False Pretenses

The difference here is what you get and how you get it. First, this crime requires that you obtain *ownership*, not just custody or possession, of something. Second, you don't take it but trick someone into giving it to you.

- Knowingly False Representation of

- Present or Past (but <u>not</u> future) Fact

- Causing Victim to Pass Title to Defendant

Essentially the defendant gets the victim to give the defendant ownership of something by lying about something important. The lie cannot be a false promise, however. The fact falsely represented must be a present or past one. So if I drop by the car dealership and convince a gullible salesperson to give me the pink slip to a new Ferrari (the parking attendant really banged up mine) by telling the salesperson that I paid his colleague in cash the previous week then the crime would be complete. If I tell him instead that I will pay him next week (knowing full well that I can't on a professor's salary) then we have a breach of contract or possibly a fraud case but not this crime.

Note that this crime does important work that larceny ordinarily does not. When the police pull me over in *my* new Ferrari after my lie has been discovered it will not do me any good to waive the pink slip at them and tell them that the car is not stolen. I am not going to jail for larceny, but for obtaining property by false pretenses. Oh, what tangled webs we weave when we deceive in order to get those shiny, flashy things we covet!

Larceny by Trick Distinguished

Earlier I mentioned that stealing something by tricking them into giving it to you is considered larceny by trick in many jurisdictions. The difference between larceny by trick and obtaining property by false pretenses is that you only obtain possession-in larceny by trick—not title and ownership.

What crime occurs when you obtain ownership by knowingly writing a bad check? Most jurisdictions treat that as larceny by trick on the grounds that title does not pass until the check is successfully cashed. So the bad-check writer walks out of the store with possession but not ownership.

On a related note, obtaining property by use of an unauthorized or stolen credit card is dealt with in most jurisdictions by a specific statute.

Forgery and Writing Bad Checks

Speaking of bad checks, two different crimes ordinarily come into play here. First, many jurisdictions have specific statutory crimes for writing a check against insufficient funds in one's bank account. These statutes require that you *know* that the check will "bounce" and that you *intend to defraud* the recipient of the check thereby. So bad arithmetic in balancing your checkbook is a defense!

Writing a bad check also is included within forgery ordinarily although forgery encompasses lots of other types of behavior as well, obviously.

- Making or Altering

- A Legally Significant Writing

- With the Intent to Defraud

Note that forgery includes altering as well as making a document. So you don't need to steal someone's checkbook and write out a check from scratch in order to be guilty. Just wait for them to write you a check and add a couple of zeroes to the amount! Both count equally as forgeries under the criminal law.

Consolidated Theft Statutes

Not surprisingly some jurisdictions have grown weary of keeping all of these common law crimes straight for judges, prosecutors, juries and the public. These jurisdictions have consolidated the theft crimes discussed into a single "theft" statute. Sometimes these consolidations change the requirements of the particular crimes in order to iron out inconsistencies or gaps. Other times the statutes simply create different sections for each type of theft crime under one omnibus statute in order to simplify charging and proof at trial.

Robbery

Think of robbery as a particular type of larceny with a particular type of assault added on. Robbery includes someone walking into a store or bank and demanding money at gunpoint and a mugger who hits you over the head in an alley and takes your money. For reasons that will become apparent, it does not include a pickpocket or someone who grabs money off a store counter and runs out the door.

- Taking the Personal Property of Another

- From Their Person or Presence

- Through Force OR

- Through Intimidation

- With the Intent to Permanently Deprive the Victim of the Property

Note first that taking another's property with the intent to permanently deprive is ordinarily larceny. So robbery is simply a more serious form of larceny. It is typically classified as a felony although unarmed robberies are sometimes classified as high level misdemeanors in some jurisdictions.

From Person or Presence

Robberies can only occur from someone's person or presence. Something in your hand or in a pocket or in contact in some other way with your body or clothing that you are wearing is considered to be on your body. Presence is a bit more complex. The key factors are proximity and control. The basic idea is that had the victim not been threatened or harmed he could have stopped the taking. Pulling a handbag from a little old lady's arm is taking it from her person. Grabbing if off the park bench that she is sitting on is taking it from her presence. Note that a number of modern statutes (including the Model Penal Code) do not require that the taking be from the person or presence.

Through Force or Intimidation

Simply snatching the little old lady's handbag from the park bench where she is feeding the pigeons is not enough by itself to make my larceny a robbery at common law. I must either use force intimidation. Note the "or." You need one or the other, not both.

Force is more than simply the physical effort necessary to take and move the object. This is why a pickpocket is not ordinarily a robber. I don't need a gun or a knife or any sort of weapon though. Punching the little old lady in the nose would be enough although I also do not need to inflict any sort of harm upon her. The tougher case is if I just snatch the bag off of her arm. Most cases hold that simply snatching something from another's grasp is not enough. If, however, the victim resists or struggles during the taking, then any amount of force sufficient to overcome that resistance will be enough for a robbery. Even a momentary tug of war would be enough. Again, no injury or harm to the victim is required—simply momentary resistance that is successfully overcome. So make sure that you make a clean grab the next time you decide to go purse snatching.

Intimidation is something entirely different. Here you do not need to even touch the victim. One must simply create a fear of harm. So if I shake my fist in the little old lady's face as I snatch her purse from the park bench she is sitting on then I have probably committed a robbery. I say probably because the law requires for a robbery to occur that the victim *actually be in fear*. Fear here means the apprehension of bodily harm though, not necessarily a state of fright. Imagine that instead of robbing a little old lady I grab the "murse" (man purse) of Shaquille O'Neal (a former NBA player who is 7'1" tall and over 300 pounds) from the bench he is sitting on. When I shake my fist at Shaquille he will probably start to laugh, but as long as he expects me to punch him in the face if he tries to rescue his murse robbery has still occurred. (I better get clean away though or there will be nothing left of me to prosecute.)

Mental State

Mental state is rarely an issue in robbery cases because the conduct essentially speaks for itself. It is hard to imagine someone accidentally threatening someone else and taking their money. Not surprisingly robbery is a general intent offense in common law terms. One need only be aware that one is threatening or hurting another and taking their property. One need not have any particular purpose to be a robber. Sorry Robin Hood, the law does not care why you rob or what you do with the money.

Attempted Robbery

Many jurisdictions have defined robbery to include an attempted robbery on the grounds that robbers should not be rewarded with a lesser conviction if their victims successfully resist or otherwise thwart the taking. So if the little old lady wins the tug of war over her purse you still get convicted of a robbery in these jurisdictions.

Aggravated Robbery

Not surprisingly, many jurisdictions have defined by statute more aggravated forms of robbery that entail harsher punishments. Typically the aggravating factors include use of a deadly weapon, infliction of bodily harm or the presence of at least one accomplice.

Burglary

Burglary was a relatively narrowly defined offense at common law that has since been expanded by statute in a number of different ways. We will begin with the narrow common law definition.

- Breaking and

- Entering

- A Dwelling

- At Night

- With the Intent to Commit a Felony or Larceny Therein

The elements that have been dropped or modified over time are the dwelling and nighttime requirements. Many jurisdictions define burglary as the breaking and entering of any structure with the requisite intent; others create different degrees of burglary depending on whether the structure was a dwelling or not. Similarly, many jurisdictions have abolished the night time requirement, and others treat night time burglaries as a more serious offense. Finally, some jurisdictions have largely eliminated the breaking requirement.

Breaking

Breaking requires a trespass. One who enters with either express or implied consent is not breaking although the law will find a "constructive breaking" if the consent was obtained by fraud or coercion. So you can't escape a burglary charge by tricking or threatening your way inside. Breaking otherwise requires some use of force against the structure itself. One does not have to actually "break" down the door or break through a window. Simply opening a door or window is enough. Even the slight enlargement of an existing opening is enough: pushing a door that is already ajar just a little bit more open or lifting up an already open window would suffice. That said, many jurisdictions have simply done away with the breaking requirement although they still require the entry to be without consent.

Entering

One need not step completely inside the structure to accomplish the burglary in order to enter. Inserting any part of the human anatomy would be enough. Imagine that you smell your favorite pie through the open window of someone's kitchen. You lift up the already open window (breaking!) in order to fit your hand in and then reach through the window to grab the pie. As soon as your hand passes through the open window you have committed the burglary. You don't even need to touch the pie! You can also accomplish the required entry with a tool or instrument, but the insertion of the tool must be to accomplish the felony or larceny intended. Using a crowbar to open the window would not count, but using a "grabber" to grab the pie (messy!) would.

Felonious or Larcenous Intent

This intent must exist concurrently with the breaking and entering. Breaking into a house just to get out of the cold is a criminal trespass, not a burglary, even if you subsequently decide while inside to steal something. On the other hand, you become guilty of burglary at the moment you and break and enter with the requisite intent. Changing your mind later does not undo your liability. So if you so much as set foot inside a structure that you "broke" into with the requisite intent, the crime is complete.

This element is satisfied if the defendant intended to commit any felony inside the structure, or if they intended to commit larceny.   Don't be confused if you see this element stated as simply with the intent to commit a felony inside. At common law all larceny was a felony.   Larceny aside, other misdemeanors won't suffice. If you break and enter to commit a misdemeanor act of vandalism, you are not guilty of burglary but of trespass (and of vandalism if you follow through).

Burglary as an Anticipatory Offense

Burglary is a great example of what scholars and judges refer to as an anticipatory offense. Like the crime of attempt, burglary is punished seriously because it anticipates a greater social harm that might happen. We all feel violated if someone intrudes into our home, but we feel a greater sense of violation if the intruder has come to do us harm or take things from us. So the law allows persons who break and enter under circumstances suggesting that they meant to do either of these things to be punished far more severely than an ordinary trespasser.

Arson

Arson, like burglary, has been expanded by modern statutes. At common law it consisted of the following.

- Malicious
- Burning of the
- Dwelling of
- Another

Most modern statutes have expanded arson to include non-dwellings and to include burning one's own structures as well.

Burning

One need not burn a building down to be guilty of arson. Burning means the combustion of some part of the structure. Slight charring would therefore be enough. Scorching is not enough though because scorching involves not combustion but discoloration by smoke or heat.

Malicious

Outside of homicide, arson is the one other place where you are likely to come across the common law mental state of malice. In the context of arson, malice means that the defendant intentionally did something that involved a substantial risk of burning. A *reckless disregard* of an obvious risk of burning would be enough.

CHAPTER 19

Inchoate Crimes: An Overview

Something inchoate is something not fully done or realized. So far we have concerned ourselves with complete crimes, but criminal law has always created liability for inchoate—incomplete—crimes as well. The three inchoate crimes that first year criminal law courses typically touch upon are solicitation, conspiracy and attempt. Attempt is the most important, but professors fit in solicitation and conspiracy as they can. Logically though it is easier to start with solicitation and conspiracy, then end with attempt.

- Solicitation is the crime of seriously asking someone to commit a crime.

- Conspiracy is the crime of agreeing with some to commit a crime or to do something illegal.

- Attempt is beginning to commit a crime.

Each of these crimes deserve their own special consideration, but it is helpful to understand a few big picture points before we delve into the details of each.

First, we obviously don't want to prosecute people for "thinking bad thoughts." If I admit to you that I was seriously thinking of stealing a candy bar, I am not admitting to any inchoate crime. We don't prosecute thought crimes for a number of reasons. People who think bad thoughts often don't act on them and are therefore neither dangerous to society nor sufficiently blameworthy to punish. There is also something distinctly creepy and scary about the idea that the government could punish you for something you are thinking of doing. We also intuitively believe that we are all entitled to our own "mental freedom" to think as we like.

These rather obvious objections to thought crimes immediately become complicated when we try to define inchoate crimes. With respect to solicitation, under what circumstances should asking someone to commit a crime be a crime itself? They might not agree; you might change your mind; nothing might ever happen. You did ask though. When should that be enough? With respect to conspiracy, what difference does it make if someone agrees with you to commit a crime? Quite a lot under the law, as it turns out. Now again, neither of you have actually begun committing any crime. Still, the law of conspiracy will cover you both if the elements of that crime are satisfied.

Attempt raises these issues most clearly. To be guilty of an attempt, you must have done something towards the commission of the crime, but how much should be enough? People begin all sorts of things intending to see them through but then change their minds or just give up. Where should the criminal law fix that "point of no return" at which you have now committed the crime of attempt regardless of whether you see it through or not? At what point do you become blameworthy or dangerous enough to condemn or deter?

Defining inchoate offenses requires a balancing act. On the one hand if we require too much to establish guilt then we lose an opportunity to prevent crime by cutting off potentially dangerous conduct and to punish people who are already sufficiently blameworthy. On the other hand, if we require too little to establish guilt then we may punish people who would never done anything further and who are not sufficiently blameworthy to merit criminal punishment.

What you will see as you work through the law of inchoate offenses is that the law makes a tradeoff. To be guilty of an inchoate offense, you must have a very guilty mind since you have a much less guilty hand than you would have for a completed crime. Inchoate offenses are what the common law terms specific intent offenses and sometimes require a greater mental state than the completed offense itself.

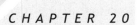

CHAPTER 20

Solicitation

Solicitation means asking, inviting, requesting, commanding, or even encouraging another to commit a crime with the intent that the person do so. At common law the crime solicited had to be a felony or a misdemeanor that constituted obstruction of justice or a "breach of the peace" (which generally meant a crime of violence or public disorder). The guilty hand is the soliciting, and the guilty mind is the purpose that the person solicited commit the crime.

An Historical Example

Solicitation is a very compact crime. It is complete once the words leave the solicitor's mouth. Let's take an example from history. In 1170, England's King Henry II got into a serious quarrel with Thomas Becket, the Archbishop of Canterbury for excommunicating another Archbishop who was loyal to Henry. This was very serious stuff, and everyone knew it. One day at court Henry yelled out "Will someone not rid me of this troublesome priest?" Four knights who heard this concluded that Henry wanted Becket dead, so they went and killed Becket.

Let's play around with this story to illustrate and the ins and outs of solicitation as a crime. Assume Henry is on trial for solicitation

- What if Henry was only joking? Not guilty of solicitation because he lacks intent. The fact that the knights thought Henry was serious and that someone died does not change things.

- What if Henry was serious but the knights did not respond to Henry's request? Not a defense to solicitation because no agreement or response of any sort is required.

- What about the fact that Henry did not direct the request to any particular person or persons? Not required as long as he has solicited someone (i.e. not just talking to himself in an empty room).

- What if Henry was serious but everyone thought he was joking? Still guilty. It is only Henry's state of mind that matters. As long as Henry intended the crime to be committed, it does not matter what those solicited thought.

- What if no one killed Becket even though they thought Henry was serious? Still guilty because crime is complete once solicitation is made with the required intent.

- What if Henry was serious, but no one heard him? Henry would not be guilty of solicitation under the common law because he would not actually have solicited *anyone*. You might argue that he was guilty of attempted solicitation, but few if any common law jurisdictions recognize "attempted solicitation."

What is key in these hypotheticals is that everything turns on Henry's state of mind. He must actually intend that Thomas be killed. It would not be enough if he were joking but had been reckless or negligent with respect to the risk that someone might think he was serious. If Henry has the highly culpable mental state of intending Thomas be killed though, the law does not care whether anyone believed or acted on his request. Solicitation doctrine punishes people who seriously ask others to commit a crime without respect to what does or does not happen next.

First Amendment Limits

"It is a free country," people say. Why then can we criminalize speech? Well, your first amendment right to free speech stops short of asking other people to commit crimes. First amendment concerns are raised, however, with respect to what constitutes a solicitation. One key issue is whether this speech is directed at a definable group. A general call to violate a particular law contained in a widely distributed leaflet or in an internet blog post might not be considered a solicitation. A targeted mailing or a post in a restricted internet chat room would more likely be seen as a criminal solicitation.

Solicitation as an Attempt?

We will return to this point when we discuss attempt liability, but the majority of jurisdictions do not consider a solicitation by itself to be an attempt of the crime solicited. A minority of jurisdictions will treat solicitations as attempts in and of themselves.

Model Penal Code

The MPC creates wider criminal liability for solicitation. First, it applies to any crime, not just felonies or certain misdemeanors. Second, it extends not just to solicitations to commit a crime but to any conduct that would either constitute an attempt or make the other person an accomplice. So if I ask you to hand me a gun so that I shoot someone, I am not soliciting a crime under the common law because your handing me a gun is not a crime in and of itself. I would be guilty of solicitation under the MPC because if you did hand me the gun after being told that I was going to shoot someone, you would be an accomplice to the shooting (as we will discuss later on).

The Model Penal Code does offer would be solicitors one consolation prize. It allows them to "undo" their solicitation by renouncing it. If a person completely and voluntarily renounces his criminal intent and either persuades the person he solicited to abandon the crime *or* prevents them from committing it then he will not be guilty of solicitation. Under the common law, there is no going back, however, as the crime is complete once the words leave your mouth (or once you hit send on your email browser).

Merger

Merger doctrine for inchoate offenses aims to avoid punishing someone twice for what is essentially the same conduct. Whenever we want to stop the state from "double dipping in the punishment bowl" we say that the lesser offense *merges* into the greater offense. Assume you solicit someone to commit a crime, they agree, and they commit the crime? Can you be found guilty of solicitation *and* conspiracy *and* the completed crime? No, the crime of solicitation *merges* into the conspiracy and also merges into the completed crime. If you solicited someone to commit a crime, and were found guilty of attempting that crime your solicitation would also merge into your attempt if both were based on the same conduct.

CHAPTER 21

Conspiracy

Conspiracy is an important but very complicated doctrine that contains many different rules. Criminal law professors often fit it in as best they can near the end of the semester. Some criminal law professors skip it altogether, finding it too difficult to quickly dip into something that has so many moving parts. Others spend a day or two trying to get across the main principles. A few give it more time because of its great importance to the practice of criminal law. This chapter will hit the fundamental concepts hard and touch on a few of the more important ancillary rules.

The Crime Is the Agreement

The first thing to get firmly in mind is that with conspiracy the crime is the agreement. A criminal conspiracy is an agreement to commit a crime. Fans of the TV show "The Office" might appreciate the following example. In one episode Dwight, a dweebishly evil character, is confronted by another employee who tells him "I know about your diabolical plan!" Dwight feigns ignorance and says "I don't know what you are talking about." His co-worker says "You left it in the printer," and hands Dwight a thick document with Dwight's name on it that is titled "Dwight's Diabolical Plan." "What do you want?" Dwight asks. "I want in," his co-worker replies at which point both of them shake hands. What I want you to remember above all things is that at common law the crime of conspiracy was complete once they shook hands (assuming that the diabolical plan was to do something unlawful). They do not need to do anything more because *the crime is the agreement.*

The idea of a criminal agreement makes conspiracy doctrine a bit tricky. The guilty mind required is the intent to agree and the intent to achieve the object of the agreement. The guilty hand required at common law is the agreement itself. Most people think of an agreement as something that exists in people's minds though. This makes conspiracy's conduct requirement what I would call a "mentalish" one.

One last thing to stress before we explore conspiracy doctrine. Conspiracy is a crime all onto itself. You might also be guilty of the crime you conspired to commit (depending on complicity doctrine to be discussed later), but you might not be because no might have done anything beyond agreeing to commit the crime. You also might be guilty of attempting to commit the crime you agreed to commit, but again you might not be because no one might have attempted anything. Conspiracy is a crime all onto itself though, and you should always analyze it separately from liability for other crimes and attempted crimes.

Policies Behind Conspiracy Doctrine

Why do we punish people for agreeing to do bad things before any of them have even attempted to do a bad thing? We might end up punishing people who might not ever end up doing anything because they either had a change of heart or were too lazy, fearful or incompetent to get things going.

One reason we punish conspiracies is crime prevention. Making it a crime to agree to commit a crime allows the police to arrest people before they can get close to doing something bad. Police surveillance and investigation is an imperfect enterprise conducted with limited resources. Following around conspirators until they begin their attempt would take up a lot of police time that is better spent doing other things. Also, the continued surveillance might be detected or circumvented in which case we risk that the crime will end up being successfully carried out at some point in the future. If a group of people agree to blow up a building, do we really want to try following them around until they buy their explosives?

The second reason we punish conspiracies is the "special danger of group activity." The criminal law considers people who commit crimes in groups to be more likely to see things through to the end and more likely to be successful in their efforts. Teamwork makes lots of things easy, including crime. A group of people can encourage one another, pool their resources and divide up the tasks involved in efficient ways. Groups can commit more elaborate crimes. They can also continue their criminal activities longer as new members add to or replace the old ones. Historically the criminal law has had good reason to fear crime committed by groups: think of organized crime syndicates, terrorist organizations, and insurrectionary movements. The government relied heavily on conspiracy law in prosecuting the Ku Klux Klan, the Mafia, and Al Qaeda.

But conspiracy law also involves special dangers to civil liberties. Criminal conspiracy law is defined so broadly that one noted judge aptly called it the "darling of the modern prosecutor's nursery." The same features that make conspiracy a great weapon against the evil and the dangerous also make it a handy club against the unpopular. Critics of conspiracy law fear that it promotes guilt by association and chills our first amendment rights of free assembly by making it possible to be convicted just for meeting with people the government deems suspicious. Because conspiracy requires little or no action on the part of the conspirator it also confers great power onto informants who can make out a case for criminal conspiracy by making up a conversation about an agreement that never existed. Finally, broad conspiracy liability may actually waste government resources in the war against terrorism or organized crime by unleashing prosecutions against hapless groups of incompetent individuals who talk big but who could never bring themselves to organize a luncheon, much less an elaborate crime.

The law strikes the balance between these competing concerns in how it defines the elements and scope of conspiracy law.

The Elements of Conspiracy: An Overview

Because conspiracy involves "mentalish" conduct both the conduct and mental state requirements deserve separate discussion. It helps though to have a snapshot of the overall crime before working through the elements. A criminal conspiracy may be usefully defined in the following way.

- An Agreement, express or implied

  o Agreement may be inferred from circumstances

- But fact finder must find a "communion of understanding," not just a coincidence of purpose—a shared and mutual understanding

- To commit a crime or—at common law and in a few jurisdictions still—an unlawful act

- To which the defendant intended to agree

- With the further intent that the object of the agreement be achieved

- Many jurisdictions including the MPC (but unlike the common law) also require an overt act in furtherance of the conspiracy in addition to the acts constituting the agreement

The Guilty Hand: The Agreement

Almost all jurisdictions today (including the Model Penal Code) limit conspiracy to agreements to commit a *crime*. At common law and in a few remaining jurisdictions one could be convicted of the crime of conspiracy if you agreed to commit an *unlawful* act. This older, broader understanding of conspiracy meant that an agreement to violate some aspect of civil law could be prosecuted criminally. For most jurisdictions today, however, this broader version of conspiracy is far too sweeping. An aggressive prosecutor could use it to obliterate the distinction between civil and criminal wrongs. Garden variety breaches of contract or tort violations could be prosecuted as crimes if two or more people agreed on the conduct constituting the civil wrong.

The most important thing to learn about the agreement element of conspiracy is that it may be implied from the circumstances. No signed contract, handshake or even express words of agreement are required. Even more perplexing, no direct communication between conspirators is necessarily required. A mere coincidence of purpose is not enough for an agreement though. There must be a *communion of purpose* by which the cases mean that the actors are mutually aware of their shared purpose.

Imagine that a mob descends on an unlucky few. People in the crowd never speak to one another, but they can clearly see one another as they surround the victims. Acting in concert permits the inference that they share an understanding that each wishes the crime to be committed, and that could be enough to find an agreement for the purposes of criminal conspiracy. Note though that simple awareness of one another's purpose should not even be enough for an agreement (although this distinction is razor thin). The understanding must be mutual in the sense that each takes the other person's purpose into account and intends the other person to take his shared purpose into account. This idea of a mutual understanding brings us into the realm of a tacit agreement. "Yeah," people in the crowd think, "we are all agreed on doing this thing." Now you have communion of purpose, not just a coincidence of purpose.

Contrast that scenario with an unlucky law professor who faces assassination by not one, but two of his disgruntled first year law students. One student walks up behind him with a knife while the other (more forthright) student walks up to his face with a gun. Each share a purpose but because they are not mutually aware they cannot enjoy the communion of purpose necessary for conspiracy.

Remember that while an agreement may be implied from very little, it still must be proved. Just because a judge allows a conspiracy charge to go to the jury does not mean that the jury will find the agreement to have been proved beyond a reasonable doubt. If a jury returns a verdict of guilty, however, it may be hard for a judge to set aside the verdict as a matter of law because it is often very easy to imply an agreement from actions that work together towards a criminal objective.

The Guilty Hand: Overt Act

While the crime of conspiracy is the agreement, a majority of common law jurisdictions as well as the Model Penal Code require an *overt act in furtherance of the conspiracy* in addition to the acts that constituted the agreement itself. (Although the Model Penal Code dispenses with this requirement for conspiracies to commit the most serious felonies.) In such a jurisdiction Dwight and his co-worker in the scenario described at the beginning of this chapter would not become guilty of conspiracy as soon as they shook hands. The shaking of hands would be an express act of agreement, not an overt act in furtherance of the agreement.

The purpose of the overt act requirement is to make sure that the conspiracy is not something that will always exist only in the minds of the conspirators. The fact that someone has taken some action after the agreement is formed provides a modest guarantee that the agreement to commit a crime is a serious one.

This overt act does not have to be the beginning of an attempt to commit the crime. It need only be performed by one member of the group and need not be a criminal act in and of itself. Imagine that after Dwight and his co-worker shake hands on Dwight's diabolical plan, his co-worker says "I am going to make a copy of your diabolical plan." That would satisfy the overt act requirement in these jurisdictions even though copying the plan is neither a crime nor enough to constitute an attempt to commit the crime planned in many jurisdictions.

The Guilty Mind: Intent to Agree and Intent to Achieve

The two intents required for conspiracy should be kept separate although the distinction seems a bit fuzzy to many. One must both intend to agree with one another as well as intend to achieve the object of the agreement.

Intent to agree is difficult to separate from intent to achieve the criminal objective. An undercover police officers posing as a hit man may intend to agree with the person asking him to kill someone for money but not intend to actually carry out the crime. For this reason undercover policeman officers ordinarily can't be found guilty for conspiracy for their actions in sting operations. Conversely, a "lone wolf" mob member in the crowd scenario described above might intend to attack the victims but not intend to enter into any sort of agreement with anyone else in the mob.

If the intent to agree issue seems to blend into the conduct issue of whether an agreement actually exists, don't worry. It does! This is what I meant earlier by saying that the "act" of agreeing is a "mentalish" act. The intent to agree is the mental state side of the "mentalish" act of agreement.

The intent to achieve the object of the conspiracy has its own wrinkles. At a minimum it means that you must have the mental state required for the crime. You and I and my roommate agree to borrow your roommate's Ferrari sports car without his permission. You plan on returning it in mint condition after speeding around for a while whereas my roommate and I plan to sell the car to cover our gambling debts. You are not guilty of conspiracy to steal the car because you lack the mental state required by theft—the intent to permanently deprive the owner of the property. My roommate and I are guilty of conspiracy because we both have that intent.

This mental state requirement also effectively rules out conspiracy for crimes that create liability for reckless or negligent results. What if you and I agree to use the Ferrari in a game of chicken with another car where we speed toward a cliff with another car in order to see who "chickens out" first. The drivers in the other car cut things too close and drive off the cliff to their deaths. Have you and I conspired to commit reckless murder or involuntary manslaughter? We intended to do something at least criminally negligent and possibly extremely reckless depending on all of the circumstances. True, but we did not intend for anyone to die. Death is a required result for any homicide crime. Conspiracy requires you to intend that the objective of the conspiracy occur, and in this case that crime requires death to occur. For this reason, many commentators observe that the only sorts of homicide one can conspire to commit are intentional killings, and probably ones that are premeditated and deliberate.

Purposeful v. Knowing Assistance

Intent can mean either purposeful or knowing behavior. Since agreeing is by definition a purposeful act, one cannot intend to agree without it being one's purpose to agree by one's actions. Whether intent means purpose or knowledge with respect to the intent to achieve the object of the agreement is a more difficult question.

Consider a supplier of goods and services. If the supplier knows that one of his customers uses what is supplied to commit a crime has the supplier conspired to commit that crime by agreeing to supply the customer? The supplier could claim "I don't care what my customers use my stuff for as long as I get paid, so I don't really intend a crime or anything else for that matter." A prosecutor might argue that people who knowingly profit from criminal activity should be found to intend that activity. Whether the supplier "intends" the crime to be committed depends on whether his knowledge alone constitutes intent or whether it must be his purpose that his supplies be used to commit the crime.

There is a split among jurisdictions as to whether knowledge alone in such cases suffices for criminal conspiracy. The split is less consequential than one might think, however, because the jurisdictions that require purpose often define it in a way that comes very close to knowledge plus some sort of special stake in the outcome. If a supplier provides something that can only be used illegally, or provides it at greatly inflated prices, or if his criminal buyers constitute a disproportionate share of his business, then courts seem likely to find that to be legally sufficient evidence of purpose.

One leading Supreme Court case suggests that providing assistance in closely regulated areas also supports a finding of purposeful assistance of illegal activities when the assistance circumvents those regulations. Assume that you have a hand held scanner that can rapidly scan the pictures of a textbook, and that you rent the scanner out to other students in the library whom you know use it to make bootleg copies of the very expensive textbooks that law school courses often require. Whether you might be found to have conspired to violate the copyright laws (which do contain limited criminal provisions) would probably depend on whether the success of your rental business seemed to depend on—or do particularly well as a result of—the illegal nature of what was being scanned. While scanners are not per se illegal, the copying of material published under copyright is sufficiently regulated that a court might find your agreements with your customers to be purposeful with respect to the violation of copyright laws. (So don't agree to let anyone use your scanner to scan this book! ☺)

Attendant Circumstances

What does it mean to intend a crime to be committed if the crime itself does not require knowledge of all the circumstances that attend its commission? An easy example from a Supreme Court case concerned a drug dealer's henchman who assaulted an undercover federal agent as part of an attempted robbery. Being guilty of assaulting a federal officer does not require that you know that the person you assaulted was a federal officer. The logic is that if you are a bad enough person to assault someone then you do so at the risk that they might end up being a federal officer. But what about the head of the drug gang who told his henchman to attack the undercover agent? Can the drug dealer intend through his agreement with his henchman to assault a federal officer without even knowing that he is a federal officer? The Court decided that conspiracy required no greater mental state with respect to the attendant circumstance of the victim being a federal officer than did the underlying statute defining the crime. This issue varies from state to state and even from offense to offense, so you would be well advised to argue it both ways on an exam unless your professor tells you otherwise.

The Corrupt Motive Doctrine

Can you conspire to violate a law that you don't know about? Ignorance of the law is ordinarily no excuse, but some courts require what is called a "corrupt motive" for conspiracy liability. These courts reason that the very idea of a conspiracy implies that you are agreeing to something with an evil purpose. The cases distinguish between regulatory offenses which are wrong because society has legally prohibited them (*malum prohibitum*) and other offenses which are clearly understood to be wrong in and of themselves (*malum en se*). One can always be guilty of conspiring to commit a *malum en se* offense such as theft. To be guilty of conspiring to commit a *malum prohibitum* offense, such as certain regulatory reporting or disclosure requirements, jurisdictions recognizing this doctrine will require either proof of knowledge of the law to be broken or proof of a corrupt or evil motive more generally.

Liability for Other Crimes

Conspiracy is its own crime, but the federal courts and many jurisdictions also will hold a conspirator liable for certain crimes committed as a result of the conspiracy. This additional liability is known as *Pinkerton* liability, taking its name from the Supreme Court case that announced the rule for the federal courts. Under this rule a conspirator is responsible for crimes committed by other conspirators if

1. The crime was committed in furtherance of the conspiracy and

2. The crime was a foreseeable consequence of the unlawful agreement.

Pinkerton liability often overlaps with ordinary complicity liability, which will be discussed in a subsequent chapter. The Pinkerton, however, doctrine can create liability for a crime that the conspirator did not aid or assist (the basis for complicity liability). For example, in the original case Pinkerton himself was held liable for crimes committed by his co-conspirators while Pinkerton was in jail.

Most crimes that are committed in furtherance of a conspiracy will be considered foreseeable. A bank robber who kills a resisting clerk during a convenience store robbery satisfies both elements. What if the same robber sees amongst the store customers someone who bullied him in high school and the robber executes the former bully without warning? That would not seem to further the conspiracy to rob the store nor be a foreseeable result of the agreement to rob it. One could argue that killing the bully eliminates a witness who might recognize the robber. That would further the conspiracy by reducing the chances of apprehension. Unless this was a very small town though the risks that one of the robbers would be recognized and then take it upon himself to kill the potential witness might not be seen as foreseeable in which case liability for the killing would not be imputed to the other conspirators.

Abandoning or Withdrawing from a Conspiracy

Unless and until someone invents a time machine, you cannot "undo" your criminal liability for conspiracy by withdrawing from the agreement or abandoning the effort once the crime of conspiracy has been committed in the majority of jurisdictions or at common law. If your jurisdiction requires an overt act, you can avoid conspiracy liability if you withdraw before the overt act is committed, however. Withdrawal is still worth doing in any event because while it may not eliminate your *past* liability for conspiracy it will cut off your *future* liability for crimes committed in furtherance of the conspiracy under the *Pinkerton* doctrine. Withdrawal in the above circumstances requires you to effectively communicate to all conspirators that you are withdrawing. In most jurisdictions you do not have to report the conspiracy to the police.

The Model Penal Code and a small minority of jurisdictions will allow you to withdraw in a way that not only cuts off future liability but also constitutes a defense to your past crime of conspiracy. Not surprisingly you have to do more than just break the bad news to all of your co-conspirators. The Model Penal Code requires that you "thwart the success of the conspiracy." (Some of these minority jurisdictions require only that you make timely warning to the authorities.)

So if you change your mind after agreeing with your roommates to rob a bank in order to pay your law school bills, make sure you call each and every one of them before they get to the bank lest they do something really bad while they are inside. If you are in an MPC/Minority jurisdiction you might want to also call the police before they get there to avoid being held liable for the conspiracy itself.

Duration of the Conspiracy

Determining when a conspiracy ends can be important for terminating Pinkerton liability for other crimes and also for beginning the running of the statute of limitations (the time period within which the state must prosecute you for the crime). Conspiracies end when the goal of the conspiracy is successfully achieved (although that achievement sometimes includes activities after the fact to avoid detection). Withdrawal from a conspiracy also ends the duration of the conspiracy for the person withdrawing. One thing that does not terminate a conspiracy is the secret intervention of the police in frustration of the conspiracy's purpose.

Merger

More bad news for would-be conspirators. Conspiracy (unlike solicitation and attempt) does not merge into either an attempt to commit the crime or the completed crime itself. Why the difference? The conspiracy itself is considered a "distinct evil" separate and apart from any crimes that are committed as a result, so you can get punished twice—once for the crime and once for the conspiracy. So if you are still thinking about robbing that bank, you might want to consider doing it solo.

Wharton's Rule

What if the offense you agree to commit requires at least two people to commit it by its very nature? Can you be convicted of both the conspiracy and the intended offense? Many offenses cannot be committed alone: bigamy, dueling, selling illegal drugs, bribery. The traditional version of Wharton's rule was that you could not prosecute people for conspiracy to commit such offenses. The modern rule is that the government has "fielder's choice." They can prosecute you for conspiracy or for the target offense, but not for both. Wharton's rule is a presumption of legislative intent, not a constitutional principle, so the legislature can provide for liability for both conspiracy and the target offense if it expresses its intent clearly. The Model Penal Code does not recognize Wharton's rule at all.

Unilateral v. Bilateral Conspiracies

What if your roommate with whom you agree to rob the bank is actually working for the police or (worse yet) is an undercover police officer herself? Since a police agent does not intend to actually ever rob the bank (or let you do the same), they are not *really* agreeing with you. You may think that they are, but no actual agreement exists since one of you is faking it. The common law's view was expressed by Justice Cardozo when he said that "it was impossible for a man to conspire with himself." The law describes such a one-sided-pretend agreement as a "unilateral" conspiracy. The common law recognized only bilateral conspiracies. Think if this as the "it takes at least two to tango" approach. The Model Penal Code recognizes unilateral conspiracies, and the modern trend has been to do the same. So check out your roommate pretty carefully before you bring up the whole bank robbing idea.

Scope of the Conspiracy

Professors who really love conspiracy will take the time to dip into a complex set of rules that determine the scope and nature of very elaborate conspiracies. Even touching on these intricate rules is beyond the scope of a short and happy guide. The fundamental issue is "who is conspiring with whom and about what?" The way most books and cases explore these issues is by three visual references: chain, spoke and wheel conspiracies.

A chain conspiracy is one where people work together in one connected process. A typical example of a chain conspiracy can be the manufacture and sale of an illegal drug that might involve a producer, a smuggler, and a distributor. A wheel or spoke conspiracy on the other hand involves a hub who sits at the center of all activity. The distributor of illegal drugs might sell drugs to a number of people who sell it on the streets. At this point, however, we need to distinguish between a wheel conspiracy in which each of the street sellers all work as part of a single organization and therefore as members of a single conspiracy and a series of separate conspiracies like the spokes of a wheel that are each connected to the same hub but that are not connected to one another by an outer rim. In the latter model, each street seller is akin to an independent contractor who enters into his own separate conspiracy with the distributor who operates as the hub for each of these separate conspiracies.

Correctly determining the scope and shape of the conspiracy affects numerous issues, most importantly Pinkerton liability for crimes committed in furtherance of the conspiracy. In wheel and chain conspiracies, you are on the hook for all crimes committed by anyone in the chain or anyone on the wheel. A spoke conspiracy means that you will be responsible only for the acts of those in your own separate conspiracy.

No simple rule of thumb distinguishes one conspiratorial structure from another, but a few general observations can be usefully made. Not every member of a single conspiracy needs to communicate with every other member. More importantly, not every member of a single conspiracy needs to either know the identity of *or even be aware of the existence of* every other member. Each conspirator must be generally aware of the scope and nature of the conspiracy, however. So don't expect every conspirator to be able to fill out an organizational chart, but do expect each one to have the sense that "we are all in this together," the sense that the fortunes of each rises and fall to some degree with the success or failure of the larger enterprise. It is this sort of "community of interest" that the courts seem to be guided by in deciding who belongs to which conspiracy.

CHAPTER 22

Attempt

In the science fiction movie *Minority Report,* government develops a "pre-crime program" that uses psychics to stop murders before they are committed. Once the psychics give the word, a SWAT team swoops in and arrests the would be killers for the crimes they were about to commit. While no such psychics exist in real life (if there were, they'd probably be in Vegas anyway) the doctrine of attempt is our pre-crime program. Through attempt law we try to identify those who are going to commit a crime and subject them to arrest and prosecution for criminal liability before the crime is completed.

Attempt doctrine raises a number of really interesting issues, including some of the metaphysical ones raised in science fiction tales such as "Minority Report." Is it prudent to punish people for something they have not yet done? How do we know they were going to go through with it? Are they blameworthy for beginning to commit the crime? Should we allow them to back out and "undo" their attempt liability if they change their mind? Alternately, why don't we just punish someone who attempts a crime the same as someone who completes it?

More concretely:

1. Where and when should attempt liability begin?

2. Should we require a more culpable state of mind for an attempt than a completed crime?

3. Are there some crimes for which attempt liability should not exist at all?

4. What do we do about attempts that were "impossible" to begin with for one reason or another?

Attempt doctrine is important as well as interesting. As the poet said, "the best laid plans of mice and men often go awry." So too with crime. Many attempt crimes and fail or do not finish, so drawing these lines around attempt liability is not just an interesting academic enterprise.

An Overview of the Elements

As is the case with the other inchoate offenses, attempt law requires a highly culpable mental state to compensate for the fact that less conduct is required of the offender. The common law generally defined a criminal attempt as an intentional act that crossed the line from preparation to perpetration of a crime with the intent that the crime be committed. The Model Penal Code modified this definition by including within the definition of attempt the purposeful commission of a "substantial step" towards commission of a crime that this was taken with the mental state required for the offense attempted. The Model Penal Code approach generally expands attempt liability by allowing a conviction on the basis of less and earlier conduct than is possible under the common law approach. While many jurisdictions still follow the common law approach, the Model Penal Code's approach has become very influential. Many states—even ones that generally follow the common law—have adopted the MPC's definition of attempt.

Sentencing

By statute, an attempt of a crime is almost always punished less than the completion of the crime. The only exceptions are crimes where the legislature writes into the definition of the crime "commits or attempts to commit" and even then the sentencing judge may use whatever discretion she has to sentence towards the lower end of the permissible range.

Complete Attempts and "Moral Luck"

One distinction has fallen largely by the way side but is still worth noting because it reveals something important about our moral intuitions about attempts. Originally at common law one had to complete "the last act necessary" for the crime to occur in order to be guilty of attempt. For example, to be guilty of an attempted murder involving a firearm you actually had to pull the trigger. If someone grabbed the gun away from you before you pulled the trigger then no attempt would have been committed.

No common law jurisdiction follows the "last act necessary" approach anymore. Here is a question worth a moment's reflection though. Why don't we punish such complete attempts just as harshly as the completed crime? If you only miss killing me because you sneezed as you pulled the trigger why should your hay fever result in a less severe punishment? You are just as blameworthy and just as dangerous (setting your hay fever aside) as if you had not missed.

The answer is that our intuitions about punishment are heavily influenced notions of harm. The actual social harm of your missed shot is much less than the actual social harm of a successful shot. Sure, I might have a few sleepless nights thinking about what a close call I had (and worrying about how many other students might be stalking me), but I am a lot better off than if I was dead. It does not seem fair to punish you the same, even though the harm is a lot less. "No harm, no foul," is not something that we just say in sports.

Philosophers describe this sort of paradox as "moral luck," a situation where consequences turn upon factors beyond your control. Defendants who commit complete attempts enjoy moral luck because they have done everything within their control to be guilty of the complete crime but end up only being guilty of an attempt. So they should really feel lucky as they serve their lesser prison sentences.

Conduct Required for Attempt

So you now know that jurisdictions permit attempt liability for incomplete attempts. But how incomplete can it be? How close does one have to come to actually committing the intended crime in order to be guilty of an attempt? Or to look at things from the other end, what is the earliest point in time at which the police can swoop in and arrest someone with confidence that the person will be convicted?

Remember that bad thoughts alone cannot constitute a crime, not even a crime of attempt. So absolutely conclusive proof that someone had decided to commit a crime would not alone constitute an attempt. The defendant must do something. But what?

Let me repeat that the line we are talking about is between preparation to commit an offense (which is not attempting it) and beginning to perpetrate an offense. Unfortunately that rule does not really tell us anything although it is worth repeating at the beginning of your exam answer. "An act of perpetration" is a really a label for a conclusion about where attempt liability begins.

Let me begin with the bad news. This is a messy area. There are a lot of different tests for drawing the line between preparation and perpetration. Sometimes different tests will even be used within the same jurisdiction. It sometimes seems like judges are "mixing and matching" between different types of cases and the different tests. Here is the good news. As a law student, this just creates more different ways for you to earn points on an attempt question because there are a number of different rules that you can apply to the fact pattern. As a practitioner, you just need to spend a little time in the library figuring out which tests are most often used in your jurisdiction.

Remember also that the earlier we draw the line the easier it is to keep society safe but the greater the risk that we are punishing someone for attempting something that she might never have gone through with. With that in mind, let's now learn the different conduct tests for attempt.

1. *Physical Proximity.* Considers the closeness to the commission of the offense in terms of time, place and ability to carry out the crime. This test focuses not on what has been done but on what remains to be done. In its strictest form, this test requires the actor to have it within his or her power to complete the crime almost immediately.

2. *Dangerous Proximity.* A variation on the physical proximity test that takes a "sliding scale approach." The more the conduct involves a danger to human life the less the proximity required. So attempting to pick a man's pocket might require me to get close enough to put my

hand into his pocket, but attempting to kill the same man might easily be satisfied if I sat in the last row of a large auditorium in which he was speaking with a knife in my pocket. Focus on the nearness of the danger, the magnitude of the harm, and the degree of apprehension felt.

3. *Indispensable Element.* Has the actor obtained control over everything that he needs to commit the offense? A sniper needs his rifle, a con artist his "mark," and a bootlegger his raw materials in order to be guilty of an attempt under this rule.

4. *Probable Desistance.* Has the actor reached the point where an ordinary person would probably have already desisted if he were not going to complete the crime? This is not the point of no return necessarily. It might still be possible for someone to pull out without incident, but it is not probable that the average person would do so. It is the point beyond which the actor is not likely to quit absence some sort of outside intervention. Bringing a prostitute to one's room, for example, would be enough conduct for an attempt to commit prostitution under this test. Like the swimmer who swam half way across the English Channel before pondering whether to turn back, the actor is considered likely to keep going.

5. *Unequivocality.* (Also sometimes called the *res ipsa loquitor* test, which is Latin for the thing speaks for itself.) This test requires conduct to reach a point where it becomes clear from the person's actions alone that they intend to commit the crime. In requiring that the conduct

"unambiguously manifest" criminal intent, this test essentially asks whether you can imagine some innocent explanation for what has been done. A person going through the pockets of an unconscious homeless person lying in the street, for example, might be looking for some information about who might be called to aid the person, not attempting to rob him.

Some jurisdictions strictly ignore any separate evidence of the person's actual intent (such as a confession) in applying this test. That would mean that our would-be pickpocket in the above example would not be held guilty of attempted larceny even if they admit that they were bent on stealing what was found in the pockets because their conduct was not unequivocal. Other jurisdictions will consider independent evidence of mental state such as confessions in deciding whether the person's conduct unequivocally manifested a criminal intent and was thereby sufficient for an attempt. So keep your mouth shut about your attempts to commit crimes!

6. *Substantial Step.* This is the Model Penal Code test that applies to incomplete attempts. Under MPC section 5.01, a "substantial step in a course of conduct planned to culminate in commission of the crime" is sufficient conduct for an attempt if it is "strongly corroborative of the actor's criminal purpose." The MPC further provides a list of examples of conduct which would constitute a substantial step if strongly corroborative of the actor's purpose:

a. Lying in wait for or searching for the victim or trying to lure them somewhere.

b. Scouting out the place where the crime is to be committed.

c. Unlawful entry of a place where the crime will be committed.

d. Possession of materials to be used in the crime which have no lawful purpose or are specially designed for the crime, especially if possessed at what is to be the scene of the crime.

e. Soliciting an innocent agent to engage in conduct constituting an element of the crime.

The substantial step test has been widely adopted, including in many common law jurisdictions. As will be illustrated in the following example, it also greatly expands attempt liability by allowing attempt convictions on lesser and earlier conduct than any of the common law tests.

Attempt Conduct Hypo

Let's use the following hypothetical to sketch out how these various tests work in practice. The suggested answers are not offered as conclusive ones. These rules are fuzzy, and there is room for argument. The answers offered illustrate the most straightforward interpretations of the rules, not the only ones.

Assume that one of my students decides to kill me after a particularly terrible class. Between the boredom and the bad jokes she decides that she would rather kill me than sit through another class session. At what point in the following chronology does she have enough conduct for attempt liability under the various tests?

1. She thinks about different ways of killing me and decides to shoot me as I get out of my car the next morning in the faculty parking lot. *No attempt liability under any test because thoughts are not conduct.*

2. She makes a to do list in her computer of things she will need to do to prepare for the crime. *Writing down the list is conduct but arguably is still just preparation, not perpetration, under any of the tests although one could make an argument under the substantial step test more easily than the others.*

3. She scouts out the faculty parking lot immediately after class and finds a nice big rock concealed in a wooded area adjacent to the lot from which she could shoot anyone in the parking lot. *This alone clearly satisfies the substantial step test, as would all of the conduct that follows.*

4. She goes home and tells her roommate that she is leaving to go camping that night and will be gone for a couple of days. *This conduct might satisfy the unequivocality test in a jurisdiction that considered mental state evidence. Lying to her roommate in order to create an alibi might be considered unequivocal in light of the to do list on her computer.*

5. She buys a hunting rifle and ammunition. *This is the first point at which one might argue that she satisfies the indispensable element test. Without the gun she could not follow through with her plan. Buying the rifle and ammunition is not an*

unequivocal act in the strict sense as hunting rifles have lawful uses.

6.   That night she parks her car in a parking lot on the opposite side of the woods adjacent to the faculty parking lot. She takes the rifle and hides behind the rock she picked out. *One could now argue that she has met even a strict unequivocality test, since bringing the gun to campus is probably illegal and no lawful purpose could be easily imagined for hiding with it behind a rock overlooking a parking lot.*

7.   She wakes up the next morning and takes a position behind the rock looking over the parking lot. *Now many would argue that she has passed the point of probable desistance. She faces the risk that her presence might be detected in the daylight. She might also be found to be dangerously proximate. Yet she has not yet loaded the rifle.*

8.   She loads the rifle. *With the loading of the rifle she clearly is more dangerously proximate to completing the offense although some courts would wait until the intended victim is present.*

9.   When she sees me drive up she picks up the rifle. *With the presence of the victim and rifle she satisfies proximity as well as dangerous proximity and the indispensable element test. Picking up the rifle seems clearly unequivocal even without considering mental state evidence.*

10.   When I get out of my car she aims the rifle at me, and switches off the safety. *No test remains to be satisfied because our modern, risk averse*

sensibilities do not require crimes to become this dangerously close to completion for attempt liability to begin. Pointing the rifle at me seems clearly beyond the point of probable desistance, is clearly unequivocal, and is as proximate as one can get without actually pulling the trigger.

Mental State Required for Attempt

Intent lies at the conceptual heart of attempt. When you say that you "tried to do something" you almost always mean that you acted with purpose. "Accidentally attempting" something is a contradiction in terms.

As with conspiracy, there are two distinct intents required at common law. One must intend the actions that constitute the conduct for the attempt as well as intending that the crime committed be carried out. With respect to intending one's actions, you obviously can't attempt to kill someone by accidentally bumping into them by the edge of a steep cliff. What if you intentionally bumped into them, however, but did so only to give them a good scare? That also would not be attempted murder because you did not intend to kill them by bumping into them.

Attempted Result Crimes

The requirement that you intend the crime to be committed requires more than might be apparent. One must intend "the whole crime," even the parts which the crime itself do not require to be intentional. Homicide crimes provide the easiest example, although the same principle comes into play in all result crimes. Depraved heart murder, for example, does not require that you intend anyone's death, only that you are recklessly indifferent to it. Depraved heart murder does require the result of someone's death, of course. Since attempt requires that you intend the "whole crime" you must also intend someone's death. For this reason most jurisdictions conclude that one cannot really attempt a reckless or negligent killing. Since you must intend death—not be reckless or negligent with respect to it—the only type of attempted murder possible is an intentional killing under this view.

This requirement sometimes creates a paradox. Imagine that two disgruntled students independently decide to attack me after they get their exam grades back. One student decides to shoot me dead. The other student decides to maim me with a knife. If the shooter kills me, he would obviously be guilty of intentional murder. If I end up dying from the knife wounds then the student with the knife would probably be found guilty of intent to grievously injure murder in a common law jurisdiction that recognized that offense. But what if I live? Only the shooter gets convicted of attempted murder, because only the shooter intended my death. The student with the knife cannot be convicted of any attempted homicide crime because he did not intend my death. (Although he will do a nice long prison sentence for aggravated assault, thank you very much.)

So the bottom line is that if a crime requires a result then an attempt of that crime requires that the actor intended that result.

Attempted Felony Murder

All but a very few states have concluded that there is no such thing as attempted felony murder. (Imagine that the butter fingered bank robber drops his gun and it seriously wounds a bank employee.) Felony murder includes unintentional killings, but to prove an attempted felony murder you would have to prove an intent to kill as described above. If you have proved an intent to kill then you have already proved attempted intent to kill murder.

Since the butter fingered bank robber did not intend to kill he cannot be guilty of attempted felony murder.

Attempted Manslaughter

There is more of a split in jurisdictions as to whether one can attempt voluntary manslaughter. Imagine that you are adequately provoked, fly into a rage, and take a shot at someone with a gun. You are so angry though that you miss the person. Are you guilty of attempted murder or a lesser crime of attempted voluntary manslaughter? A great majority of states have concluded that attempted voluntary manslaughter does not exist because you cannot "intend to lose control in the heat of passion," which is essentially what voluntary manslaughter requires. A minority of states reason, however, that the only intent you must have is the intent to kill and that it makes no sense to convict someone one who intentionally attempts to kill after having been adequately provoked of the same crime as one who intentionally attempts to kill for no good reason at all.

Attempted involuntary manslaughter is generally not recognized as possible for the same reasons described earlier. Since manslaughter requires the result of death, one must intend—not be grossly negligent with respect to—death in order to be guilty of attempting that crime. Attempting to intentionally kill someone is murder, not involuntary manslaughter.

Attempted Reckless or Negligent Conduct Crimes

Things get more complicated with respect to whether one can attempt a crime that requires reckless or negligent conduct but not any sort of result. If the police arrest someone who was about to engage in a dangerous drag race on city streets should the driver be convicted of attempted reckless driving? Here, there are just not enough eggs to make an omelet, by which I mean that there are too few cases to describe either position as majority or minority. The few reported cases go both ways. Some cases allow attempted reckless or negligent *conduct* offenses on the grounds that one need only intend the conduct that constitutes the reckless or negligent conduct. In the drag racing example, that would be intending to drive a car really fast through city streets just for thrills. Other cases reason that you can't intend to be reckless or negligent, that you either intend a harm or you don't, but that you can't intend to be unaware of a risk or intend to consciously disregard it. So leave the car racing to the professionals just to be on the safe side.

Purpose v. Knowledge for Attempt Intent

Does intent to commit a crime mean that you do so knowing or purposefully? What if you tried to detonate a bomb to blow up your worst enemy knowing that the blast will kill innocent bystanders. Are you guilty of just one count of attempted murder or many? The answer is unclear in common law jurisdictions, which means that you can earn points on an exam for arguing the question both ways!

Attendant Circumstances

Do you have to be intentional with respect to all the circumstances that must attend the offense that you are charged with attempting? Returning to the hypo concerning assaulting a federal law enforcement officer, do you have to intend to assault a federal officer or just intend to assault someone *who turns out to be a federal officer unbeknownst to you*? There are precious few cases on this point, but the scholarly consensus seems to be that the mental state requirements for attempt do not require anything more with respect to attendant circumstances than is required for complete commission of the offense itself. So if assaulting a federal officer does not require proof that you knew the person you were assaulting was a federal officer then neither does attempting to assault a federal officer.

Model Penal Code Mental State Requirements for Attempt

The Model Penal Code diverges from the common law approach to mental state requirements for attempt in a few ways. First, belief that a result will occur is sufficient for an attempt of an offense that requires a result. So in the bomber hypothetical, a defendant who knew that bystanders would be killed would be liable under the MPC for attempted murder of all such bystanders. Second, the MPC makes clear that attempt imposes no additional mental states for attendant circumstances than exist for the complete commission of the offense.

Renunciation or Withdrawal

Thomas Wolfe said that you can't go back home. Can you go effectively go back in time and "undo" your criminal liability for an attempt you have already committed? What if you have already crossed the line separating perpetration from preparation but have a change of heart? Imagine that the law school assassin described above gets as far as pointing her rifle at me before deciding not to go through with it. If she goes home and confesses all to her roommate can she still be convicted of attempted murder?

The common law did not recognize a defense of renunciation or withdrawal to attempt liability, and most common law jurisdictions that have ruled on the matter do the same. So our soft-hearted or indecisive would-be sniper described above probably needs to pack her toothbrush for prison. Those few jurisdictions that recognize the defense (which includes the Model

Penal Code) require the withdrawal to be complete and voluntary. Complete means that you have decided to never commit the offense, not to postpone or reschedule it. Voluntary means essentially that you had a true change of heart, not that you were discouraged or frustrated by some setback or difficulty. So in the example above, if my disgruntled law student decided not to shoot me because she saw me pet a kitten then she would have a defense if she were in a jurisdiction that permitted withdrawal. If she changed her mind because she noticed a surveillance camera over the parking lot then that would not count as a truly voluntary withdrawal. In no event, however, can one withdraw once one has completed an attempt. So if she takes one shot and misses, and then changes her mind when she sees me shield the kitten with my body from the next shot she is still stuck with the attempt liability for the first shot. (Although it is lucky for me that she is a cat person.)

Even in a jurisdiction that does not recognize withdrawal you should remember that a decision not to complete an attempt can be used to argue that the person never really intended to commit the crime in the first place and therefore had never really attempted the crime. If I were defending my would-be-parking-lot assassin I would argue that even though she pointed the rifle at me she never really did so with the intent to kill me. She was still wrestling with her conscience and thinking about it all along. The farther along one gets with the attempt conduct the harder it becomes to make this argument, but it is "worth a shot."

Impossibility

This doctrine really is a bit of a mind bender. The issue is whether someone should be guilty of attempt if success was impossible. The short version of the story is that judges originally thought factual impossibility was not a defense and legal impossibility was a defense. Over time, however, it eventually became clear that the distinction between factual and impossibility was not workable. Now most jurisdictions have come to recognize that impossibility is not a defense, and whether you think if it as factual or legal does not matter. But, I am getting ahead of myself. To really understand how this doctrine works we have to retrace the steps of common law judges as they wrestled with this issue.

Factual vs. Legal Impossibility

Assume that my homicidal law student decides to sneak into my house and shoot me to death while I sleep. She bursts into my bedroom in the dead of night, and shoots into my bed at the form beneath the blankets. Unbeknownst to her I have become quite paranoid after years of thinking up homicidal hypotheticals for my criminal law class, and I have taken to sleeping in my bedroom closet while leaving a manikin under my blankets to fool would be assassins.

Has my homicidal student committed attempted murder? Early common law judges said yes. They would concede that it is impossible to kill me (or anyone) by shooting a manikin but would point out that the law student was as morally blameworthy as a murderer. The only thing that made the crime impossible was the fact that I was not in the bed as she pulled the trigger, and this fact makes no difference to her blameworthiness or dangerousness. These common law judges called this sort of situation factual impossibility, and they ruled that factual impossibility was not a defense to an attempt charge.

Now consider a second type of case. A man buys a horse at a really cheap price and believes that the price is so low because the horse is stolen. If the horse was in fact stolen he would be guilty of the property crime of knowingly receiving stolen property. He is wrong though. The horse is not stolen; the seller is just desperate. Is the buyer of the horse guilty of attempted receipt of stolen property? Common law judges used to say no. This was a case of legal impossibility because whether the property was stolen or not is a matter of law. These judges reasoned that you can't be guilty of attempting something that is not a crime, and it was not a crime to buy this horse. So legal impossibility they reasoned was a defense to an attempt charge.

The Breakdown of the Distinction Between Factual and Legal Impossibility

Well, a middle category of cases soon developed. And common law judges applying this rule came to different conclusions as to whether the impossibility was legal or factual. One man tried to pick another man's pocket, but the pocket was empty. Was the first man guilty of attempted pickpocketing? (Technically this would have been called attempted grand larceny because it involved trying to steal something from another's person, but we will just call it pickpocketing for present purposes.) Think about this for a minute before you read on. Whatever you decide, can you see why some people might decide it differently?

Some judges decided this was a clear case of factual impossibility and would find the person guilty of attempted pickpocketing. Like the student shooting the manikin, this crime was not possible because of the fact that the pocket was empty. Not so fast, said a number of other judges. They said this was a case of legal impossibility because there is no such crime as picking an empty pocket. (Putting your hand into someone else's pocket is a minor physical trespass but pickpocketing/grand larceny requires that you take something.) Since you can't be guilt of attempting something that is not a crime, it is not a crime to try to pick an empty pocket under this view.

More and more examples of this middle categories of cases came along over the years, and judges eventually realized that you could characterize just about any type of impossibility as legal or factual. Was my homicidal student's attempt factually impossible because the bed was empty or legally impossible because there is no such crime as murdering a manikin? Was the circumstance that the horse was not stolen a fact or a legal circumstance?

The Model Penal Code and Pure Legal Impossibility

The drafters of the Model Penal Code eventually cut through this confusion with a simple principle. We should take the circumstances of the act as the attempter believes them to be in deciding whether they have committed an attempt. If I was in the bed instead of the manikin—as the homicidal student believed—then she would have been guilty of murder, so she becomes guilty of attempted murder. If the horse was in fact stolen—as the horse buyer believed—then he would have been guilty of receiving stolen property, so he becomes guilty of attempted receipt of stolen property.

There was one limit to the Model Penal Code's principle of taking the world as the actor imagined it to be, however. We will take the world as the actor imagines it to be, but we won't take the *law itself* to be as the actor imagines it to be. Let's assume for example that after taking some sort of professionalism pledge on the first day of law school you believe that it is actually a crime to come to class unprepared. Are you guilty of the crime of attempting to come to class unprepared if you do so? No, because there is no such crime. Well, are you guilty of the crime of attempted coming to class unprepared because you thought you were committing a crime? No, that would be crazy. There is no such crime, and we are not going to invent one just to indulge your paranoid conscience. Wait, you might ask, aren't you blameworthy and perhaps dangerous because you committed what you thought to be a crime? No, society answers, you are only blameworthy or dangerous if you think you are doing something that actually is a crime. What if you thought that singing out of tune was a crime? Are we going to prosecute you for that, too? (I would be in a lot of trouble because I can't carry a tune to save my life.)

The coming-to-class-unprepared/singing-out-of-tune category is what the Model Penal Code commentary calls instances of *pure legal impossibility*. This is the only type of impossibility that the Model Penal Code recognizes. The crime contemplated is impossible because it is *imaginary* in all respects.

An Example

Here is a less fanciful example of the distinction. Imagine that you believe it to be a crime to sell alcohol to someone who is under the age of 30. (You have seen those signs in the supermarket saying that they card people who are under the age of 30, so you assume that 30, not 21, is the drinking age.) Consider the following hypotheticals.

- You sell someone alcohol whom you believe to be 29 and who is 29. Are you guilty of attempting to sell alcohol to someone who is under the age of 21? No, because you did not believe them to be under the age of 21 and selling someone alcohol who is 29 is not a crime.

- Now imagine that they are 29 but that you believed them to be 20. (Lucky them, they must really have stayed out of the sun.) Now you would be guilty of attempting to sell someone who is under the age of 21 alcohol because while we won't take the law as you imagine it to be (i.e. the drinking age) we will take the world as you imagine it to be (i.e. the age of the person you sold to), and that makes what you did an attempted crime.

The Modern Approach

The end of this long and complicated story is that judges in most common law jurisdictions have come to realize that the MPC got it right. Impossibility (legal or factual) is not a defense to an attempt charge. In figuring out whether they are guilty of an attempt we take everything as they imagine it to be *except the law itself*. This means, by the way, that the guy who thought he was buying the stolen horse that was actually not stolen is now considered guilty of attempting to receive stolen property.

Inherent Impossibility

There is one final rule worth mentioning, not because it is ever likely to come up in real life, but because you may wake up in the middle of the night wondering about it the night before your final. What about someone who just got into the Harry Potter stories a little too much and who came to believe that he, like Harry, has magical powers. Unlike Harry, however, he is not blessed with a saintly disposition. He uses a killing curse against someone fully believing that the curse will kill. Is Evil-Wanna-Be-Harry guilty of attempted murder? The answer would seem to be yes because 1) killing someone is a crime so he is not committing an imaginary crime; and 2) if his curse had the power to kill then the person would be dead. This situation is referred to as a case of "inherent impossibility" because it is inherently impossible to commit murder in this way. The MPC provides that while such an actor is guilty of attempted murder the sentencing judge should take the inherent impossibility of success of such a scheme into consideration during sentencing. So Evil-Wannabe-Harry gets a reduced sentence but not an acquittal. Maybe he can earn money making wands in prison.

CHAPTER 23

Complicity and Liability for Crimes of Others

Complicity is not a crime in and of itself like conspiracy: it is a *way of being guilty of a crime.* This simple point is worth belaboring at the outset. If you are an accomplice to a bank robbery that you are guilty of the crime of . . . wait for it . . . bank robbery! And you receive the same prison sentence as a . . . wait for it again . . . bank robbery! This might strike you as uncontroversial because you probably imagine a team of armed robbers running around in the bank waiving guns around. What you will soon learn, however, is that you don't need to do much to become an accomplice to a bank robbery or any other crime as long as you do it with the right frame of mind. Even bit players in the cast of characters get the same full liability for the crime being committed as those enjoying the starring roles (although a judge might sentence them differently within the range permitted for the offense). Your chicken-hearted getaway driver parked at the curb outside will also be guilty of armed robbery. So will your sainted mother who made you a bag lunch before you set out to rob the bank that day. At least you will have a lot of company in prison.

Overview of the Elements

Complicity has both guilty hand and guilty mind requirements. In the simplest terms possible, an accomplice is one who

- Even Slightly Assists or Encourages (but who does actually assist or encourage)

- Another in the Commission of a Crime

- With the Intent to Assist or Encourage and

- With the Intent that the Crime Assisted or Encouraged be Committed.

Timing is of the essence for a would-be accomplice, however. You cannot be an accomplice if you come into the picture after the crime has already been committed. On the other hand if you have intentionally assisted in or encouraged the commission of a crime and change your mind you are generally out of luck because your complicity was complete at the moment of assistance or encouragement.

Philosophical and Policy Considerations

Why do we expand criminal liability so greatly through complicity? Why would even a slight act of assistance or even a slight act of encouragement subject one to the full weight of punishment for a crime that someone else actually committed? The utilitarian answer is that we fear the effectiveness and dangerousness of group criminality and defining complicity broadly allows us to deter group crime by making sure that all members of the group can be fully punished. In terms of blameworthiness, broad complicity prevents highly culpable individuals from hiding their guilt behind the work of others.

Yet broad complicity liability raises many troubling issues. So little conduct is required that complicity depends very heavily on getting the mental state of the offender right. Since mental states are often inferred from circumstances, a real danger exists that some hapless individual who was helping the wrong people at the wrong time will suffer criminal liability that he does not deserve. Moreover, in failing to meaningfully distinguish between great and small acts of assistance and between mere encouragement as opposed to real action, complicity arguably fails to distinguish the half-hearted offender from the committed criminal, the merely bad from the truly evil. The man who points the gun is arguably a worse and more dangerous person than the person who writes the bank robbery note, but each share equally in liability for bank robbery under complicity doctrine.

Common Law Terminology

The modern approach is to treat anyone who intentionally assists or encourages the crime equally and to not make distinctions between types of accomplices. The common law took a different approach. Learning the different types of accomplice at common law is useful both because the old terminology still crops up in cases from time to time and because these terms usefully describe the full range of accomplice liability.

- *Principal in the First Degree.* This is the main actor, the one who often "does the crime" although he may be assisted by others. Ordinarily he will be present at the scene of the crime during its commission. There also may be more than one principal in the first degree. If three men run into a bank waiving guns and demanding money all three would be considered principals in the first degree at common law.

- *Principal in the Second Degree.* These are the "helpers" or encouragers of the principals in the first degree. They also generally must be present at the scene when the crime is committed. The getaway driver who sits behind the wheel of the car outside of the bank would be a principal in the second degree. So would a lookout who stood outside looking for police cars and listening for sirens. Neither threatens anyone with a gun nor takes anything from anyone—necessary elements for armed robbery—but they help people who do and are guilty of armed robbery as a result.

- *Accessory Before the Fact.* These are the "helpers" or encouragers who are not present at the scene of the crime and who ordinarily did their part before the crime began. So your loud mouth roommate who got you all fired up on the idea of robbing the bank would fit the bill. So might your otherwise saintly mother who worried that you might not take the time to eat a nutritious lunch the day of the robbery unless she packed one for you. Neither could be bothered going with you to the bank, so neither would be considered principals in the second degree. Think of them as the "stay-at-home" types.

It bears repeating that all of the above would be considered accomplices both at common law and in all modern jurisdictions. They are all bank robbers.

There is one final category of "helper" at common law that needs to be discussed so that you will understand one of the important limits of complicity liability.

- *Accessory After the Fact.* This is the "Johnny-Come-Lately" crime. An accessory after the fact is someone who knowingly and intentionally helps another to avoid arrest, trial or conviction of a crime after it has been convicted. So your old college roommate drops by your apartment after the bank robbery. You mention that you just robbed a bank and that the police are looking all over for you. Your former roommate says that he does not think you would do very well in prison and offers to let you spend the night at his place. He is an accessory after the fact because he knows you committed the bank robbery, and he intends by letting you spend the night to help you avoid arrest.

You must remember that *an accessory **after** the fact is **not** an accomplice.* As willing and helpful (and blameworthy and dangerous) as they are, they came into the picture too late to be an accomplice. (At common law they were accomplices but this is not the rule anywhere anymore.) Since accessories after the fact are not accomplices they cannot be liable for the crime that has already been committed, so your good old college roommate is not guilty of bank robbery. What do we have as a consolation prize for our Johnny-Come-Lately helper? An accessory after the fact is guilty of the *separate* crime of being an accessory after the fact, a crime that has been created in many jurisdictions just for this purpose.

Once you have learned the common law terminology remember to burn the main point into your brain. Principals in the first degree, principals in the second degree, and accessories before the fact are all considered accomplices today and are all therefore all equally guilty of whatever crime has been committed.

Acquittal of the Principal

These old common law distinctions made a difference when some but not all of the accomplices were acquitted. Specifically, acquittal of the principal in the first degree—the primary "doer" of the crime—barred conviction of the principal in the second degree and the accessories. Virtually all jurisdictions have abandoned this rule although a few may still bar conviction of a second degree principal or an accessory before the fact if the principal in the first degree was acquitted *in the same trial* in order to avoid an inconsistent verdict. So today any sort of accomplice can be tried and convicted regardless of whether other accomplices have been convicted or acquitted just as long as the prosecution proves that the crime assisted or encouraged did take place.

So your mother can be put on trial for making your lunch before the bank robbery even though you are safely—and selfishly—counting your ill-gotten gains in some country from which you cannot be extradited to face trial. The prosecution has to prove, of course, that the bank was robbed in order to convict your mother of bank robbery, so your name will definitely come up. But you don't have to be convicted for your mother to go to prison for bank robbery. Just imagine though all the nasty things the jury will say about you before they send your Mom packing off to prison. Fine son or daughter you are!

The Guilty Hand: Assistance

The basic rule is that even a slight act of assistance will make one an accomplice, but you must *actually* assist. Your assistance though does not need to be essential to the crime. So the prosecutor does not have to prove that but for your assistance the crime would not have been committed.

Let's imagine that I am present during your robbery of the bank, and that I recognize you as a former student who has obviously fallen on hard times (and who probably is going to end up doing hard time). You have your hands full with your shotgun as you are walking into the bank, and I realize that you are going to have to put the shotgun down in order to open the door. I helpfully open the door for you. That slight act of assistance, if done with the requisite mental state—would be sufficient to make me an accomplice to your bank robbery. Now would you have gone ahead and robbed the bank anyway even if I had not opened the door for you? Of course! It is very unlikely that having walked up to a bank carrying a shotgun that you would have let an unlocked door stand in your way. But my act of assistance need not be a but for cause of your crime (i.e. but for my assistance the crime would not have been committed). My act need only slightly assist you, which it did since you did not have to put down and pick up your all-important shotgun.

Note that while it might be of slight assistance, the act must actually assist. Imagine now that I ran and opened one door while you went through the other door oblivious to my efforts to assist. This attempt to assist would not make me an accomplice in the vast majority of jurisdictions (MPC jurisdictions being the exception, which we will discuss later). Even though I have an equally blameworthy mental state in both cases and even though even slight assistance is enough to make one an accomplice I would not be guilty of anything since I did not actually assist.

The Guilty Hand: Acts of Encouragement

This one throws a lot of people for a loop. You can be guilty of a crime just for applauding. Now imagine that instead of opening the door I loudly applauded your efforts once you announced "this is a robbery." (How melodramatic of you.) I do nothing to help, but I clap wildly as I deliver a rambling speech about the vices of capitalism, high finance and banks that are "too big to jail." Assuming the requisite mental state, I have just committed bank robbery along with you.

The rule is simple. *Inciting, soliciting, inducing or encouraging* is sufficient conduct for complicity. Once again, the encouragement need not be a but-for cause of the crime. "Thank you very much for the applause," you say, "but I am not your student anymore and don't need your approval to rob this bank." An *attempted* act of encouragement is not enough, however. If I am standing outside the bank, waiving at you through the window and cheering wildly but you neither hear nor see me I am, once again, not an accomplice.

One less obvious issue arises when an actor is encouraged by an attempt to assist. As discussed earlier, attempting to assist someone does not alone make one an accomplice. If you know of my attempted assistance, however, you may be *actually encouraged* by my failed attempt. So if in the example above you see me open the other door to the bank, that could be enough to make me an accomplice even if you go through a different door. The resulting encouragement of a failed effort to assist can be enough to make one an accomplice.

Solicitation and Conspiracy

At this point you may be asking yourself about the relationship between the crime of solicitation and complicity. Asking or inducing someone to commit a crime is enough conduct to make you an accomplice to the crime. As you may remember from an earlier chapter, the crime of solicitation merges into any crime in which you are complicit. So Henry's guilt of solicitation when he implicitly asked someone to kill Thomas Becket merged into his guilt of murder once the knights acted on his request.

Mere Presence Not Enough

Some of the most difficult cases in this area deal with people whose presence is alleged to assist or encourage the crime. The basic rule is simple enough. *Mere presence is insufficient conduct for complicity.* Indeed, one might quibble whether being somewhere is actually conduct at all but instead a state of being rather than an act of doing. Deciding when presence is *mere* is not always so easy though.

Imagine now that I am standing in the bank when you come into rob it. Seeing me there you immediately feel encouraged. You remember my anti-bank diatribes in class and feel encouraged knowing that at least some people might approve of what you are doing. Perhaps you also think that if things go badly that I might pitch in and help out in some way. Do your thoughts about my presence make me an accomplice? No, that would not be very fair to me. Do my prior anti-bank diatribes combined with my presence make me an accomplice? No, unless I specifically encouraged you to rob a bank, in which case my presence might actually be superfluous to my complicity (see above).

Even if I were secretly glad that you were robbing the bank or were secretly planning to help you if things went badly I would still not be an accomplice. Secret wishes or plans do not change the fact that I am merely present and doing nothing as you rob the bank.

Presence can be enough for complicity when coupled with some prior statement or understanding that encourages the principal actor. If I told you previously that I would help out if needed my presence would make me an accomplice even if I never ended up doing anything. Similarly, telling someone during a crime that you won't interfere could be seen as an act of encouragement that could also be sufficient for complicity (if the statement was made with the required mental state).

Assistance by Omission

As discussed previously, no general duty exists to prevent a crime or to interfere with one in progress. Absent one of the legal duties described in the earlier chapter on the voluntary act requirement, you can just sit and watch a crime take place without fear of becoming an accomplice. Just as failure to act in the face of a legal duty can sometimes constitute a crime, so too can failure to act in the face of a legal duty make someone an accomplice. A police officer who watches a shoplifting unfold, a mother who watches her child being beaten, and even a property owner who watches criminal activity take place on his premises may become an accomplice to the crimes committed if they have the requisite mental states.

Aiding and Abetting

Why use simple, easy to understand words when fancy legal ones are at hand? Doubtless you have heard the terms "aid and abet" to describe conspiracy. Originally the two words each meant something different. Aid meant to assist, and abet meant to encourage or incite. (The root of abet literally comes from the word "bait" and referred to the practice of "baiting" animals to get them to do something.) Alas, the two terms have come to be used largely synonymously, so thing are not quite that simple anymore.

The Guilty Mind

There is a bit of confusion here among the courts. To be specific, there are two different ways of stating complicity's mental state requirement in common use, a traditional rule and an alternate one that takes into account special issues arising from complicity in crimes requiring only a reckless or negligent state of mind. Most professors and most textbooks spare you as much of that confusion as they can. Following that approach, we will learn the traditional rule and then learn the alternate rule. To paraphrase Einstein, we make things as simple as possible but no simpler.

The traditional rule is that an accomplice must intend to assist or encourage the person in the conduct that constitutes the crime and further intend that the crime encouraged or assisted be committed. So when I open the door for you as you go into the bank I can't be doing it absent-mindedly; I must be opening the door *for you*. I must further intend by so doing that you are going to rob the bank. So when your Mom makes your lunch the morning of the bank robbery she does not become a bank robber unless she intends that you rob the bank. (That should make you feel a little better.) Note that it is practically impossible to have the second mental state if you don't have the first. It is hard even for law professors to come up with realistic examples where someone did not intend their act of assistance or encouragement but intends a crime to be committed.

Purpose v. Knowledge

Once again we confront the issue of what intent means. Is it enough if you know that you are assisting a crime or must it be your purpose to assist a crime? If your Mom knows that you are robbing a bank the day that she makes your lunch, should that be enough? Let's assume she does not want you to rob the bank— what mother would?—but she does not want you to go hungry— what mother wouldn't?—yet she knows that having your lunch made in advance will make it easier for you to rob the bank (hard to do drive through at a fast food restaurant when the police are chasing you). Should this knowledge be enough to make her an accomplice to bank robbery?

While early cases held that knowledge that you were helping someone commit a crime was sufficient, the majority of courts now hold that purpose is required. The line between purpose and knowledge becomes blurry in many cases though (as it does with respect to the meaning of intent in conspiracy).

The cases that typically raise this issue concern providers of legal services to people who use them for illegal purposes with the full knowledge of the provider. A hotel owner rents rooms to prostitutes, or a merchant sells sugar to a moonshiner, each knowing full well that they are assisting illegal activity. The position of the provider is that they are indifferent to what paying customers use their goods or services for and therefore cannot be purposeful with respect to the crimes eventually committed as a result.

While the case law is a bit of a muddle two trends are evident. First, courts tend to find providers of legal goods and services to be purposeful with respect to resulting crimes—and thereby to be complicit—when the provider can be said to have some sort of *stake in the venture*. Perhaps criminals constitute a disproportionate share of his business, or he charges inflated prices, or he literally gets paid out of the proceeds from the crime. Second, some courts require only knowledge with respect to serious crimes that involve danger to life.

Even where a jurisdiction does not specifically lower the requirement for complicity from purpose to knowledge for more serious crimes, juries are much more likely to find purpose when danger to human life is involved. Imagine that I ask you to give me directions to someone's house after tell you that I am planning on killing the person who lives there. If you give me the directions a jury would doubt whether you were purely indifferent to whether I killed the person and would more likely conclude that you also wanted the person dead. So the purpose required for complicity is more likely to be found from knowing assistance for serious crimes than for minor ones.

Some jurisdictions deal with the knowledge issue by creating a stand alone offense of "knowingly facilitating a criminal offense." Such crimes are offenses onto themselves, however, and do not make the facilitator guilty of the crime assisted.

Complicity for Recklessness or Negligence

Can you be an accomplice to a crime that requires only recklessness? If you give your car keys to someone you know to be drunk, are you an accomplice to involuntary manslaughter if they kill someone while driving your car? Involuntary manslaughter requires recklessness or criminal negligence depending on the jurisdiction. It was reckless or at least negligent of your friend to drive drunk. Can you be said to have intended him to be reckless or negligent when you gave him your keys? If you intended him to kill someone when you gave him your keys that would be murder, not manslaughter. Many have argued that you cannot be an accomplice to his negligence because it is conceptually not possible for you to *intend recklessness or negligence*. A number of courts have found complicity in such cases, however. One leading treatise even states that the overwhelming majority rule is to recognize complicity for reckless or negligence crimes. Another treatise, however, describes the cases as more mixed. So pay attention to how your professor characterizes this split and adopt whatever terminology she uses to characterize it.

In many cases of recklessness or negligence involving multiple actors, however, complicity is not the only or even the best way of finding criminal liability. For example, arguably you were negligent or reckless to give your car keys to an obviously intoxicated driver and could be found directly liable for involuntary manslaughter without resort to a theory of complicity.

The Alternate Rule for Complicity Mental States

Some courts, professors and textbook authors favor a different way of expressing the mental state requirements of complicity because of the issues raised by complicity for reckless/negligent crimes.

- Intentionally assist or encourage with

- The mental state required for the crime assisted or encouraged

By changing the second requirement from "intending that the crime assisted or encouraged by committed" to "with the mental state required for the crime assisted or encouraged" these sources eliminate the apparent paradox involved in "intending recklessness/negligence. Such a statement allows for complicity in recklessness/negligence by importing the mental state requirement from the underlying crime into the mental state required for the accomplice. So you could be an accomplice to involuntary manslaughter in the drunk driving case if you were grossly negligent in giving the driver your keys.

It is important to recognize that the traditional rule already required that an accomplice have the mental state required for the crime assisted or encouraged. You can't intend for someone to engage in larceny, for example, without knowing that the property taken is the property of another. By not requiring that the underlying crime be intended, however, this alternate rule reduces the mental state required for complicity to the mental state required for the offense itself, something that does not matter when the underlying crime requires intentional conduct anyway but that does matter when it only requires reckless or negligent conduct.

Needless to say, follow the lead of your professor and/or textbook.   Until and unless you become either a judge or a law professor, you don't need to choose sides in this somewhat arcane dispute.   For now, you just need to learn what your professor expects you to learn.

Natural and Probable Consequences

At common law an accomplice was said to be liable not only for the crime assisted or encouraged but also for any other crimes that were the "natural and probable consequence" of the crime assisted or encouraged.   Under this rule an accomplice to an armed bank robbery would be liable for murder if one of the robbers shot a bank teller.   An accomplice to shoplifting, however, would not be liable for murder if his accomplice killed a security guard who tried to apprehend him, as one would not think of lethal violence as a natural and probable consequence of what is usually a stealthy crime of theft typically punishable as a misdemeanor.

The leading treatises seem to agree that this remains the established rule today in the majority of jurisdictions but one treatise questions how widely it really applies.   The easiest examples are ones that are already covered by the felony murder rule as would the bank robbery example described above.   One author notes that application of the natural and probable consequences rule outside the context of felony murder or misdemeanor manslaughter tends to involve very special cases involving unusual circumstances.   Some courts have clearly rejected the rule in cases that don't involve dangerous felonies. For example, a defendant who helped falsify a company's books was not found liable for the subsequent filing of a false tax return using the falsified records, an offense that most would agree is a natural and probable consequence of accounting fraud. (Once you have cooked your books you might actually run a greater risk of being caught if you did not incorporate them into your tax return.) Look to see how widely your professor or textbook applies this rule.

Also, don't forget about possible Pinkerton liability under conspiracy law if crimes are committed in furtherance of a conspiratorial agreement. (See above in the chapter on conspiracy.) In reality, a conspirator will often *also* be an accomplice, but this is not necessarily the case. Someone who agreed to a crime, but did not assist in anyway and did not offer any direct encouragement to any of those who committed it might nonetheless but liable for the crime in a jurisdiction that recognized Pinkerton liability. The harsh nature of expanding criminal liability so widely is, of course, one of the reasons why so many jurisdictions reject this sort of conspiracy-based complicity. Still, you usually get points on an exam for identifying each theory of liability separately when both apply.

Exam Tip: Felony Murder and Complicity

One of the reasons law professors love felony murder exam questions is because they require knowledge of many different doctrines. Felony murder fact patterns involving multiple defendants require you to apply both felony murder and complicity doctrines. Could your Mom be guilty of felony murder for making your lunch the day of the robbery if one of your fellow robbers kills someone during the robbery? If she intended to assist in the robbing of the bank when she packed the lunch, the answer is yes in most jurisdictions that have a classic felony murder rule. You only come up with this answer if you see how these various doctrines connect with one another, and that is one of the principle challenges of a criminal law exam.

Abandonment/Withdrawal

Unlike conspiracy, some jurisdictions will allow an accomplice to "undo" their crime by withdrawing from or abandoning the crime assisted or encouraged. Such withdrawal requires you to do everything you can to "undo" your acts of assistance or encouragement. If you have supplied materials you must get them back. If you have offered shelter you must revoke the invitation. If you only encouraged the commission of the crime then you need only communicate your change of heart to those involved. So, yes, this means that your poor mother is going to have to chase you through the street to get the bag lunch back to escape liability for bank robbery. If you can't take back the assistance or encouragement given you may have to try to thwart the crime by informing the police or taking equivalent preventative measures on your own. So if Mom can't catch up to you before you rob the bank she will have to "drop a dime" on you and call the police. If the crime is already complete or reached a point where it simply can't be stopped then withdrawal has come too late to constitute a defense.

Some jurisdictions impose additional requirements upon such a withdrawal. In such jurisdictions withdrawal must be truly voluntary in the sense that it is not motivated by new developments that make the crime more difficult or dangerous. It also must be complete in the sense that one is not postponing or rescheduling the crime.

Even if a jurisdiction does not accept withdrawal as a defense to complicity, it may allow it to cut off liability for further criminal acts by one's accomplices. This means that the withdrawing accomplice would not be held liable for crimes that are the natural and probable consequence of the crimes committed. Many courts take this approach.

Model Penal Code

The Model Penal Code departs from the common law approach in a number of important ways. The common theme among these differences is the greater importance that the MPC places on the mental state of the offender. In places the MPC requires more in the way of mental state and less in the way of conduct than the common law.

As noted earlier, the MPC rejects Pinkerton liability for foreseeable crimes committed in furtherance of a conspiracy of which the defendant was a member. The MPC also rejects liability for crimes that are the natural and probable consequences of the crime assisted or encouraged. The MPC specifically provides for complicity liability, however, for one who agrees to aid, but the resulting liability is for the crime one agreed to aid, not all crimes in furtherance of that crime as would be the case under Pinkerton liability.

Unlike the common law, the MPC creates complicity liability for one who merely *attempts to aid*. So if you don't even see the lunch your mother packed for you on the kitchen counter, she can still go down the river for bank robbery because she was trying to aid you in your bank robbery. It gets worse! The MPC recognizes complicity liability for one who attempts to aid in the commission of the offense *even if the party you intended to assist never even attempted the crime.* So even if you chicken out of the bank robbery your Mom still goes away for bank robbery for making you that lunch. So you could be not guilty of anything (if you had not taken the substantial step required for an attempt), but your Mom becomes guilty for a bank robbery that was never attempted or completed. Now don't you *really* feel badly!

On the bright side (for defendants, that is), complicity under the MPC requires purpose. It is not enough to knowingly assist or encourage; one must do so with "the purpose of promoting or facilitating the commission of the crime." (MPC 2.06(3)(a). This means that the prosecutor must prove that your mother did not just know that you were going to rob the bank the day she made your lunch. It must be proved that she provided you with lunch for the purpose of helping you rob the bank. Maybe there is a Thanksgiving dinner in your (post-prison) future after all!

The MPC came down on the side of the prosecutor, however, with respect to the issue of reckless and negligent crimes. The MPC specifically provides that with respect to results that an accomplice need only have the mental state required for the offense assisted or encouraged. So you could easily be an accomplice to involuntary manslaughter if you handed your car keys to an intoxicated driver and he killed someone as a result.

Finally, the MPC clearly provides for a defense of abandonment. To qualify one must 1) neutralize their assistance or encouragement or 2) warn the police in a timely manner or 3) try some other way to prevent the crime assisted or encouraged.

Vicarious and Enterprise Liability Distinguished

Two different types of criminal liability need to be distinguished from complicity liability. (Neither gets much attention in first year courses.)

Vicarious liability refers to the situation where one person is held criminally responsible for the acts of another. Such vicarious liability is today created by statute. The most common scenario is an employer being liable for the criminal acts of his employees. One such statute holds one who runs a liquor store criminally responsible for any sales by his employees of alcohol to those under the legal drinking age. Such statutes often create only misdemeanor liability. Other statutes create liability for certain employee actions only when the employer knows or should know of those actions.

Enterprise liability on the other hand refers to the criminal liability of corporations and other such legal entities. The corporation itself is found guilty despite their being "no body to kick and no soul to damn." Ordinarily such liability exists only when the board of directors or high ranking officers engage in criminal conduct.

Vicarious and enterprise liability may exist alongside of complicity liability in a fact pattern, but remember to analyze each separately in your exam answer. More issues, more points!

CHAPTER 24

Defensive Force

Self-defense is the classic justification defense. People intuitively believe that the innocent have a right to protect themselves from violence. People also intuitively understand that there is an important difference between self-defense and retaliation, between attacking someone out of fear and attacking someone out of anger. One of the main purposes of the criminal law is to reduce violence by stopping people from taking the law into their own hands, but the law cannot be everywhere. A person should not have to choose between allowing himself to be hurt and breaking the law. So the criminal law justifies what it usually forbids—private violence—when a person is rightfully protecting him or herself or another innocent party.

Distinguishing self-defense from ordinary violence is all very fine in theory. In practice, drawing the line between justified and unjustified force is often far from easy. Fear and anger go hand in hand. When we are afraid of people we often also hate them. Also, deciding how early people can use force to protect themselves is a very tricky business. If we make it too easy to lawfully use force people will become more afraid of one another, more likely to use force in anticipation of the other person using force, and we could easily spiral into the sort of chaotic, Hobbesian battle of all against all that the criminal law is supposed to prevent.

These issues and a host of others make the doctrines justifying defensive force interesting and important. Lawyers who practice criminal law deal with self-defense issues all the time. Don't be lulled by the intuitive nature of these doctrines, however. One needs to think systematically through a range of issues—not just latch onto the first one that jumps out at you.

Justification v. Excuse

Before we work through the elements, let's review the distinction between justifications and excuses. We refer to a defense as a justification when society approves or tolerates your conduct. We say that you were justified in your actions because you did not do anything wrong. An excuse, in contrast, involves a wrongful act but one committed under circumstances that relieve you of criminal (but usually not civil) liability for what you did.

Self-defense is generally thought of as the paradigm example of a justification. Society approves of defensive force. We want you to defend yourself against wrongful force. We will eventually see, however, that the distinction is not all that clear depending on how we define some of the elements of self-defense.

Overview of the Elements

Defensive force doctrines cover both the justified use of force to defend others as well as one's self. The rules for each are largely the same with a few important differences. To avoid the cumbersome repetition of the phrase "defense of self or of others" we will just refer to both as "self-defense" until later in the chapter when we learn the special rules that do apply to using force to protect others.

Generally speaking you can only use force when you reasonably fear an imminent harm. The amount of force you use must be reasonably proportionate and necessary under the circumstances. You also must not be in the wrong to begin with, which means that you did not start a fight with someone else and were not committing a crime. So violent bullies and criminals can't claim self-defense when they are attacking or stealing from someone.

With that very general understanding let's use the following checklist to systematically analyze the issues raised.

Justifiable Defensive Force must . . .

- *Be used against an unlawful force*

- *Be used as the result of a reasonable fear*

- *Be used as the result of an actual fear*

- *Be used in the face of an imminent harm*

- *Be necessary*

- *Be reasonable in the amount of force used*

- *Not be used by an initial aggressor*

- *Not be used when you should retreat*

Once you learn to use this checklist you will be able to defend yourself against any self-defense fact pattern on an exam!

Used Against an Unlawful Force

If you go shoplifting and get caught, you don't get to punch the security guard in order to get away. When the security guard tells you to stop and you run, he lawfully is allowed to grab you by the arm. You can't lawfully use any force in response because his force is lawful. What if the security guard throws you to the ground and starts kicking you? Now you can defend yourself because his excessive force has ceased to be lawful.

The basic idea here is that only one person in a conflict can be lawfully using force at a time. If the security guard lawfully got to grab you, and you lawfully got to punch him, then society would end up with a lawful fist fight. This is not good, since a goal of the criminal law is to reduce violence, not sanction and promote it.

The security guard example is intended to be obvious, but the principle also can apply to any conflict between two private citizens. If you someone puts some hard but legal blocks on you during an intramural football game you cannot lawfully punch them in self-defense. Their blocks are lawful because the law implies your consent to be subject to them when you agree to play football.

Things get more serious when deadly force is involved and when one of the two parties involved makes a mistake. Imagine that your bone-headed friend decides to break into your house late at night and stand over your bed with an axe as a Halloween prank. If you start shooting at him out of reasonable fear he cannot defend himself with the axe because your use of force is lawful, even though mistaken. (We will discuss why your mistaken but reasonable belief is good enough for lawful self-defense later.)

We will return to this idea that the criminal law can only privilege one person at a time to lawfully use force when we deal with the initial aggressor rules and with the special rules that apply to the use of defensive force against law enforcement officers.

Reasonable Fear

The reasonableness of one's fear is the moral foundation of self-defense. There are all sorts of reasons one might be afraid, but we don't want to license force based on unreasonable fear. Imagine that someone goes to the door on Halloween night after hearing his doorbell ring and opens fire on a group of teenagers wearing masks. Perhaps this is an exceptionally timorous person who forgot that it was Halloween. He may have actually been in fear for his life, but his use of force would not be justified because we would not consider his fear to be reasonable. Without the reasonableness requirement we would legally be at the mercy of the most fearful people in our society.

A Reasonable Fear Does Not Have to Be Correct

On the other hand, your fear need only be reasonable, not right. Now imagine that you as you walk across campus one night you are confronted by someone wearing a ski mask and pointing a gun at you while telling you to get down on your knees and pray for your life. You happen to be carrying your field hockey stick, so you smash him over the head with it. It turns out that he is a participant in a role-playing game called "Assassin," and he mistook you for the game player he was supposed to attack. The "gun" was a completely realistic looking toy. You are not guilty of felonious assault (or even murder if he dies) because you reasonably feared that he was going to kill you.

We justify force used reasonably but mistakenly because we don't want you to have to take the chance of facing down what might be a real gun in the hope that it is a toy. If everyone has to wait until the first shot is fired to make sure that the gun is real, then innocent people may die out of fear of going to prison. So while no one is happy about "reasonable mistakes" where people are hurt or killed, society has decided to tolerate—if not approve— such reasonably mistaken uses of defensive force.

A Fear Can Be Unreasonable but Correct

To be reasonable, the grounds for fear need to be apparent to the defendant. Sometimes a fear can be reasonable in an abstract sense but not a reasonable basis for the use of force because the defendant does know now what makes the fear reasonable.

In one episode of the animated TV series "The Simpsons," Springfield suffers a plague of Zombies. Homer's hated goody- two-shoes neighbor Flanders chases after Homer and his family as they try to escape in the family car asking if he can nibble Homer's ear. On noticing Flanders's approach Homer whirls and shoots Flanders dead. When Bart exclaims that "Mr. Flanders was a zombie," Homer replies "he was?" In such a case Homer would not have a claim of self-defense to homicide (putting entirely aside the issue of whether killing a member of the "undead" can be homicide) because his fear of Flanders could not be reasonable if he did not know that Flanders was a Zombie.

On a less comic and more typical note, imagine that a subway rider shoots a fellow passenger on a hunch that he was about to be robbed because the fellow passenger "looked at him funny." As the shooting victim is being taken away in an ambulance a knife falls out of the victim's pocket and he admits to the medics that he was about to rob the shooter. The shooter would have no claim of self-defense because his fear was correct but unreasonable since the shooter had no reasonable way of knowing that he was going to be mugged. The criminal law takes this position to stop people from "gambling" unreasonably when they use force.

Who Is the Reasonable Person, and What Is Reasonable Fear?

Any time you see a reasonableness standard you should ask the question, "reasonable to who?" Who is the person whose fear must be reasonable in order to enjoy a right of self-defense? A person of what age, gender, physical size and strength? Is the reasonable person a frail 98 pound weakling, or a heavyweight Mixed Martial Arts fighting champion or some mythical "average" person in between? And under what circumstances is your fear to be judged? What time and place? Asking someone for money on the first tee of a golf course at an elite country club is one thing; asking someone for change in a dark alley of a high crime neighborhood is arguably another. Do we imagine some fear-neutral time and place? Most of these questions find no clear answer in the law. Instead we look to jurors or prosecutors to exercise reasonable discretion.

The reasonableness of one's fear becomes an issue when force is used pre-emptively to some degree. Once an attack is ongoing, the reasonableness of one's fear is beyond question. One need not wait until an attack begins, however, to have a fear that the criminal law recognizes as reasonable. In movies set in the wild west the "good guy" would wait until the "bad guy" reached for his gun before shooting. The criminal law does not always require you to wait that long because it does not assume that the good guys will always be faster than the bad. Deciding how long you must wait before your fear becomes reasonable, however, is difficult.

Much ink has been spilt by judges and legislators trying to define reasonable fear in a way that is both sensitive enough to context to be fair and yet clear enough in general to be predictable. The consensus view allows the following factors to be taken into consideration in determining whether a fear is reasonable.

- Physical attributes of the defendant using the defensive force

- Physical attributes of the person against whom defensive force was used

- Knowledge the defendant has about the person against whom defensive force was used

- Any relevant past experiences of the defendant

For example, a woman who has been raped before in a dark alley sees a man walking behind her in a dark alley approach her. She recognizes him as a heavy drinker in a bar she just visited. He is much bigger than she is and that night made sexually threatening remarks to her in the bar. She quickens her pace, and he breaks into a run catching up to her. She turns and shoots him in the face with pepper spray. Was her fear of being sexually assaulted reasonable? Juries in most jurisdictions would be invited to take all of the above facts into account in deciding whether she was reasonable in fearing that he would sexually assault her.

A few courts go even farther and incorporate even more subjective factors into consideration. Such courts tell juries essentially to see things from the defendant's perspective, and that that perspective includes more of the defendant's individual characteristics. Under such a standard a person who was the victim of and witness to extensive abuse as a child would be held to a different (and probably lower) standard than one who had never suffered violence. In the hands of these courts the "reasonable person" standard would become in this case the "reasonable person who had been violently abuse as a child" standard.

Granted, the line between of these two approaches may seem thin. Under the first approach, the alley rape of the woman leaving the bar would be taken into account but the prior child abuse of the second defendant would not be. The difference is that the woman in the first hypo finds herself once again vulnerable to attack in a dark alley, which makes her past experience relevant to our assessment to the reasonableness of her fear in the current case. The child abuse of the second defendant would not ordinarily be considered relevant to the reasonableness of his fears as an adult, even though the fearfulness of his early childhood might have stayed within throughout his adult life.

All courts, however, draw the line against what the MPC might call "morally idiosyncratic" beliefs or traits. A person who was excessively fearful of people of other races, however, would not be entitled to a "reasonable racist person" standard because "reasonable racism" would be considered a contradiction in terms.

Most courts draw the line against incorporating the personal characteristics of the defendant into the reasonable person standard because doing so makes the reasonable person standard too subjective. We all have our fears, but the criminal law requires us to master our irrational ones. The Model Penal Code goes so far as to instruct jurors to assess reasonableness from the point of view of a person "in the actor's situation," but leaves it up to the jury to decide exactly what that should include.

Subjective Reasonableness as a Standard for an Excuse

> "I'm pretty much not afraid of anything. Except clowns . . . I'm not really sure where the fear comes from. My mother says it's because when I was a kid I found a dead clown in the woods. But who knows."
>
> "Modern Family's" Phil Dunphy

Many have noted that the more individualized and subjective a jurisdiction makes self-defense's reasonable person standard the more self-defense becomes an excuse as opposed to a justification. Imagine that Phil Dunphy punches out of fear a circus clown who gets too close to him during a birthday party. Since society does not consider clowns to be dangerous and "clown fear" to be reasonable, such an act is not something that society can approve of or tolerate the way we tolerate more reasonable mistakes such as shooting the game player pointing the realistic looking toy gun. The rationale for incorporating Phil Dunphy's fear of clowns into the reasonable person standard is to excuse him for his unjustified use of force out of sympathy and understanding for the childhood trauma that created his irrational fear of clowns.

One difficulty with excusing people for using force on such a basis, however, is finding a principle upon which one can distinguish good unreasonable fears from bad ones. What if the fearful defendant had been traumatized as a child not by a clown but by someone of a different race? Transforming self-defense from a justification into an excuse also removes an important incentive for people to master the fears that society as a whole does not find to be reasonable. It subjects the potentially innocent objects of those fears to force that may have been reasonable from the defendant's perspective but which was unreasonable from the wider perspective of more average people living in our society. Clowns are people, too!

Actual Fear

Fear must not only be reasonable but actual. Usually the two go hand in hand, but occasionally one comes across a fact pattern where a person has a reason other than fear to use force against another. Going back to Homer's shooting of Flanders described above, imagine that Homer had instead said in response to Bart's observation that Flanders was a zombie "who cares?" If Homer shot his do-good neighbor just because he hated him and not because he feared him then Homer would have no valid claim of self-defense.

Imminence of Harm

Timing is everything in self-defense. You cannot use force against harms that took place in the past or that will not occur in the immediate future.

In the movie "Pulp Fiction," John Travolta's and Samuel Jackson's characters survive a fusillade of bullets from an attacker. Their attacker empties his gun, and they can clearly hear it clicking as he pulls the trigger again and again after he is out of bullets. All of his bullets missed though. After Travolta and Jackson's characters exchange a momentary look of surprise they shoot their attacker dead. Their use of force is clearly not self-defense but simple retaliation because the harm is past, not imminent.

The more difficult issue is how close to happening a future harm must be in order to justify defensive force. The general idea is that we don't want people to act rashly and end up engaging in unnecessary violence, yet we don't want them to have to wait until it is too late to avoid injury. Forcing lawful defenders to absorb the first blow in a fight might put them at a disadvantage from which they might never recover.

While imminence does not require you to wait until an attack begins, it does preclude responding with force to an attack that is not going to happen right now. The farther in the future the threatened harm the greater the possibility that it will never happen or that you have some reasonable recourse other than violence. Having someone tell you that they are going to kill you the next time they see you clearly does not justify using defensive force that very moment. It might justify using it the very next time you see them although if you have not sought the police in the interim the finder of fact may wonder whether you really believed the initial threat was real. Even having an irate fan tell you during the seventh inning stretch of a baseball game that they are going to beat you up after the game does not justify you hitting them preemptively. Especially given how slow baseball games can be! Somewhere between the next inning and the next pitch, however, things get murky and imminence becomes a jury question.

Immediacy v. Necessity

What if someone threatens you in the future, but your only chance to respond to the threat comes long before that. Fans of the book and movie *The Princess Bride* may think of this as the "Dread Pirate Roberts" problem. Every night for a number of years the Dread Pirate Roberts told Wesley his cabin boy "Good night, Wesley, nice work today, I'll most likely kill you in the morning." Now imagine that Wesley could have easily killed Roberts in his sleep, but that he was no match for Roberts once he was awake. Does Wesley have to wait until the *harm is imminent* or does the *necessity of imminent action* satisfy the imminence requirement? It seems unfair and unwise to force Wesley to let sleeping pirates lie but in point of fact Roberts never did follow through on his threat and eventually groomed Wesley to be his replacement.

This fanciful example illustrates a very real issue that arises in a number of very real contexts. A hostage whose life is being held for ransom would be justified in killing his captor long before the ransom was due if it seemed to be the only way to avoid being killed. The necessity of taking immediate action would justify not waiting until the actual harm was more imminent. This works only because the ransom makes the prospect of death at some point in the future sufficiently likely and the captivity of the hostage rules out any obtaining help from the police or any other course of action. A far more controversial application of this same principle involves a battered spouse who effectively believes herself to be hostage to her batterer. This specific issue will be discussed along with other domestic violence issues below.

Some jurisdictions (including those that follow the Model Penal Code) deal with this issue by requiring that the use of force only be *immediately necessary* instead of requiring that the harm be imminent. Such a standard allows the hostage, and in some cases the battered spouse, to use force more pre-emptively than they might be able to under a strict interpretation of imminence.

Necessity of Force

One may not use force in the face of an imminent harm if one does not have to. Returning to the seventh inning stretch scenario described above, imagine that the enraged fan who threatens to beat you up after the game is an intoxicated, elderly and somewhat infirm person. After the game while you are standing next to each other and hemmed in on all sides by the fans standing around you he throws a punch at you. He is so slow though that you easily duck the punch. Now visibly out of breath he takes a second, slower swing but you easily duck that punch too. He is now even more out of breath, and you see the police approaching him from behind reaching out to grab him. As he begins a third, even slower swing you punch him right in the face, knocking him down. Now you shouldn't feel very good about yourself (even if he is a Yankees fan), but you will feel even worse when the police officer (who has been going to law school at night and read this book) arrests you for misdemeanor battery. You don't have a valid claim of self-defense even though you reasonably feared an imminent harm because your use of force was not necessary. You could have easily ducked the third punch, and the police were about to grab him anyway, so your punch was not necessary.

This necessity requirement makes sense if you remember that self-defense legalizes violence, something that the criminal law generally forbids and tries to reduce. So self-defense limits a person to using only what force is necessary, even though that person faces a wrongful, unlawful attack. You don't "get to hit the old man" just because he swung at you. We don't want you hitting people just because they made you mad, even if the other person "has it coming to them" in society's view. Instead, we want you to report that person to the police and have them prosecuted. That way private violence goes down, not up. Self-defense is not a license for righteous retaliation, but an exception to the criminal law's general prohibition on violence narrowly drawn to keep violence overall to a minimum while allowing the righteous to do what is *necessary* to protect themselves.

Exam Tip: Reading Fact Patterns Carefully

I imagined the above scenario in the crowded stands of a major league baseball game because I wanted to avoid dealing with the issue of retreat. If you imagine yourself hemmed in by people in the seats around you then running away is not an option (although ducking clearly was). The reason I wrote a possible retreat out of the problem was to isolate the general requirement of necessity from the particular sub-issue of retreat, or "stand your ground." I draw attention to this not to show you how clever I am (although it was a little clever, wasn't it?) but to demonstrate a big part of how law school professors write their questions.

Law professors create fact patterns specifically to raise some issues and to exclude others. This is important because it makes a difference as to how we grade your answers. If you write on and on about whether a duty of retreat exists and what the scope of that duty would be on this fact pattern you probably would not be earning any points because this fact pattern was written to exclude that issue. As much as you might want to show me that you know all about the retreat rules I am about to explain in the next section you are out of luck because I decided to write that issue out of the question when I hemmed you and the old man in between the other fans. Instead, you should briefly describe why factually retreat was not an option to show me that you did consider the issue before writing about necessity—the issue that I did write into the problem.

Don't fight the facts either! Sometimes students will get hung up on whether the facts are realistic or by some particular fact that offends their world view. For example, some people might be annoyed by the idea that you have to let this old guy keep swinging at you. They might be bothered by a legal rule that forces you to risk the possibility the next punch might connect. They might further imagine that most fights probably do not involve elderly, infirm men whose punches you can evade with relative safety. Such a student might "fight the facts" in this question by arguing that it was necessary to hit the old man because his next punch might have connected before the police grabbed him. Fair enough. I would give you a point for considering this possibility, but you would lose a lot more points by not noting that the defendant ducked the first two punches *easily* and that each punch was getting *slower and slower*. So analyze the facts that the professor gives you, not some other set of facts that comports with how you think the world is or should be. Remember that professors write fact patterns not to mirror or model reality but to test your understanding of often very complicated legal doctrines. Also remember that your number one goal in writing your answer is to show that you do know the law well and that you can apply it well to any set of facts, even strange ones that might never happen in the world as we know it.

Stand Your Ground and the Duty to Retreat

What if you weren't hemmed in by people all around you in the baseball problem described above? Do you have to run away from the old man rather than hit him? Or let's make things a little more dramatic. Imagine that you see your former freshman year college roommate at your 60 year college reunion. He hated you then, and he hates you still. He seems to have spent the last sixty years hating you even more because after you and he have been arguing for a while about old slights that have been festering for years he grabs a really sharp carving knife from the meat tray at the buffet and screams that he is going to kill you. Time has not been kind to him, however, because he is now wheelchair bound. He begins to wheel quickly toward you waiving the carving knife. As luck would have it you have kept in pretty good shape and just won the 100, 400, and 800 meter races in your state's "Senior Olympics." As luck would also have it you are lawfully carrying a concealed handgun. Can you shoot him dead, or do you have to run away?

Applying the principle of necessity, it would seem that self-defense law should require you to "retreat" in both instances even though you did nothing wrong and face a wrongful aggressor. This in fact was the position that the early common law took where one had to "retreat to the wall" before using deadly force.

American jurisdictions as a whole have always taken a different view. Retreat was considered ignominious and dishonorable. No jurisdiction requires one to retreat in the face of an imminent, wrongful harm before using non-deadly force. So even if you could run away from the elderly intoxicated baseball fan you don't have to in any jurisdiction because the punch you threw is not ordinarily considered deadly force. A majority of jurisdiction do not even require you to retreat before using deadly force. You could shoot your knife wielding former roommate as he wheels towards you in his wheel chair. In these jurisdictions requiring retreat is considered to be inflicting a second wrong on the wronged party. Why should you have to run away from your hateful former roommate when you did nothing wrong?

A minority of jurisdiction (including the Model Penal Code) do require you to retreat before using deadly force *only if you can safely do so*. You could be prosecuted for murder if you shot your former roommate instead of running away from him. These jurisdictions reason that even the life of a wrongful aggressor is worth sparing, and a safe retreat by an innocent victim of aggression is not too big a price to pay for avoiding an unnecessary loss of life.

It bears emphasis that only a minority of American jurisdictions ever required retreat under any circumstances, and that no jurisdictions has ever required someone to endanger themselves by retreating. (This is why I made you a track star in the hypo above so that there would be no doubt that you could safely get away if you wanted to.) Furthermore, you have to be actually aware of your safe avenue of retreat for the obligation to exist at all. Retreat is usually not therefore an issue if you are facing a gun because no one can safely outrun a bullet.

A number of states have recently passed "Stand Your Ground" laws eliminating any obligation to retreat and sometimes expanding one's right to stand one's ground, so one might be forgiven for assuming that most jurisdictions used to require retreat. In some cases, these new laws expanded the right to stand your ground and not retreat by creating pretrial hearings at which one's immunity from civil and criminal prosecution on self-defense grounds could be established.

The Castle Exception

Your home is your castle, and no one has to run out of their castle. Even the minority of jurisdictions that require you to retreat before using deadly force do not require you to retreat if you are in your own home. Some jurisdictions have broadened this exception to include one's car and one's place of work. What if the person attacking you lives or works with you? While some jurisdictions do require retreat before using deadly force against a co-occupant, the recent trend is decidedly in favor of not requiring retreat from the home in cases of domestic violence. (Some of these same jurisdictions do require a workplace retreat from a co-worker though.)

Proportionate Force

A corollary to the necessity requirement is that force used in lawful self-defense must be necessary and proportionate to the harm that is imminent. Even if you could not safely duck the old man's punches in the baseball hypothetical, punching him might have been unnecessary if you could have safely restrained him until the police got hold of him. You cannot use deadly force against non-deadly force, and fact finders will sometimes draw further distinctions between levels of non-deadly force. So you may not be able to punch someone who is pushing you, and you ordinarily can't stab someone who is punching you. Any force that threatens *death or serious bodily injury* may be lawfully met with deadly force. You can shoot your college roommate who is going to stab you because force does not have to be exactly equal to be proportionate. (It is his problem that he brought a knife to a gunfight.)

Whether force is deadly will sometimes depend on the circumstances. Deadly weapons aren't always required. Age, size, and strength and training all matter as does the specific nature of the attack. Details matter. An unarmed attack by Chuck Norris, the former martial arts TV and movie star who is the subject of numerous jokes about his power ("when the bogey man goes to sleep he checks under his bed for Chuck Norris") could constitute deadly force even though Norris is now in his seventies.

Initial Aggressor Rules

If you start it, you don't get to end it, or—to be a little more precise—you ordinarily don't get to claim self-defense against someone you have attacked. The person who "starts it" is called the "initial aggressor" in the law of self-defense. Aggressors ordinarily don't enjoy a right of self-defense. So if it was necessary to punch the old man at the baseball game who attacked you (maybe the old man was Chuck Norris!) then he can't claim self-defense with respect to any subsequent punches he throws since he was the initial aggressor.

Note that being an initial aggressor does not mean that you are just being a jerk. If you insult a Yankee's fan, and he throws a punch at you, he is the initial aggressor, not you. Being an initial aggressor does not always require actual violence though. One can become an initial aggressor by threatening imminent harm. If midway through your heated argument with the hated Yankees fan he raises a clenched fist and says he is going to "knock your block off," then he is the initial aggressor. If his punch reasonably seemed imminent then you can punch him in self-defense, and he won't be able to legally punch you back.

Can an initial aggressor ever *regain* his right of self-defense? This is where things get a bit more complicated. It is a lot easier for the enraged old man than it is for your knife wielding college roommate because there is only one way for a "deadly initial aggressor" (one who uses deadly force) to regain his right of self-defense. *A deadly initial aggressor must completely withdraw from the conflict and communicate that withdrawal to the victim of his initial aggression.*

So assume that your college roommate has been slashing away at you with his knife. You pick up another carving knife from one of the other trays. Your college roommate wheels back away from you and tells you that he quits. You have been cut, however, and are very mad. You chase after him with your knife. Your college roommate can now legally stab you with his knife because he has regained his right of self-defense through his complete and clearly communicated withdrawal. To allow you to kill him with impunity would be to legalize a retaliatory killing because you no longer face an imminent harm.

Note, however, that most jurisdictions require you to both withdraw and clearly communicate that withdrawal. This reduces the chance of a misunderstanding. You might otherwise think that your opponent is just resting up for another attack. Note that you don't necessarily have to put down your weapon and accept the initial aggressor's withdrawal at face value. (He might be a liar as well as an initial aggressor.) But you do need to cease your attack unless and until you have a reasonable fear that he is going to continue the attack.

A non-deadly initial aggressor has a second way of regaining his right of self-defense (in addition to the sort of withdrawal just described). A non-deadly initial aggressor may regain his right of self-defense if the victim of his initial aggression responds with deadly force. Some jurisdictions (including the Model Penal Code) immediately restore the initial aggressor's right of self-defense at this point. So if you shove someone for no reason, and they pull out a knife and try to stab you, you can pull out a gun and shoot him, even though they were the initial victim. You, of course, can still be prosecuted for the misdemeanor battery you initially committed, but at least you don't have to choose between letting him stab you and going to prison for murder.

Other jurisdictions, however, require a non-deadly initial aggressor to retreat if possible when faced with deadly force from his victim. In these jurisdictions you would need to run away from your knife-wielding, shove-victim. You could only use deadly force if he chases you down, and you have no other choice. Some jurisdictions will find a non-deadly initial aggressor who faces a deadly force response guilty not of murder but of manslaughter if he kills his victim without first retreating. Such "split-the-baby" manslaughter is one form of what is called "imperfect self defense."

Protection of Property and Home

You can use reasonable force to protect property. This means that you can't use deadly force to protect your property, since human life is considered more valuable than property (even the life of a would be thief or vandal). So you can run out and grab someone you see breaking into your car, but you can't shoot them on sight.

What if you grab someone who is breaking into your car, and they start punching you. Can you punch them back? Of course! You are not an initial aggressor because your initial use of force (grabbing them) was legally justified by your right to use reasonable force to protect property. Your auto burglar does not legally get to punch you for grabbing him because he has no right to defend himself against your *lawful* use of force.

The line between protection of property and protection of self becomes blurry when the property at issue is one's home, however. Depending on the circumstances, a person breaking into one's home may or may not also create a reasonable fear of imminent harm to your safety. Details matter here. If you wake up in the middle of the knife to find an intruder looming over your bed holding a knife all juries would find use of deadly force justified on the grounds that you reasonably feared for your life. If, on the other hand, you discover your no-good-crack-addicted neighbor stealing a bicycle out of your garage one morning you can't shoot him because these circumstances don't present the same fear of imminent death or serious bodily injury. Many jurisdictions, however, have created a rebuttable presumption of a reasonable fear of serious bodily injury if you confront someone who has broken into your home. If the burglar raised his hands and said "don't shoot, "or if he was a clearly unarmed child, the jury might find this presumption to be rebutted, and your use of deadly force would not be lawful self defense.

Along similar lines, "spring guns" or other lethal traps that expose intruders to death or serious bodily injury are not lawful means of protecting your property. Since they ordinarily operate automatically in your absence it is not possible for you to claim that you were in reasonable fear at the time, and the death or serious injury involved is not justified by the protection of mere property.

Protection of Others

The principles discussed with respect to self-defense apply to the defense of others. The most important distinction between self-defense and the defense of others concerns the mistaken use of force. A typical fact pattern involves a Good Samaritan who uses force to help someone he mistakenly believes to be the victim of a wrongful aggression. You punch a scruffy looking man whom you saw tackle someone else to the ground but soon discover that the man you punched was an undercover police officer chasing a purse snatcher.

A minority of jurisdictions apply what is called the *alter ego* rule, which means that the Good Samaritan steps into the shoes of the person she was defending. Since the undercover officer was using lawful and non-excessive force against the fleeing purse snatcher, the purse snatcher had no right of self-defense against the officer. Since the purse snatcher had no right of self-defense, neither doe his alter ego, the Good Samaritan who steps into his shoes. Without a lawful basis for self-defense the Good Samaritan is guilty of the crime of hitting the police officer.

The majority of jurisdictions now find the alter ego rule to be too harsh. They base the Good Samaritan's liability on the reasonableness of his belief in the need for defensive force, so one using defensive force on behalf of another needs to just be reasonable, not correct, in their fear of imminent harm to the party protected. Under that standard, the scruffiness of the undercover officer would work in favor of the Good Samaritan by suggesting that it was reasonable that he thought the officer was a mugger or wrongful assailant. This is also the Model Penal Code's rule.

Imperfect Self Defense

Usually self-defense operates as an all-or-nothing defense. If one acts in lawful self-defense one is guilty of no crime; if not then one suffers the full weight of criminal liability for the force used. This principal can operate harshly in homicide cases. One who shoots another out of a genuine but unreasonable fear becomes guilty of murder for an intentional killing. Some jurisdictions have created a middle category of liability between guilty and not guilty in homicide cases that is called imperfect self-defense and which results in a conviction for manslaughter, not murder.

Different types of imperfect self-defense exist in different jurisdictions although all create manslaughter liability. These are the three most common versions.

1. *One who kills out of an actual but unreasonable fear.* You shoot the mask wearing treat-or-treating teenager at your doorstep on Halloween night out of a sincere but unreasonable fear.

2. *One who unreasonably but actually believes that deadly force is necessary.* A police officer shoots a charging unarmed assailant because the officer forgot that he had his Taser on his gun belt.

3. *A non-deadly-force initial aggressor who fails to retreat in the face of deadly force from his victim.* You shove someone, they pull a knife, and you fail to run before shooting them in a jurisdiction that does require retreat under these circumstances.

As we will learn later, jurisdictions that follow the Model Penal Code create more than one type of imperfect self-defense liability by distinguishing reckless fears from unreasonable ones.

Special Issues: Domestic Violence

Domestic violence has raised difficult issues for self-defense doctrine. The most common scenario involves women who kill the husbands and boyfriends who batter and abuse them. Such killings can be usefully divided up into two categories: confrontational and non-confrontational homicides.

Confrontational homicides occur when the woman kills while she is being assaulted or just before she believes she is going to be assaulted. These killings can usually be analyzed under ordinary self-defense principles. Evidence of the man's prior violence against the woman is ordinarily admitted to establish that the woman's fear on this occasion was a reasonable one.

The more difficult self-defense issues arise in the relatively rare non-confrontational homicide cases. In these cases when women kill their batterers during a lull in the violence or sometimes even while her batterer is asleep. Ordinarily, nothing could seem less imminent than an attack from someone who is asleep and nothing less necessary than killing him instead of calling the police.

In both of these types of cases, battered spouse syndrome evidence has been accepted by some courts to provide the jury with a better understanding of how the principles of reasonable fear, imminence, and necessity should be applied to such violence. Battered spouse syndrome is a complex phenomenon, but generally describes a state of learned helplessness in which the battered woman feels that her abuser is all powerful. Expert evidence in this area also usually describes a cycle of violence with distinct phases that involves a buildup of tension followed by battering. Cycle of violence testimony can help woman establish that they reasonably believed violence was imminent because of the telltale signs of building tension. The learned helplessness testimony explains to the juror why a battered woman reasonably might believe that no one can help her and that her only chance of defending herself against her spouse is through a pre-emptive attack before he assaults her or in extreme cases when he is asleep. Such evidence is used in different ways in different jurisdictions and remains controversial when used in non-confrontational homicides.

Exam Tip: Other Syndromes

Self-defense cases involving actors who arguably suffer from a syndrome are great subjects for policy oriented exam questions.

Professors who have covered battered spouse syndrome in class but who want to assess their students' ability to think creatively often raise new types of syndrome issues on their exams. Post-traumatic stress syndrome based on military service, early child abuse, or sexual assault are three subjects that raise interesting and difficult questions.

Model Penal Code

The Model Penal Code follows the common law approach to self-defense in many respects. The MPC takes the following positions on the splits among common law jurisdictions discussed earlier.

- A person must retreat if he can safely do so before he uses deadly force.

- An initial aggressor who initially uses non-deadly force regains his right of self-defense if the victim of his initial aggression escalates the conflict from non-deadly to deadly force.

- A person may use force when it is *immediately necessary*, even if the actual harm feared is not yet imminent.

- The reasonableness of a person's fear is to be judged on the basis of a person in the actor's situation.

These differences have been explained above in the sections dealing with reasonableness, imminence, retreat and initial aggressors. The most important difference between the Model Penal Code and common law jurisdictions deals with actual but unreasonable fears.

Actual but Unreasonable Fears

An actual but unreasonable fear is a partial defense to criminal liability under the MPC. As discussed earlier, some common law jurisdictions recognize an imperfect form of self-defense in homicide cases that results in not murder but manslaughter liability. The Model Penal Code goes several steps further, applying the concept of imperfect self-defense to all crimes and making distinctions between different degrees of unreasonableness.

Under the MPC an actor cannot be guilty of a crime requiring purpose or knowledge if he used force out of an *actual* fear of unlawful harm. If that fear was recklessly formed, however, the actor can be guilty of a crime requiring a reckless state of mind. If the fear was formed with gross negligence, then the actor can be found guilty of a crime requiring gross negligence. The result is a rejection of the all or nothing approach of many common law jurisdictions in favor of an approach that calibrates one's liability to the culpability of one's mental state.

Return to the scenario of the fearful resident who kills the trick-or-treating teenager at his doorstep on Halloween night. Assume the jury accepts that the resident was actually afraid that the masked teenager was a deranged killer. If the jury concludes that the resident was criminally (grossly) negligent in not realizing that the teenager was a harmless trick-or-treater then the jury can find the resident guilty of negligent homicide. If the jury concludes that the resident consciously disregarded a substantial and unjustifiable risk that the teenager was harmless then the jury could find the resident guilty of reckless homicide (manslaughter under the MPC). If the jury concludes that the resident was so reckless as to be extremely indifferent to human life in shooting without further investigation then they could find him guilty of extremely reckless murder under the MPC.

Instead of facing the all or nothing choice between a conviction for murder and a not guilty verdict, the MPC permits the jury to convict the defendant of a crime that matches how unreasonable his fear was.

Exam Tip: Look for Breadth and Depth

As will be discussed in the final chapter, some exam questions contain lots of issue and other contain fewer issues that require more in depth discussions. (Impossible questions require both, but remember that they are equally impossible for the person writing next to you.) Self-defense fact patterns lend themselves easily to both types of question. A fight sequence can contain multiple moments at which the reasonableness of fears can change over time, the role of initial aggressor can change, obligations to retreat can come and go, and questions about the necessity and proportionality of the amount of force used can arise. Self defense fact patterns can also raise interesting questions about how individualized our standard of reasonable fear should be, how imminent the harm must be, and what role psychological syndromes should play in reasonable fear. Don't be afraid of these issues! See them as opportunities for you to show what you know.

Duress and Necessity

Duress and necessity are two different doctrines that both law students and judges sometimes confuse. They usually play a small part in the typical first year criminal law course, if they are covered at all.

Duress is generally thought of as an excuse. Here is a classic example of duress. Your first year criminal law professor becomes progressively more annoyed at the person sitting next to you in class, who smirks whenever the professor gets particularly serious about something and—even worse—never laugh's at any of the professor's jokes. One day when this student is being particularly dismissive, the professor pulls out a gun, points it **at you** and orders **you** to slap the student hard across the face. To make things perfectly clear the professor says that he is going to shoot **you** if you don't slap the student. You slap the student. After the cheering from your classmates dies down (the student really did get on everyone's nerves), someone calls the police. The professor and you are both arrested. You have a perfect defense though. Your criminal responsibility for the misdemeanor battery is *excused* because you committed the crime under duress. The professor, on the other hand is guilty not just for felonious assault for pointing a gun at you but also for the misdemeanor battery on the smirking student that he forced you to commit!

Necessity is generally thought of as a justification. Here is a classic example of necessity. To recover from the terrible stress of having your life threatened by one of your first year professors you go cross-country skiing one day. A freak storm suddenly develops, and you get caught in a terrible blizzard. Unable to see your hand in front of your face you become hopelessly lost. Night begins to fall. Just when you think all is lost, you see a cabin in the woods. (Not the one from all the horror movies; that would be a homicide fact pattern.) You stagger up to it and bang on all the doors and windows, but no one answers. Once night falls it gets unbelievably cold and you realize that you may freeze to death if you spend the night outside. You break into the cabin and survive the night watching Netflix and drinking some beer you find in the refrigerator. You would be found not guilty of criminal trespass under the doctrine of necessity because your breaking into the cabin is considered to be a lesser evil than your dying in the snow. (You are guilty of stealing the beer, however, because no one ever died of lack of beer.)

One must at the outset distinguish both of these defenses from other defenses that arise from a failure of proof with respect to one of the required elements. The law student committed a voluntary act when she slapped her fellow student and when she broke into the cabin. She also had the mental state required for assault/battery and for trespass respectively. Duress and necessity come into play after the prosecutor proves the guilty hand, the guilty mind, and any required result.

Elements of Duress

The defense of duress is sometimes referred to as the defense of coercion. The defense existed at common law. A number of jurisdictions have reduced it to statutory form, but there is a great deal of variation from one state to another. States that are common law jurisdictions generally apply it even in the absence of a statute. For these reasons it is harder than usual to generalize about the elements of duress. That said, the following description tracks what how common law jurisdictions define the elements of duress.

1. *A threat to kill or seriously injure the defendant or a third party unless the defendant commits the crime.* At common law the threat had to be to the defendant or to a member of his family, but many modern statues include any innocent third party.

2. *The defendant reasonably believed that the threat would be carried out if he did not commit the crime.*

3. *The threat coerced the defendant to commit the crime.* Not all jurisdictions require this element. Some require only that the defendant reasonably believed the threat as mentioned above.

4. *The threat was of an imminent/immediate/instant/impending harm.* Lots of variation in the words used here, but you get the idea. A threat of harm in the non-immediate future is insufficient because then you could presumably get help. (See below.)

5. *No reasonable alternative existed.* No time to call the police, and no other way to nullify the threatened harm or warn the intended victim.

6.   *The defendant has "clean hands."* This means that the defendant did not do something wrong in the first place that exposed him to the threat such as participating with others in committing a crime or joining a criminal organization. The idea here is that you should have known when you signed up to commit a crime with others that they might threaten you at some point if you did not do your part.

The common law was quite clear that duress could not be a defense to murder. So if your crazy law professor puts the gun to your head and puts a knife on the desk in front of you and tells you to kill, not slap, the smirking student then you just have to take the bullet! If this last limitation on the defense seems a bit harsh to you, you have plenty of company on that point. A number of jurisdictions have abandoned this limitation and will allow duress to be a defense to a homicide crime.

Most jurisdictions also limit duress to harms emanating from human forces. In these jurisdictions one cannot be "under duress" from natural forces or from a situation. Someone must threaten you, not something. Note also that orders from a boss or a commanding officer do not constitute duress (unless he points a gun at your head as he gives them).

Duress Under the Model Penal Code

The Model Penal Code takes a different approach, and a number of jurisdictions have followed their lead.

• Duress is not limited to imminent threats of death or serious bodily injury but includes any coercion that a "person of ordinary firmness" would be unable to resist. This also opens up duress to include threats of future harms although the harm must be of bodily injury or death.

- The person endangered does not have to be the defendant or a member of his family.

- Duress can be a defense to murder or a defense to a crime other than the one required by the person making the threat. (See below under prison escapes.)

The Model Penal Code also deals with the common law's clean hands/no fault requirement in a more nuanced way. If one recklessly or negligently exposed one's self to the threat then one can be found guilty of a crime requiring a reckless or negligent mental state. As with self-defense, the MPC's aim here is to calibrate one's criminal liability to match the culpability of one's mental state. So check the membership rules next time you join a criminal street gang!

Prison Escapes

Duress defenses are not infrequently raised in certain types of prison escapes. An inmate will claim that he had to escape custody (often a minimum security facility where he can just walk away) in order to avoid being killed, badly beaten or sexually assaulted. Jurisdictions split on whether the defense raised is one of duress or necessity. The fact that human forces are at work suggests duress, but the threatened inmate is not being ordered to escape but is committing the lesser evil of escaping to avoid the greater evil of death or felonious assault, which suggest necessity. In either event, most courts require the inmate to promptly turn themselves in once they have escaped the facility and also require some showing that the inmate could not have eliminated the threat by reporting it earlier.

The Model Penal Code facilitates use of the duress defense in prison escape cases by providing that the defense extends to any crime that the threatened harm causes one to commit. So if your prison gang orders you to kill someone, you can just escape instead and raise duress as a defense to the escape. You don't have to kill the person in order to raise the defense.

Elements of the Necessity Defense

Necessity is messier and vaguer than duress. It did not seem to exist at common law but has always been a part of American criminal law. In the absence of a statutory definition, a general common law definition applies. Some states have defined it by statute although many of those definitions are vague. A once clear line between duress and necessity has gotten fuzzy, and the Model Penal Code and a number of jurisdictions have expanded the defense.

Necessity can generally be broken down into three interconnected elements.

1. *The defendant faces an immediate danger that presents a "greater evil" than the "lesser evil" of the crime he is committing.* Note that the evil avoided must be greater in the eyes of society, not just in the eyes of the actor. So our blizzard-stranded law student is ok since society considers her life more important than the integrity of the cabin.

2. *The crime committed must be the most reasonable way of averting the greater evil.* If our law student could have safely called for help on her cell phone (what a cell phone commercial that would make!)

then she would not have a defense to breaking into the cabin.

3. *The defendant must have "clean hands."* This means that the defendant neither created the emergency herself nor was otherwise at fault. I made the blizzard a freak storm to write this issue out of the hypo. If the storm had been predicted in a weather report that the law student failed to check she would not have a defense to the trespass charge.

Note that a necessity defense can be ruled out by statute. The legislature gets to balance the evils on behalf of society. For example, a legislature's explicit decision to prohibit the use of marijuana even for medical purposes rules out an argument by users that their medical use of marijuana is the lesser evil than suffering without it.

Necessity defenses have been raised in a variety of different situations with varying degrees of success. Some of the more notable examples include the following.

*   Needle exchange programs to control the spread of AIDS that violate restrictions on the distribution of hypodermic needles

*   Homeless people violating city ordinances against sleeping outside

*   Inmates escaping prisons to avoid dangerous or intolerable conditions

*   Parents kidnapping adult children from brainwashing cults

*   Some acts of civil disobedience

Relatively few necessity defenses are successful although the outcomes can be difficult to predict given the vagueness of the standards and the fact-specific nature of the inquiry. A city without homeless shelters might be hard pressed to overcome the defense brought by the homeless because of the lack of reasonable alternatives to sleeping on the streets. Needle exchange activists on the other hand might have a difficult time establishing the imminence of the harm when infection by a shared needle is a matter of probability, not certainty.

Sometimes the line between necessity and duress becomes hard to draw. As discussed above, courts have split on whether the prison escape cases come within necessity, the key point being whether necessity is restricted to responses to human forces or only natural ones.

Necessity as a Defense to Murder

The most famous necessity case is a favorite of many textbook authors. In *Regina v. Dudley and Stephens*, two seaman killed and ate a third to avoid dying of starvation and thirst on a lifeboat lost at sea. One of the principle issues raised was whether the killing of one was a "lesser evil" than the "greater evil" of the death of the remaining sailors and thereby justified under the doctrine of necessity. The court denied the defense. Although acknowledging that the temptation of the starving, dying men was overwhelming and conceding that the man killed would have died anyway, the court refused to either justify or excuse the killing. The court's opinion can be read many different ways, but one of the simpler points was that necessity stops short of justifying the killing of an innocent person. The idea that necessity is not a defense to an intentional killing seems to be generally accepted. Although troubling counterexamples have been raised from time to time (including most notably the unexecuted decision on 9/11 to shoot down a hijacked plane filled with innocent passengers before it could be crashed into a government building in the nation's capital) no judicial case has yet ruled to the contrary.

Necessity Under the Model Penal Code

The MPC roughly follows the common law approach but expands the defense in a number of ways. First, the defense is not limited to natural forces but includes human ones, so prison escape cases may qualify. Second, the need not be imminent although it still must not be reasonably avoidable. Finally, whether fault on the part of the defendant in creating the impending harm bars raising the defense depends on the degree of fault involved and the mental state required for the crime charged. One who recklessly creates a hazard remains criminally liable for any crime requiring a reckless state of mind, and one who is grossly negligent remains liable for crimes requiring gross negligence. Finally, commentary to the code suggests that necessity might justify taking one life to save more lives although no case so holding yet exists.

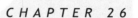

CHAPTER 26

Insanity and Related Defenses

Should someone be criminally punished if as the result of mental illness he believes that God has ordered him to kill someone, or that the person he killed has been beaming radio waves into his head, or if he feels an overwhelming compulsion to attack the next person who speaks to him? Welcome to the world of insanity!

Insanity is the classic excuse. Retribution and deterrence both presume a person's ability to make rational choices. How can you be morally responsible for your behavior when through no fault of your own your mind tricks you into seeing things that are not there and hearing things that are not said or believing things that are beyond rational belief? And how can such a person be deterred?

Insanity seems like the perfect excuse because it destroys the ability to make meaningful choices. Yet America's individualistic culture has always been very skeptical of excuses in general. "It is not my fault that I never learned to accept responsibility," the joke goes. We have also been particularly hard on those claiming excuses based on mental illness. Opinion surveys consistently show that most people see insanity as a "fake excuse" built on fabricated evidence of mental illness. Yet mental illness is all too real, and the idea that it makes a difference to criminal responsibility is not a modern notion but a very old one.

The insanity defense is hard to establish, rarely asserted, and even more rarely successful. Still, it remains an important doctrine to study because it describes an outer boundary to our notions of personal responsibility and raises fundamental issues about the purposes of punishment.

Related to insanity but different in its standards and consequences are the doctrines of diminished capacity and partial responsibility. They operate in a small minority of jurisdictions but are worthy of brief discussion.

Overview of the Elements of Insanity

Insanity is a legal concept, not a medical one. Doctors diagnose patients with various mental illnesses and disorders, but medical science does not define sanity or insanity because it has no need for such a definition.

Society needs a definition of insanity for two different purposes. First, society needs a civil definition of insanity to determine when a person may be committed involuntarily to a mental institution (although people who are subject to involuntary commitment are not generally referred to as insane anymore). This definition is a somewhat empty one: it generally provides that a person may be involuntarily committed when they are a danger to themselves or others. Second, society needs a criminal definition of insanity to decide when a person should be *excused from criminal responsibility* for their actions. Law, not medicine, supplies both definitions because the question is ultimately not a scientific one but a philosophical and policy question. For your criminal law class you need only learn the second definition, which continues to be referred to as insanity.

Most jurisdictions have settled on one of two definitions of insanity although important variations of each test exists: the M'Naghten test and the Model Penal Code test (also referred to as the "ALI" or American Law Institute test).

The M'Naghten test dates from the common law and defines as insane one who as a result of mental disease or defect fails to

1. Know the Nature and Quality of his Act *or who fails to*

2. Know the Difference between Right and Wrong.

The M'Naghten test is generally described as a *cognitive* test because it define insanity solely in terms of a defendant's ability to know things.

The MPC test in contrast adds a *volitional* test which concerns a defendant's ability to control his actions. The MPC test defines as insane one who as the result of mental disease or defect lacks the

1. Substantial Capacity to Appreciate the Criminality or Wrongfulness of his act *or* who lacks the

2. Substantial Capacity to Conform his Conduct to the requirements of the law.

In addition to adding a volitional component the MPC also requires less of an impairment than the M'Naghten test. Under M'Naghten, one must *not know* which implies a complete lack of capacity to know. In contrast, the MPC test is satisfied if one lacks the *substantial capacity* to satisfy either the cognitive or volitional prong.

Note that both tests require a mental disease or defect although each requires more than the existence of that condition. You can't be insane without a mental illness, but the existence of mental illness does not necessarily make you insane.

Procedural Background

A variety of procedural issues surround the insanity defense. While outside the scope of what is taught and tested in most first year criminal law courses, these issue provide useful background. Substantial variation exists between jurisdictions, but a few general observations can be made.

Those found to be insane during criminal proceedings are usually involuntarily committed to a mental institution. This means essentially that they are locked up in a mental hospital. You might wonder how society can lock people up if they have been found not guilty on grounds of insanity. The answer is that this confinement is civil in nature and not considered criminal punishment. The defendant's confinement to the hospital is not done to punish him but to treat the mental disease or defect that produced his insanity. Mental illness is not the only ground for such civil commitments. A person with a dangerous contagious disease can also be civilly confined for treatment under certain circumstances. Like a patient with a contagious disease the criminally insane will be released from his civil confinement when he is no longer a danger to himself or others.

The nature of involuntary commitment is one reason why so few defendants present insanity defenses. For a variety of reasons many would rather face imprisonment for a definite term than an open ended commitment to a hospital that only ends once they have been "cured."

The other important procedural consideration is burden of proof. Insanity is an affirmative defense. In all states a defendant most present some initial mental health evidence in order to raise the defense. The burden then used to switch to the prosecution to prove the defendant's sanity at the time of the crime beyond a reasonable doubt. This is still the case in a minority of jurisdictions. A majority of jurisdictions now require the defendant to prove insanity by a preponderance of the evidence (which means roughly a 51% probability) although the federal courts and some others require proof by clear and convincing evidence.

Whatever the burden of proof, most jurisdictions allow for three different verdicts in an insanity case: guilty, not guilty, and not guilty by reason of insanity. The straight not guilty verdict is necessary because the state might not be able to prove the defendant guilty beyond a reasonable doubt regardless of the defendant's sanity. (The defendant might not be the person who committed the crime, for example.) Not guilty by reason of insanity means that prosecution proved beyond a reasonable doubt that the defendant committed the crime except for the defendant's insanity. A guilty verdict means that the defendant committed the crime and was sane.

A substantial minority of jurisdictions have created a very different, fourth option: guilty but mentally ill. This verdict subjects the defendant to a prison sentence but allows the defendant to be treated while in prison. Even if cured, however, the defendant must finish their sentence. Proponents of this fourth option argue that it reduces improper insanity verdicts by giving the jury a way to recognize the mental illness of the offender while still finding them to be sane and criminally responsible. Critics point out that it is at best unnecessary—since all inmates found guilty may receive psychiatric care—and at worst a cruel trick since the jury may believe that the verdict entitles the inmate to psychiatric care (which it does not).   Critics also argue that the temptation to use this verdict to "split the baby" between guilty and insane will encourage juries to find insane defendants to be sane.

Competency Distinguished

Insanity should be distinguished from being mentally incompetent.   Insanity deals with one's mental condition at the time the crime was committed.   Incompetency in contrast concerns one's mental condition at the time of trial.   It is a violation of constitutional due process to put a mentally incompetent person on trial. The standards for incompetency and insanity are also different. A defendant is incompetent if he 1) is unable to assist his attorney prepare or present his defense or if he 2) does not understand the nature of the proceedings against him. To use some extreme examples, a mentally ill defendant who was incapable of coherent speech would fail the first prong, and a defendant who believed that he was a king and the trial an effort to depose him from the throne would fail the second prong.

Being found incompetent to stand trial does not result in one's release.   One is confined and treated until one is competent and then put on trial.   A person who never regains competency might never be tried or released.

Mental Disease or Defect

The foundation for any insanity defense under any of the tests is that the defendant must fail the cognitive or volitional test as the result of a *mental disease or defect*.   There are a lot of reasons, for example, why a person might not be able to distinguish right from wrong or be unable to control his impulses. Maybe he was raised as a child to be an evil person by evil parents.

Such a condition would not make a person insane because being brought up by evil parents is not a mental disease or defect.

No clear legal definition of mental disease or defect exists although disease is generally thought of as something that can either be cured or managed by treatment (such as schizophrenia) whereas a defect is a permanent condition (such as a condition caused by a traumatic brain injury). In this area, the law defers largely to medical science although some widely recognized diagnosis is generally required. Any mental disorder would do including organic brain damage and basic intellectual deficiencies (e.g. extremely low IQ). A brain tumor that impairs thinking could also suffice. Theoretically so could syndromes such as postpartum depression or post-traumatic stress disorder. In practice, however, only extreme forms of psychosis are ordinarily enough to satisfy either the M'Naghten or the MPC test. One may be grossly impaired by any number of conditions in any number of ways, but to not know what you are doing or to not know right from wrong usually requires a gross distortion of reality and to not be able to control one's self requires a gross impairment of control.

One group of disorders has been expressly excluded from the definition of mental disease or defect in all jurisdictions: psychopathy and sociopathy and any condition whose only symptom is the tendency to commit criminal or anti-social acts. Criminality itself does not constitute insanity. Also, some jurisdictions require a "severe" mental disease or defect in order to rule out mere neuroses, personality disorders or low level impairments resulting from the habitual use of alcohol or illegal drugs.

M'Naghten Test

The M'Naghten test is the majority rule among American states and a version of the rule is used in the federal system. The test has two cognitive prongs. You are insane if you satisfy either one. Once again, the predicate for either prong is that your lack of knowledge is the result of a mental disease or defect.

- Not know the Nature and Quality of the Act or (if you did know this)

- Not know the Wrongfulness of the Act

While distinct, these prongs are clearly related. If you don't know what you are doing, you clearly cannot know that it is wrong. Borrowing an example from a particularly tragic case, imagine that you believe the police officer you shoot as she approaches your car is not a human being but an alien invader. If you don't know that you are shooting a human being the question of whether you know that it is wrongful to kill a human being under these circumstances becomes moot. Now imagine that you believe that the police officer is a human being who is working with the alien forces to kill or enslave human beings. You know that you are killing a human being but arguably you can't know the wrongfulness of that act if you believe that you are protecting yourself and other human beings from death or enslavement at the hands of an alien race.

Note that both prongs require a lack of knowledge. Narrow and broad definition of knowledge exists among the states applying this test. The narrow definition interprets knowledge in a formal way as referring to a mere intellectual awareness. You satisfy this definition if you can describe in mechanical terms what you did and acknowledge that you were doing something considered to be wrong. The broader interpretation of know requires that a person be able to more fully appreciate the significance of what was done, to grasp its consequences and meaning in the grand scale of things. Some refer to this broader meaning of know as affective or emotional knowledge.

For example, in the early eighties John Hinckley tried to assassinate President Ronald Reagan in order to attract the attention and affection of the actress Jodie Foster, with whom Hinckley had become deeply obsessed as the result of a mental illness.   Hinckley clearly satisfied the narrow definition of knowledge. He knew that he was trying to kill the president of the United States. He also knew that he would be imprisoned for it. That may, in fact, have been part of his plan to win the affections (or at least the attention) of Ms. Foster. But one could argue that Hinckley failed the broader definition of knowledge under M'Naghten. Did he really think that killing the President was going to get him a date with Jodie Foster? That a famous actress, or anyone for that matter, would be romantically intrigued with someone just because they assassinated the head of our government? Hinckley's failure to "see the big picture" through his psychosis arguably makes him insane under the broader—but not the narrower—definition of knowledge under M'Naghten.

Most M'Naghten jurisdictions have not defined "know" with any specificity, but some research suggests that the broader understanding of "know" is usually applied.

Different interpretations also exist as to whether "wrongful" in M'Naghten's second prong refers to legal or moral wrongfulness. A defendant kills his next door neighbor because of a paranoid delusion that his neighbor has been poisoning all of the defendant's food. The defendant might recognize that the killing would be considered legally wrong but not consider it morally wrongful because of the danger and pain he has suffered at the hands of his neighbor. Jurisdictions are split on whether legal or moral wrongfulness is required for insanity under M'Naghten. The difference in any event may not be as great as it seems because courts that use moral wrongfulness for the test define wrongful in terms of societal standards, not the defendant's purely personal sense of moral right or wrong. So if our delusional defendant understands that society would consider the killing of his neighbor-poisoner to be wrongful then he would not be insane, even though the defendant himself believes the killing to be a righteous one.

Arguing About Delusional Beliefs

One of the truly "crazy" aspects of making arguments about insanity is that lawyers and students often find themselves making arguments from within the delusional belief system of the mentally ill actor. Riffing off of the TV show "Heroes," a person who believes that he must "kill the cheerleader to save the world" would be acting morally in subjecting himself to life imprisonment or execution in order to save the rest of humanity. Here the delusional beliefs arguably makes the actor incapable of knowing that killing the cheerleader is wrongful because it can't be wrongful to save the world!

Prosecutors sometimes also argue from within a defendant's delusional complex. Arguably Hinckley was not insane but sociopathic in being willing to kill Ronald Reagan just to get Jodie Foster to answer his love letters. Hinckley had something he wanted, and he killed in order to get it. Such behavior does not mean that he was incapable of distinguishing right from wrong; it means that he disregarded right from wrong in order to pursue his own selfish ends. Under this view, the fact that his means and ends were delusional does not change the fact that he knew he was doing wrong.

Arguing within a delusional complex can be dangerous for a prosecutor, however, because it draws even more attention to the utter irrationality of the defendant's thinking. Actresses don't date assassins. People who think otherwise seem "crazy." Often, a stronger argument for the prosecution is to point out non-delusional albeit not entirely rational reasons for the defendant's behavior. For example, mentally ill people sometimes kill those who annoy or offend them. If a defendant claims a delusional complex of persecution by a neighbor he kills, a prosecutor could argue that the defendant killed the neighbor because the defendant was short-tempered and overly sensitive, not delusional. Remember that a criminal act need not be entirely rational in order to be sane. (If mere irrationality was a defense, we would have to let a whole lot of people out of prison.)

Deific Commands

Courts have wrestled with difficulty with the not uncommon psychotic delusion psychotic that God has commanded you to perform a criminal act. M'Naghten has been applied to such "deific commands" in different ways. Some jurisdictions treat deific commands as an exception to the requirements of M'Naghten. This interpretation would find Abraham to be insane if he labors under a psychotic delusion that God wants him to sacrifice his son Isaac, notwithstanding Abraham's understanding that his society will consider the killing to be morally and legally wrong. On this reading, God has commanded the actor to do something wrongful. The alternate interpretation treats deific commands as falling squarely within M'Naghten's definition of insanity. On this reading, one who believes he is carrying out a command of God will believe that his act will be seen by society as morally right and the actor is therefore incapable of understanding its wrongfulness. This reading treats God as the ultimate source of moral standards.

Deific commands also raise interesting philosophical questions about the relationship between religious thought and conventional notions of rationality. One person's devoutly held religions belief might be another person's psychotic delusion. Many people talk to God, but claiming that he or she talks back to you can either be an authentic religious experience or an auditory hallucination depending on one's point of view. Ultimately such claims are evaluated not philosophically but sociologically though. A deific command that you kill or commit a criminal act is more likely to be considered evidence of mental disease than divine inspiration.

M'Naghten Criticisms and Responses

It is easier to understand the Model Penal Code test if one first understands the following two tests that developed in response to criticisms of the M'Naghten test. The MPC test can be understood as an attempt to find a middle ground between all of these approaches.

The Irresistible Impulse Test and the Role of Volition

One of the principal criticisms of the M'Naghten is that it ignored the way in which mental illness often impairs volition as opposed to cognition. Regardless of what you know to be true or right, your ability to control your behavior might be impaired by your disease or defect. A person tortured by continual auditory and visual hallucinations may lose the necessary willpower to resist impulses they know to be irrational. Organic brain damage may directly impair impulse control. Even milder neurological conditions may create a fractured, disordered interior world that weakens a person's ability to govern their emotions.

Since your ability to control your behavior is an essential foundation for both your moral blameworthiness and your ability to be deterred by the threat of punishment, an insanity test that ignores control is arguably deeply flawed. In response to these criticisms some jurisdictions added a volitional test to the M'Naghten's cognitive one. Some courts described this as the *irresistible impulse test*, which means that the defendant suffered a disease or defect that disabled him from controlling his conduct. Other courts phrased this volitional test in terms of *the loss of one's power to choose between right and wrong* or the *destruction of one's will.*

These volitional tests were criticized from two directions. Some argued that they demanded too much by seeming to require a complete loss of self-control. Others argued that any impulse or urge is capable of being resisted and that the degree of one's self control is in any event too difficult to medically assess. Advocates of deterrence argued that the harder an impulse is to control the greater the need to reinforce control with the threat of criminal punishment. Critics of deterrence argued in turn that people who lack the ability to control their behavior can not be deterred by any amount of punishment.

The Durham "Product" Test and the Scope of Psychiatric Expertise

A second and distinct criticism of M'Naghten is that it restricted psychiatric testimony too much. Rather than confining psychiatric testimony to narrow, semi-philosophical questions about one's ability to know right from wrong or the nature and quality of acts, an insanity test should invite medical experts to share the full range of their understanding of a mental disease or defect affected the defendant. In response to these criticisms, some jurisdictions experimented with what was essentially a cause and effect test. A person was insane if their unlawful act was *the product of mental disease or defect.*

The product rule greatly widened the scope of psychiatric testimony in insanity cases because any symptom or condition that might have caused the behavior was now relevant. Since many mental health conditions involve a range of symptoms this test allowed expert witnesses to give a jury the fullest possible picture of the defendant's mental condition.

The principal problem with the product test was its "emptiness." It asked the jury to decide whether an act was or was not a product of mental illness. This seemed too open-ended. Some described it as a "non-rule." For one thing, the test failed to define whether the mental illness could be one cause among many, a primary cause, or an exclusive cause of the defendant's behavior. John Hinckley would never have shot Reagan but for his obsessions and delusions about Jodie Foster. Does this mean that his act was "a product" of his mental illness? Should that alone make him insane? The rule provides no guidance to the jury on these key questions. Ultimately calling an act a "product" of mental illness operates more as a label for a conclusion than as a standard for evaluating behavior.

Many feared that expert psychiatric testimony would now play too great a role in the juror's deliberations because the juror deliberations might just focus on whether the defendant had a mental disease of defect. Others feared that the absence of more definite criteria to guide the deliberations of the jury would result in arbitrary and inconsistent verdicts.

Before abandoning it altogether some jurisdictions narrowed this test somewhat by defining mental disease or defect in a way that essentially foreshadowed what would become the Model Penal Code test.

The Model Penal Code's Substantial Capacity Test

The Model Penal Code test defines insanity in a substantial minority of jurisdictions. The MPC test emerged from the debate about the limitations of the M'Naghten test. In addition to adding a volitional component to a M'Naghten like cognitive test it also made a series other more nuanced changes. Section 4.01 of the Model Penal Code defines insanity in the following terms.

1.   A person is not responsible for criminal conduct if at the time of such conduct as a result of mental disease or defect he lacks substantial capacity either to appreciate the criminality [wrongfulness] of his conduct or to conform his conduct to the requirements of law.

2.   As used in this Article, the terms "mental disease or defect" do not include an abnormality manifested only by repeated criminal or otherwise anti-social conduct.

As noted earlier, the test requires only the lack of a substantial capacity with respect to the cognitive prong of insanity, not a complete failure of knowledge as does M'Naghten. Likewise, the volitional component requires only a lack of substantial capacity—not a complete inability—to conform one's conduct to the requirements of law. The use of the phrase substantial capacity tracks the broader definition of "know" described earlier in the discussion of the M'Naghten standard. Likewise the use of the word "appreciate" also invites a full consideration of the emotional and affective nature of a defendant's mental condition, not just a sterile intellectual assessment of what he believes to be true or real. Since the mentally ill are often plagued by conflicting and sometimes incoherent thoughts and emotions, these changes invite a much more nuanced assessment of criminal responsibility by the finder of fact.

Likewise, the cognitive prong of the MPC test requires only the *lack of a substantial capacity to conform one's conduct* rather than an inability to resist an impulse or control one's behavior as was the case with some of the other volitional tests used. In addition to requiring a lack of substantial capacity instead of a total inability, this volitional prong speaks to an actor's ability to *conform* as opposed to control his conduct. Practically speaking, these changes means that a mentally ill person need not "snap" or "explode" in order to be found insane under this prong. A brooding, confused defendant who wrestled with himself before acting could be more easily found insane. The more lengthy conflicted nature of his thought process arguably reveals some capacity for control but not a *substantial capacity*. Furthermore, some ability to control his behavior (by lying in wait for a victim, for example) would not be inconsistent with his ultimate inability to conform his behavior to the law.

Note that with respect to the cognitive prong the Model Penal put the word "wrongfulness" in brackets after criminality in order to avoid taking a stand on the controversy over whether legal or moral wrongfulness was at issue. The Model Penal Code left it up to each jurisdiction to decide which was appropriate.

Finally, the second paragraph of the Model Penal Code test clearly rules out sociopathy or psychopathy as a basis for insanity. Arguably a classic sociopath or psychopath—one unable to experience empathy towards another—lacks substantial capacity to appreciate the wrongfulness of his actions (he may still be intellectually aware that they are illegal and criminal). The best way of understanding the exemption of sociopathy and psychopathy is that such a complete lack of empathy is itself the core of both dangerousness and blameworthiness. It is what most people think of as the essence of evil, something that we choose not to excuse even if it is the result of a mental disease or defect.

The Hinckley Verdict and the Return of M'Naghten

Rarely does one criminal case have as big an effect on criminal law doctrine as the Hinckley case did. Hinckley was tried for the attempted murder of Ronald Reagan in federal court, and the federal courts at that time used the MPC's substantial capacity test. After Hinckley was found not guilty by reason of insanity an enormous backlash against the MPC test ensued. Congress changed the federal standard and a number of states switched back to the M'Naghten test.

The Hinckley case provides a nice illustration of the difference between the two tests. As discussed earlier one could certainly argue under M'Naghten that Hinckley did not "know" what he was doing or its wrongfulness in the sense that he did not really appreciate its significance. Such an argument is much easier under the MPC's substantial capacity test, however. The prosecution's argument was that Hinckley wanted to kill Reagan to become famous, a bad reason to be sure but a reason nonetheless. The defense was able to argue under the MPC test, however, that Hinckley could not *fully appreciate* just how wrongful his act was because of his delusional obsession with Jodie Foster. Hinckley believed that killing the president would make him infamous. Hinckley appreciated the wrongfulness of the killing to this extent, but he was unable to appreciate that this would not make him attractive or interesting to Jodie Foster. His inability to fully grasp the wrongfulness of his act reveals not a complete lack of capacity to know what he was doing was wrong but a *lack of substantial capacity to appreciate its wrongfulness.*

Diminished Capacity and Partial Responsibility

Diminished capacity and partial responsibility are two terms that have sometimes been used interchangeably to refer to doctrines that mitigate or rule out guilt on the basis of mental health conditions that fall short of insanity. The broad version of this doctrine allows for a defense to any crime. The narrow form allows for arguments that may reduce premeditated and deliberate murder down to intentional murder or intentional murder down to voluntary manslaughter. Following one leading treatise and a trend among some courts we will refer to the broad form of this defense that potentially applies to all crimes as diminished capacity and the narrow form that potentially applies only to homicide crimes as partial responsibility since the very term "partial responsibility" admits of some remaining criminal liability.

Diminished Capacity

A small number of jurisdictions follow the Model Penal Code in allowing evidence of some mental condition short of insanity for the purpose of establishing that the defendant did not have the capacity to form the mental state required for the offense. In reality, however, it is very difficult to find examples in the cases of conditions which if proved would not support a finding of lack of cognition or lack of volition sufficient to establish insanity. The significance of this doctrine may lie in the different allocations of the burden of proof involved. Imagine that a defendant wishes to put on evidence of a mental condition that leads him to lash out violently at people when he is in a crowd. Since many jurisdictions put the burden of proof of an insanity defense on the defendant, he might have to prove his lack of volition if pleading insanity. In a diminished capacity jurisdiction, however, the prosecution would have to prove his general or specific intent (depending on the charge) beyond a reasonable doubt and would have to in the process disprove the defense's evidence that he possessed no such intent.

Some jurisdictions will admit evidence of diminished mental capacity to disprove specific intent (usually requiring purpose or knowledge) but not general intent crimes (usually requiring recklessness or negligence).

While one may think of diminished capacity as disproving mental states, the actual standard is a bit different. Diminished capacity means that the mental condition prevented the defendant from forming the required mental state or "negated his capacity" to form it.

Partial Responsibility

In practice use of mental diseases or defects short of insanity to disprove one's capacity to form a required mental state is most common in the context of homicide, and a few jurisdictions have limited such evidence to the homicide context. Evidence of a brain disorder that impaired a person's ability to plan or deliberate might be admitted to disprove (or negate) premeditation and deliberation in a first degree murder case. Similarly, a mental condition that resulted in explosive anger might be used to negate the malice of intentional murder and permit a verdict of only voluntary manslaughter in these jurisdictions.

Exam Tip: Figuring Out the Type of Question

There are two very different types of exam questions that insanity and/or diminished capacity fact patterns give rise to. First, professors can easily create traditional issue spotting fact patterns that require the student to apply one or more definitions of insanity. These sorts of questions often test the student's ability to make creative arguments from the facts, including arguments that require the student to argue from within the actor's delusional complex. Second, professors can ask policy questions that require the student to argue for/against different definitions of insanity in different settings. Syndrome evidence, for example, such as post-traumatic stress disorder, or postpartum depression or psychosis or even battered spouse syndrome can all be used to explore fundamental issues of criminal responsibility through the doctrines of insanity and/or diminished capacity.

Tips for Writing Law School Exam Answers

Read the first part of the earlier chapter titled "Thinking Like a Lawyer and Learning Like a Law Student" if you have not already done so. There I discuss much of what you need to know about law school exams as well as how to prepare for exams during the course of the semester. In this short chapter I share tips on *exam writing*.

Needless to say, law exams come in all shapes and sizes. Professors write and grade them differently. Figuring out how your professor likes to test is key. The best way to do that is to look at your professor's past exams, take them under simulated test conditions, and then compare your answers to any model answers or top scoring answers available. That said, there are some general observations about how most professors test and about the most common law student mistakes that are valuable to know.

363

The Most Important Tip: Bird by Bird

Let me get all Zen on you for a moment. "When is an exam question not a question?" (Get into a lotus position and pause for meditative silence.) When it is not one question but many.

Even a fact pattern that contains a single question such as "what criminal liability exists on these facts?" can best be thought of as a series of questions. There may be multiple actors who are criminally liable. There may be multiple crimes for each actor that should be considered. Each crime will have a number of different elements (guilty mind, guilty hand etc.). Many of these elements will be defined by rules that themselves contain a number of elements. A number of defenses might also apply that themselves contain a number of different elements.

This, of course, is what makes law school exam questions overwhelming for many students. There is so much going on! What do you do? Where do you start? Why did you sign up for this abuse?

In her book on writing, Bird By Bird, the author Anne Lamott tells a story about the panic and frustration her little brother experienced as a child when assigned to write an essay about birds. He ran to their father in tears, telling him that there were just too many birds to write about and asking what he should do. "Just take it bird by bird," was the father's answer, which became not just the title of Lamott's book but also the theme of her advice about writing.

Since a law exam question is not one question but many the best way to think about the answer is a series of separate but logically related answers. Some issues are harder to spot and analyze than others, but none are impossible as long as one does not get overwhelmed by the number of issues. Just take the analysis issue by issue, rule by rule, element by element by element, bird by bird. Don't think of writing one big answer: think of writing a whole bunch of little answers.

How to Write About an Issue

Each of these little answers follows the same basic structure.

- Identify the issue raised by the fact pattern

- State the rule(s) that deals with that issue

- Apply that rule to the relevant facts

- State a conclusion about how and why the judge or jury will resolve the issue

The simplest way of writing through this structure is to do so in the order listed above. People refer to this approach by the acronym IRAC that stands for the following.

- Issue

- Rule

- Application

- Conclusion

Some authors and professors prefer a slightly different approach that goes by the acronym TRAC.

- Thesis

- Rule

- Application

- Conclusion

Each offers its own advantages. IRAC allows one to think through the problem as one writes because it does not commit the exam writer to a conclusion until the end of the paragraph. TRAC requires the student to decide upon a conclusion at the outset because the thesis statement states both the issue and the conclusion (which is also restated at the end). TRAC offers the advantage of communicating one's conclusion earlier to the reader. You should go with the approach one's professor prefers or with the one that feels more comfortable to you in the event that your professor has no preference.

Finally, don't assume that each element of the analysis always requires a single sentence. Sometimes application requires multiple sentences. Sometimes one can state the application, and conclusion all in one sentence.   Often one can combine a statement of the issue and a statement of the rule in a single sentence.   Sometimes one can write the rule and application together in a single sentence, and so on.   It depends on the complexity of the issue involved. Getting a feel for how you write your way through this analysis is key to writing efficiently and comes from practice. The most important thing is to make sure that all elements of the analysis clearly appear in each mini-answer.

Burglary as an Example

Let's return to the burglary hypothetical from the very first chapter. You snuck into your neighbor's apartment when they were away to steal something. The door was slightly ajar. You tried to slip through but your butt hit the door pushing it slightly more open. Assume that before you slipped through the door you were heard to say "I have got to play that new video game she has but can't afford to buy my own."

Let's consider two basic issues raised by this simple fact pattern.

- Issue: Did D commit a breaking?

- Issue: Did D intend to commit a felony or larceny inside the neighbor's apartment at the time of the breaking and entering?

Simply *identifying* and *separating* these issues from one another is much of the work. The next step would be to discuss the applicable rule. Let's consider two issues raised by these facts.

- Issue: Did D commit a breaking?

- Rule: The slightest enlargement of an opening in a door or window constitutes a breaking.

- Issue: Did D intend to commit a felony or larceny inside the neighbor's apartment?

- Rule: Larceny Requires an Intent to Permanently Deprive the Rightful Possessor of personal property.

One then needs to apply the rules to the relevant facts.

- Issue: Did D commit a breaking?

- Rule: The slightest enlargement of an opening in a door or window constitutes a breaking.

- Application and Conclusion: When D's butt hit the open door and swung it further ajar he enlarged an existing opening and thereby committed a breaking for the purposes of the crime of burglary.

- Issue: Did D intend to commit a felony or larceny inside the neighbor's apartment?

- Rule: Larceny Requires an Intent to Permanently Deprive the Rightful Possessor of personal property.

- Application: A jury could infer from his statement that he had to play the new game that he intended to steal the video game at the time he broke and entered the apartment.

Here is where things get interesting, however. The first issue is a one-sided issue. There is simply no further reasonable argument to be made on this issue. Opening the door further with his butt constituted a breaking. The second issue is a two-sided issue, however, because a reasonable argument can be made on the other side of the issue.

- Issue: Did D intend to commit a felony or larceny inside the neighbor's apartment?

- Rule: Larceny Requires an Intent to Permanently Deprive the Rightful Possessor of personal property.

- Application: A jury could infer from his statement that he had to play the new game but could not afford it that he intended to steal the video game at the time he broke and entered the apartment.

- Application: On the other hand, a jury might infer that D only intended to use the video game but not permanently deprive his neighbor of it. Note that D said "I have got to play that new video game" not "I must have that new video game."

At this point, all the heavy lifting has been done. The role the conclusion plays is just to state clearly what flows from the application.

- Issue: Did D commit a breaking?

- Rule: The slightest enlargement of an opening in a door or window constitutes a breaking.

- Application: When D's butt hit the open door and swung it further ajar he enlarged an existing opening and thereby committed a breaking for the purposes of the crime of burglary.

- Conclusion: D did commit a breaking.

For the two-sided issue, the conclusion plays a more important role although not as important as you might think.

- Issue: Did D intend to commit a felony or larceny inside the neighbor's apartment?

- Rule: Larceny Requires an Intent to Permanently Deprive the Rightful Possessor of personal property.

- Application: A jury could infer from his statement that he had to play the new game but could not afford it that he intended to steal the video game at the time he broke and entered the apartment.

- Application: On the other hand, a jury might infer that D only intended to use the video game but not permanently deprive his neighbor of it. Note that D said "I have got to play that new video game" not "I must have that new video game."

- Conclusion: A jury would find that he had intended to steal the video game because a person is not likely to enter another's apartment without permission simply to use video game equipment

  OR

- Conclusion: A jury would find that he had intended to steal the video game because the fact that he only had to sneak in through an already open door combined with the ambiguity of his statement about playing the game raises a reasonable doubt as to whether he intended to steal as opposed to borrow the game.

If a reasonable argument can be made either way then you must factor that into the rest of your analysis, which means that you must analyze the rest of the issues "in the alternative." For example, assume that the defendant with the "burgling butt" ended up causing the death of someone inside the residence. This raises the issue of felony murder liability that depends in turn on the defendant being guilty of the underlying burglary. Even if the student concludes that no burglary liability exists, she should write an alternate analysis that discusses felony murder liability on the assumption that a burglary will be found to have been committed. A two-sided issue means that one must travel down both forks of the path. The good news is that you earn points for each analysis!

The Real Importance of the Conclusion

Practically speaking the conclusion often helps the professor understand your application better. Sometimes under the stress and time pressure of exam writing students won't completely articulate how they think the rule applies to the facts. They might say something vague like "but D only said "I have got to play that new video game" thinking that it is self-evident that playing does not necessarily mean taking. Well, the professor knows this side of this issue but cannot be sure that the student knows it just from that sentence. When the student goes onto state in her conclusion "therefore the mental state required for burglary does not exist" the professor now understands more clearly how the student sees the rule applying to the facts.

Hopefully you are thinking at this point that this is something that you can do. Yes, it is! Although doing it thoroughly and efficiently over and over again on a number of issues under test conditions requires practice as well as a working knowledge of the rules themselves.

Dealing with Alternate Rules

As you have already seen, many times you will learn more than one rule for a specific issue. Some jurisdictions, for example, have completely abolished the breaking requirement. Other jurisdictions define a breaking as a significant enlargement of an existing opening. When your professor or your textbook have given you more than one rule for an issue you should apply both unless the question itself rules out one of the rules (by statutory language included in the question usually).

One-Sided v. Two-Sided Issues

One of the most difficult issues that first year law students confront is distinguishing between one-sided and two-sided issues. Sometimes law students will see two-sides where there is really only one and discuss really spurious issues out of fear that they may be missing something. For example, whether an entry occurred in the case of the burgling butt is a one-sided issue. The rule defining that elements provides that an entry occurs when any part of the human anatomy enters the dwelling. So in our hypo stepping through the door constitutes an entry. You get no points and will actually lose points with some professors if you say "on the other hand, a judge might find that stepping into the room is not sufficient for burglary" (because that is inconsistent with the law) or "if he had not stepped into the room he would not have entered" (because that is inconsistent with the facts).

Just because an issue has only one side, however, does not mean that you should skip it. *You get points for discussing one-sided issues* because your consideration of even obvious issues shows the professor that you are thinking systematically.

Here is an important rule of thumb that describes how most professors write their exams. *Not all issues in an exam have two sides, but all exams have two-sided issues.* Learning the law well enough to tell one from the other is a big part of what you must do during the course of the semester.

Policy Issues

Sometimes a professor will write policy issues into an exam. A policy issue exists where how the law applies to the facts implicates larger questions that go beyond the particular case at hand. Often these policy questions are the subject of extended discussion during the semester. When you run across such an issue, you should take your time and show the professor that you understand this connection by making a policy argument. Policy issues almost always have two sides, so you will earn more points if you discuss policy arguments on each side of the issue.

Large-Scale Organization

Now that you understand the small-scale organization of how to discuss an issue, you may be wondering how you should organize all of these "mini-essays" into one large essay.

Sometimes your professor will tell you how to organize your answer by the call of the exam question itself. A professor might, for example, tell you to analyze crime by crime or defendant by defendant, for example. If so, follow that organization!

In the absence of any suggested large scale organization for the question you should just pick one that makes sense to you. Crime by crime, defendant by defendant, conduct issues and then mental state issues—which organization you choose does not matter. What does matter is that you have some sort of organization. Having some sort of organization helps the professor follow your analysis. It also helps you think through the issues involved and makes it less likely that you will miss a major issue or set of issues.

Also, unless your professor tells you otherwise feel free to you use titles, headings, and captions to separate one section from another. Anything that makes your analysis easier to follow and that saves you time writing is worth doing.

Your large-scale organization does not need to be perfect. Professors understand that you write your answer under time pressure. But you should not just jump from one issue to another in helter skelter fashion. That suggests panic to the reader and makes it less likely that they will give you the benefit of the doubt when one of you issue discussions is less than entirely clear.

Using the Rules to Organize Your Answer

Whenever possible let the law organize your analysis for you. The simplest way to do this is by following the elements of a rule as well as the elements of a rule within a rule. Recklessness for example involves the following elements.

- Conscious disregard of a

- Substantial and

- Unjustifiable risk under

- Circumstances that involve a Gross Deviation from a reasonable standard of care.

An easy and logical way to organize this issue is by going through each element of the rule defining recklessness. The substantiality of the risk element is in turn defined in terms of the magnitude of the harm times the probability of its occurring. So when you get to that element you will introduce this new sub-rule which involves two further elements. Depending on the facts you may actually write a sentence or paragraph on each, one discussing whether the harm was great enough and one discussing whether it was probable enough.

In the abstract this may seem a bit mind boggling. Have you ever seen a "Russian egg" which contains a smaller egg within it, which in turn contains an even smaller egg within it and so on? Well law school exam issues often involve an egg that contains two or eggs within it, and each smaller egg may contain a host of sub-eggs and so on. Once you get over the shock of dealing with so many issues, however, you will eventually learn that this world of rules within rules within rules actually makes it easier to organize one's thinking and writing about complex issues, not harder!

Letting the rules organize your answer is one of the keys to writing well-organized answers quickly and efficiently without skipping any issues. If you see the issues and know the rules, the answers start to write themselves!

Common Mistakes

Now that you have an idea of what to do on a law school exam, let's talk a bit about what *not to do*. Exam-writing, like sports, is done under pressure, and students make mistakes under pressure. Some of these mistakes might strike you as "rookie" exam-writing mistakes that you have not made on an exam since the freshman year of college. Well, under the stress of dealing with these very different types of exam questions some students find themselves making mistakes that they have not made since freshman year. Other types of mistakes flow from the essentially different nature of legal analysis.

Don't Run Away from Trouble

Many smart, well prepared students make this mistake. They see the difficult, multi-sided issue that the professor has written into the problem to test her students' ability to make arguments on more than one side of an issue. What happens too often at this point is that the better prepared the student is the greater the crisis in confidence they experience. A student who outlined every single case and note in the textbook will worry that there is some case or rule that she missed. She may avoid addressing this issue altogether or write about it in a superficial way to avoid revealing her confusion or ignorance. The tragedy is that the source of the student's confusion is that she understands the issues all too well. She sees no clear answer because there is no clear answer.

This multi-sided issue is often a gold mine on an exam. Every argument you raise on each side of the issue is worth points. So don't avoid these complexities, write about them! Go from one argument to the next, confident in the knowledge that you are earning points for each one. So when you see this sort of trouble on an exam, don't run away from it. Run towards it!

Don't Freak Out if You Can't Get to Every Issue

A different sort of challenge concerns the number of issues. Sometimes students feel like they are engaged in an endless game of "whack a mole." For every issue that they address two or three more pop up in their mind as they write. Too many issues to whack in too little time!

On these sorts of questions be confident that you don't have to get every issue. Sometimes professors put more issues in a question than anyone can address in the time allotted. They do this because different students see different issues and to make sure that there is a wide enough distribution of scores to make the grades easy to curve. But take comfort in the fact that the grades are curved. You don't have to get every issue to get the top grade in the class. You just have to get more issues than anyone else.

If you confront a question with an overwhelming number of issues remember the not so funny joke about the two campers and a bear. The campers emerge from their tent in the morning in their socks only to see an enraged grizzly charging toward them. One camper immediately drops to his feet and starts putting on his boots. The other camper looks at him incredulously and says "you can't outrun that bear!" "I don't have to" the now fully shod camper replies. "I just have to outrun you." Likewise you usually don't have to solve every one of your professor's little exam puzzles to do well on her exam.

Don't Give the Professor an "Outline Dump"

The heart of legal analysis as you have seen is the application of legal rules to facts. The most efficient way to do this is by doing things "bird by bird," identifying one issue, describing the rule that applies to that issue, discussing the facts that determine whether or not that rule has been satisfied and then offering an immediate conclusion.

Sometimes students panic though. Instead of taking things one issue at a time, they just start typing rule after rule from their outline. Professors refer to this as an "outline dump." Outline dumps earn little or no points. Simply writing the rules that generally apply to the fact pattern one after another is not offering an analysis. The professor cannot tell whether you *really* understand the rule unless she sees identify the issue that the rule relates to and you apply the rule to the relevant facts.

Some students maintain that outline dumps help them organize their thinking. They will then go on to write issue by issue. You don't have time to do both. Do the issue by issue analysis that will earn you the maximal number of points in the minimum amount of time.

Don't Give the Professor a "Fact Summary"

On a similar note, some students will summarize the key facts from the fact pattern before beginning their analysis. This sort of "fact dump" earns the writer no points and is often seen as an act of panic. You may have picked out all the most important facts, but the professor cannot tell if you understand the legal significance of each fact unless they see you discuss it in connection with the issue and the rule that makes it important. Once again, some students maintain that summarizing the facts helps them organize their thinking. Once again, you do not have time for that. Do your organizing in your head or on a separate piece of paper. The professor knows the facts because she wrote them. She will not give you points for simply restating them. She will give you points when you discuss them as part of a discussion of a specific issue.

Don't Ignore the Call of the Question

The professor may have narrowed the scope of the question. Instead of simply saying "discuss all issues of criminal liability," he may have said "discuss all liability for homicide crimes, or even more specifically "discuss felony murder liability." Sometimes students cannot resist the temptation to go beyond the call of the question. These students know something about the issues left out of the call of the question and hope to impress the professor by showing what they know. Big mistake! Your professor left those issues out for a reason. She wanted you to focus on other issues. She cannot grade all the exams consistently and fairly if she awards points for issues that most students do not address because they were excluded from the question. Ignoring the call of the question also makes you seem careless, which will hurt you when the professor is deciding whether to give you the benefit of the doubt about something you wrote about an issue that was included within the question.

Don't Ignore Time Budgets

Virtually all professors give time budgets or point allocations for each question. A three hour exam involving three questions might allocate 60 points or minutes to each question. Students sometimes ignore these allocations. A student might recoil in horror from question one but think that she know the issues involved in question two cold. This student might decide to spend lots more time on question two than question one thinking that her time is better spent writing about what she knows better.

Ignoring the suggested time budgets is almost always a mistake. First, your professor will not give you more points on a question than she has allocated. So you can't get sixty-five points on a sixty point question. (You can't even get sixty-one points.) Grading a whole stack of exam papers consistently and fairly is hard enough for us as it is. Grading exam papers consistently and fairly is impossible if we start awarding "extra" points to some questions and answers. So you can't earn extra points by "overwriting" one question.

Students who ignore time budgets also usually loose more points than necessary on the questions that they shortchange. All questions contain some easy issues as well as many hard issues. Students who slight hard questions often lose points because they don't get to the "low hanging fruit."

On a similar note, the professor wrote that question for a reason—they cared about the doctrines and issues covered. Making a serious attempt to deal with the issues raised will earn you some meaningful points even if you get many issues and rules wrong. Completely blowing the question off will often result in a disastrous score because the professor will conclude that you either know even less than you do or (even worse) that you just don't care.

Don't Start Writing Too Early

I guarantee you that at least once during your first year exams you will hear someone begin typing their answer before you have even finished reading the question. What is that student doing? They are panicking. Don't join them in their panic. You must give yourself enough time reading through and thinking about the fact pattern to spot all the major issues. You don't need to see every issue before you start writing, but you do need to see every major group of issues. Once you start writing you will see new issues related to the ones that you are writing about, but you are less likely to see a wholly unrelated set of issues that you did not see before you started writing.

An easy way to check yourself is to look over the fact pattern before you start writing. Are there whole sets of facts that do not seem to have anything to do with your analysis? If so, the chances are good that you have missed some big issues. Take a breath and think about those facts a bit more before you start writing.

The other reason to take enough time to see all the major issues before you start writing is to get a sense of how you should allocate your time as you write. If you see three sets of major issues, and you have only addressed one half way through the time allotted then you know that you need to move on. You can only make these judgments about this as you write if you have already gotten an overview of the issues to be covered.

Don't Start Writing Too Late

Don't waste time writing out a complete outline before you start writing your answer. A list of major issues and arguments is usually enough. What you write before you begin writing your answer is simply a mnemonic device to keep you from forgetting something important as you write. Just write enough to jog your memory as to what you need to address in the text of your answer. You don't have time to sketch out your analysis fully before you start to write.

Also, while you should try to *see* the major issues before you start writing you should not try to figure every issue out before you start writing. You will figure out the issues as you write your way through them using the analytical structure described above.

Don't Write Overall Introductions or Conclusions

What would be the point of that? Since an essay question contains a whole set of related sub-questions, the only overall answer possible is usually "it depends." Overall introductions and conclusions are usually a waste of desperately needed time. Just jump write into the issues and start earning points.

Don't Spend Time "Writing Pretty"

There is a place in legal writing for beautiful, elegant prose that avoids the clumsy repetition of the same legal terms over and over again, but that place is not a law school exam answer. You need to write fast, clearly and succinctly. Taking time to make it elegant is wasting time.

For the same reason feel free to make reasonable use of abbreviations and symbols. "D" for defendant and "P for prosecutor. Some professors accept "OTOH" for "on the other hand."

The humorist David Sedaris has a book titled "Me Talk Pretty Some Day." Well, you not write pretty on law school exam. You write fast. You write pretty some other day.

If You Panic, It Will Wear Off

It is possible that at some point during your first year exam that you might panic. Your heart rate zooms, you keep reading the same words over and over again, you can't seem to think of anything. Don't worry. The exam has triggered your fight or flight response. Your brain is confused because it thinks that you should be running away from or fighting something. This is a purely physiological response to all the adrenaline that is coursing through your body, and it will wear off after a few minutes. It would wear off faster if you ran up and down the corridor outside the classroom, but that would probably raise a few eyebrows. When the adrenaline wears off you will remember everything you studied and you may actually feel a little bit extra calm.

Practice, Practice, Practice

There is a very old and very bad joke about a concertgoer who was looking for Carnegie Hall in New York City, a famous concert hall where only the best musicians play. The concertgoer happens to stop someone who is a concert violinist on the street and asks her "how do you get to Carnegie Hall?" The violinist answers "practice, practice, practice!" Well, the same can be said of learning to write law school exam essays well. As I stressed in chapter 1, this is a very different type of essay. You will get better at it if you practice doing it before you actually have to do it. So resist the temptation to keep adding minor details to your outline and force yourself to outline and even write a couple of answers to past exam questions. You will thank yourself later.

Some students cannot bring themselves to work through old exam questions because they find doing so too stressful. When you work through an old exam question you are confronted with what you do not know. What these students fail to realize is that doing exam questions is not just a way of finding out what you don't know but is also a very effective way of *learning* what you don't know.

Our brains remember things that are associated with strong emotions, especially stress. When you work through an exam question and then go over the answer afterwards you are literally burning those issues and rules into your brain by creating new neural pathways that will light up if and when you confront a similar issue on the actual exam. For this to work, however, you must actually try to answer the question under the stress of simulated test conditions and then either get the question right or wrong. Your brain can't be tricked into creating the new pathway by simply looking at the question and then reading over the top scoring answer. It is the stress of first trying to solve the puzzle on your own that burns the right answer into your brain.

A Last Bit of Good News

The stress and hard work of preparing for and taking law school exams is not pointless suffering. It is purposeful suffering! To really learn to think like a lawyer requires you to be able to apply not just one rule to a fact pattern but a whole framework of rules. Confronting a complex fact pattern on an exam mimics in an albeit artificial way what lawyers must do when they analyze the facts of a case. Synthesizing the rules you learned in the course into an outline puts you in a position to do exactly that. Doing so over and over again as you prepare for and take the exam under stressful conditions will change the way your brain works in a really useful and important way. In the process you will also earn the academic credits you need to get that law degree! So don't *just* worry, be happy! ☺